CERTIFICATE IN TEAM LEADING
NVQ Level 2

James Alan Parker
Eleanor Crosby

MATCHED TO THE
QCF

CERTIFICATE IN TEAM LEADING
NVQ Level 2

HODDER
EDUCATION
AN HACHETTE UK COMPANY

Picture credits

Every effort has been made to trace the copyright holders of material reproduced here. The author and publishers would like to thank the following for permission to reproduce copyright illustrations:

- Figure B11.2 © Yuri Arcurs – Fotolia
- Figure C1.1 © Andres Rodriguez – Fotolia
- Figure D1.3 © Yuri Arcurs – Fotolia
- Figure D10.2 © joé – Fotolia
- Figure D11.2 top left © Pavel Losevsky – Fotolia; top right © xy – Fotolia; bottom left © IS2 from Image Source/Alamy; bottom right © goodluz – Fotolia
- Figure D12.3 © Yuri Arcurs – Fotolia
- Figure E15.2 © diego cervo – Fotolia.

Orders: please contact Bookpoint Ltd, 130 Milton Park, Abingdon, Oxon OX14 4SB. Telephone: (44) 01235 827720. Fax: (44) 01235 400454. Lines are open from 9.00 to 5.00, Monday to Saturday, with a 24-hour message answering service. You can also order through our website www.hoddereducation.co.uk

If you have any comments to make about this, or any of our other titles, please send them to educationenquiries@hodder.co.uk

British Library Cataloguing in Publication Data
A catalogue record for this title is available from the British Library

ISBN: 978 1444 15438 2

This Edition Published 2012
Impression number   10 9 8 7 6 5 4 3 2 1
Year   2016, 2015, 2014, 2013, 2012

Copyright © 2012 James Alan Parker and Eleanor Crosby

Hachette UK's policy is to use papers that are natural, renewable and recyclable products and made from wood grown in sustainable forests. The logging and manufacturing processes are expected to conform to the environmental regulations of the country of origin.

Cover photo © Soren Hald/Cultura/Photolibrary.com.
Illustrations by Peter Lubach.
Typeset by Pantek Media, Maidstone.
Printed in Italy for Hodder Education, An Hachette UK Company, 338 Euston Road, London NW1 3BH.

Contents

INTRODUCTION

This guide has been designed as a resource to help you understand and complete the Level 2 NVQ Certificate in Team Leading. It is also a resource for anyone wanting to improve or feel more confident about their team leading skills.

The Level 2 NVQ Certificate in Team Leading is suitable for those who lead a team. You may not be the line manager but you will be leading your team, large or small, towards the achievement of a common goal. The qualification will enable you to recognise and acknowledge the skills, knowledge and understanding required to be an effective and inspirational team leader, trusted by your team and your line manager.

To achieve the Level 2 NVQ Certificate in Team Leading, you must complete the **three mandatory units** which cover the basic skills needed by a team leader in any environment:

- A1 Managing personal development
- D1 Develop working relationships with colleagues
- E11 Communicate information and knowledge.

You will also choose **one** of the two options below:

- D5 Plan, allocate and monitor work of a team *
- B5 Set objectives and provide support for team members. *

Finally, you will study **one** further unit from the remaining options, depending on your job role:

- B11 Manage or support equality of opportunity, diversity and inclusion in own area of responsibility *
- C1 Support team members in identifying, developing and implementing new ideas *
- D10 Manage conflict in a team *
- D11 Lead and manage meetings *
- D12 Participate in meetings
- E10 Make effective decisions *
- E12 Manage knowledge in own area of responsibility *
- E15 Procure supplies *
- F17 Manage customer service in own area of responsibility. *

The units marked * are Level 3 units from the Level 3 Certificate in Management and will be automatically accredited, should your job role allow, if you wish to progress to the next level.

Each unit of the qualification has a number of areas of learning called learning outcomes (LO). Each LO is broken down into a number of assessment criteria (AC). The assessment criteria address both performance and knowledge. To achieve the qualification you need to show that you have met each of these ACs.

How to use this guide

Throughout each chapter there are learning features that will help you build the knowledge and then the evidence you need to gather for each unit. The features are:

- **Introduction to the unit and its learning outcomes** giving an overview which should help you choose which optional units are best suited to you and your job role.

- **Assessment criteria** are explained and some theory is given to help develop your knowledge and understanding.

- **Case studies**, consisting of typical scenarios faced by team leaders with questions to stimulate your thought processes about team leading situations. There is no requirement to record your answers to the questions in writing, unless instructed by your tutor or assessor.

- **Development activities** with questions to help you think about team leading situations that you have experienced and how you would like to develop your skills. There is no requirement to record your answers to the questions, unless instructed by your tutor or assessor. However, your reflections might provide you with prompts and reminders later when you are gathering evidence to prove your competence. The activities have been written as if you have a 'virtual advisor' sitting beside you in the absence of your assessor or tutor, interpreting the knowledge requirements, providing you with support, reminding you of what the standards are asking of you and to help you refresh and test your knowledge and understanding.

- There may be some **Examples** of documentation that you could use.

- **Further information** sources have been suggested and some links provided. As a team leader or manager you will be carrying out your own research and continuously developing your skills and the skills of your team. These sources can add to your own list or become stepping stones to further and wider learning.

- Each unit concludes with a set of questions to **Test your knowledge** – questions related to the knowledge and how you apply it in your work role. This can help both to summarise your learning and to confirm your understanding of the unit, and will provide valuable evidence for your qualification. You and your assessor can agree which questions will be useful and whether the answers should be given in writing or verbally.

- Some suggestions for **Pulling it all together and gathering evidence**, which can be agreed with your assessor.

● Finally, an **Evaluation** asking you to reflect on your learning from completing the unit. Again, this does not have to be recorded in writing, although it could be very useful to record the answers to use in reviews with your line manager, supervisor, assessor or tutor, or possibly in a job interview. Documenting your learning throughout your working life is an effective way of showing that you use experience to influence your performance and behaviours. This section also looks at how your organisation has benefitted from the developments in your leadership skills.

As you work through the book, you can use the notes section at the end to jot down your ideas and reflections.

How to achieve the qualification

To achieve an NVQ you must prove you are competent and consistently meet the nationally agreed standards or assessment criteria. You will need to be registered with a centre, college or training provider that offers the Level 2 NVQ Certificate in Team Leading, and you will need an assessor.

There are many ways you can prove you are competent; you and your assessor will agree the most appropriate method that suits the needs of you and your workplace. This may be a mixture of:

● Observation: your assessor could observe you working and interacting with your team and other colleagues. This is a good way to capture performance evidence.

● Questioning: your assessor can ask how and why you do certain things. This can cover knowledge, understanding and some criteria that are difficult to observe.

● Discussion: a planned discussion can cover a large area of work spanning a period of time. You can show your assessor examples of your work and discuss incidents you have dealt with as a team leader.

● Product evidence: you can show your assessor examples of work you have produced, for example agendas and minutes of meetings.

● Personal statement or reflective account based on the activities in the unit. This evidence shows how and why you have taken a particular action and therefore shows your knowledge and understanding. If you can get a witness to verify it happened in the way you say, then it can also be evidence of performance.

● Case study, such as an account of a customer incident. You may, if you prefer, write about a situation rather than discuss it. You may need a witness to verify that it happened in the way you say.

● Witness testimony from your line manager or members of your team confirming your competence, either in writing or recorded as a discussion with your assessor.

It is a good idea to include a range of evidence from different sources. You can be as innovative with your evidence as your organisation, assessor and resources will allow, so if permitted you could use video, photographic or recorded audio evidence.

The evidence that you present should cover as many of the performance criteria as possible and cross-refer to other units, so you will need to discuss this with your assessor at the beginning of the qualification. Your assessor will make an assessment judgement on the suitability of the evidence that you present and will have the final say as to what is acceptable.

In some cases you will not be able to include work product evidence because of confidentiality or data protection regulations. In this instance you can ask your manager or a colleague to confirm that the evidence exists and was produced by you.

Presenting your evidence

You and your assessor will need to agree the most appropriate way of presenting your evidence, but here are some suggestions:

- An electronic portfolio: you could upload your evidence to e-portfolio software or simply store the evidence in electronic format on your PC, with a back-up on a memory stick or a CD.
- A paper-based portfolio: you could build a folder with hard copies of your evidence.

Involving other team members

You will need to involve your line manager or supervisor from the beginning of the Level 2 NVQ Certificate in Team Leading. They will be able to provide development opportunities, alongside your assessor, support and review your progress and confirm your competence in a way that will help you to successfully complete each unit and contribute towards the overall performance of the organisation. It may also be beneficial to find a mentor in your workplace, an experienced team leader, who can pass on their knowledge and be a role model for the type of team leader you want to be.

Other qualifications

As mentioned previously, most of the optional units of the Level 2 NVQ Certificate in Team Leading will count as units towards the Level 3 NVQ Certificate in Management.

Some of the chapters in this book may contribute towards some of the knowledge aspects of the Team Leading Technical Certificate, which is a requirement of the an Apprenticeship programme.

MANAGING PERSONAL DEVELOPMENT

Introduction and learning outcomes

Learning outcomes for Unit A1:

1. Be able to identify the performance requirements of your work role.

2. Be able to measure and make progress against objectives.

3. Be able to identify gaps in your own performance skills and knowledge.

4. Be able to carry out and assess planned development activities.

These learning outcomes say what you will have learned by the end of this unit. Each learning outcome is further broken down into assessment criteria, which we will look at in detail in the following sections of this unit.

This Unit Guide is a resource to help you gather the evidence you require to achieve Unit A1. It can be used as a learning resource if you are new to the role, are studying team leading in preparation for work or as a refresher if you are already an experienced team leader.

You and your assessor will agree what you need to do to meet the assessment criteria and show you are competent. This Unit Guide provides some theory to develop your understanding of managing your own development, gives some case studies for you to examine and then an opportunity for you to reflect, with a virtual adviser, on how you can develop your skills and gather evidence of competence. Some ideas are provided in the 'Pulling it all together' section at the end of this unit.

So, the purpose of this unit is to develop the skills and knowledge you need to manage your own developement. Let's start by looking at the following.

Why we need to keep developing

You may be thinking your school days are over, or maybe you have been doing your job very well for many years. So why do you need to keep on improving?

Let's begin be looking at these three reasons:

● to keep up

● to get better

● to move on.

We all need to keep up with the ever-changing working environment; organisations develop new products and services, they change the way they work, and they introduce new technologies. Employees are expected to be flexible and develop new skills to meet the changing needs of the workplace.

Improving your skills and knowledge helps you get better at the job you do, and this brings more job satisfaction. It is rewarding to have the respect of your colleagues and the recognition of your manager for doing your job well.

The workplace also offers an opportunity to develop a range of skills and knowledge that will help you move on in the future. Job-specific skills and knowledge can help you progress in your career and transferable skills such as communication and people skills can help you change your career.

Developing your skills and knowledge is an ongoing process. Once you have completed one cycle, there will inevitably be further changes and more development needs. This cycle of continuous improvement can represent the learning of a lifetime.

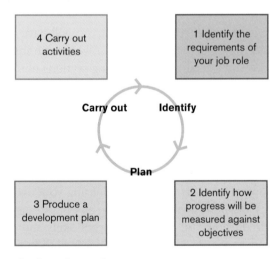

Figure A1.1: The cycle of continuous improvement

Learning outcome 1 – Be able to identify the performance requirements of your work role

In this section we will explore each of the assessment criteria in more detail to develop your knowledge and understanding.

Assessment criterion 1.1 Outline work performance requirements with those you report to

Step one in the Cycle of Improvement is to identify exactly what is expected of you in your job role and agree this with your line manager.

Most jobs have a written job description and a person specification which outline your role and the personal qualities you will need to do your job. These are an important part of the recruitment process. You may have seen these when applying for your job or been given a copy during your induction.

If you do not have a formal job description, there are many other ways in which job requirements are agreed:

- You may be asked by a manager or colleague to do certain jobs.
- You may discuss workloads at a meeting.
- You may offer to do a particular job.
- There may be some jobs where *you* decide what needs to be done.

It is important to identify:

- **what** is expected of you
- **what** resources you need to do the job
- **where** you get the resources from
- **when** is the deadline for the work to be completed
- **who** you can refer to if you have a problem.

The consequences of not knowing this information mean you will not perform to standards or meet deadlines and this affects your colleagues, your line manager and the organisation as a whole, all of whom depend on you.

The case study below provides an opportunity for you to read about a team leader or team-leading scenario. The case study highlights some of the issues discussed. You can use this to reflect on the situation and answer some questions. You do not have to write down your answers unless your tutor or assessor has asked you to do so.

CASE STUDY 1

Michael has worked in a large DIY store for a year and has been asked to supervise two 16 year olds, Jen and Pip, who have started working on Saturdays.

Michael shows the new recruits around the store, but when Jen asks if she can take her lunch break early, he says he doesn't know and will have to check with his line manager.

Pip asks what they need to do that first morning and Michael tells them both to look busy until someone asks them to do a job.

What do you think?

1. How do you think Jen and Pip are feeling on their first day at work?
2. How might Michael be feeling in his new role as team leader?
3. What could go wrong that morning? And how might that affect the organisation?
4. Give examples of clear performance requirements you would have written to avoid this situation recurring.

DEVELOPMENT ACTIVITY 1 with your virtual adviser

I am here to demystify the assessment criteria and help you relate what you have learned to your own job role. We will look at what you are currently doing and how you can develop your skills and have a real impact in your workplace.

Draw up a simple table with three columns. In the first column write **Where am I now?** and, as if you were explaining to me, make a few notes about your strengths and weaknesses when planning work for your team. Be specific and provide some examples. Be honest with yourself – this is not part of your assessment and identifying weaknesses is the first step to making improvements.

The questions below may help you.

Where am I now?
Tell me about how you discuss your role and your responsibilities with your line manager.

1. In addition to your job description, how do you find out what is expected of you?
2. Do you know exactly what to do in all areas of your work or are there some grey areas?
3. How do you agree deadlines for the work?
4. How is this communicated?
5. What decisions can you make and what do you refer to your manager?

Now, in your second column, write the heading **Improvements** and in the third column **Action**.

Improvements and action

Are there any areas where your planning could be improved?

What action do you think you could take to make those improvements happen?

Some of the changes you have identified might affect the way things are done in your organisation and you may need to discuss them with your line manager. Some changes can be made by you. Remember, small changes can make a big difference.

When you plan to make a change, remember to make your new objectives SMART!

You can discuss the notes you have made with your assessor. They may provide evidence of your competence.

Learning outcome 2 – Be able to measure and make progress against objectives

In this section we will explore each of the assessment criteria in more detail to develop your knowledge and understanding.

Assessment criterion 2.1 Identify ways that progress will be measured against your own work objectives

Once you have identified exactly what is expected of you, you need to know how your progress will be measured.

Organisations set themselves key performance objectives for different aspects of the business, for example:

- sales targets
- financial targets
- waste management targets.

These are then cascaded down as targets for the manager, the team and then each individual within the team. Each person makes a vital contribution to the overall success of the organisation.

Objectives will work better if they are SMART, that is:

- Specific
- Measurable
- Achievable
- Realistic
- Time bound.

An objective that is not specific leaves everyone unsure of exactly what they need to do, for example:

- Train staff.

whereas a SMART objective is more likely to succeed:

- To send all Team Leaders on the Team Leading training event in April.

It is difficult to know whether an objective has been met unless that objective can be measured, for example:

- Improve your work output.

You may think you have improved, but your manager may not agree. A measurable objective might be:

- Increase the number of phone calls made from 20 a day to 30 a day.

If objectives and targets are not achievable or realistic, what effect will this have on the team or an individual?

- Double profits in the next month.

Being able to achieve a realistic goal is more likely to motivate teams and individuals and give everyone a feeling of job satisfaction.

Lastly, the element of time and deadlines. If an objective is open ended, will it ever be achieved? Are you more likely to prioritise a piece of work that needs to be completed by Friday or one which has no deadline?

If the job you are doing has several stages and needs to be completed over a period of time, it is essential to break it down into smaller chunks and identify milestones along the way. Milestones are like checkpoints in the middle of your work which you use to measure whether everything is going according to plan.

Imagine you are running a marathon and you set off, hoping to run the 26 miles in 5 hours. If you don't have any means of telling the time or knowing what distance you have travelled, it will be very difficult to pace yourself or stay motivated. There is a high chance you will not achieve your goal. But if you can check your time at each mile of the race, and you have run each mile in approximately 10 minutes, you will know you can succeed.

You can build milestones into your work plan to measure whether you are on track. You need to identify the key stages and when they should be achieved in order for the next stage to go ahead on schedule. This way, you can measure your performance and be confident that you will achieve on time.

The case study below provides an opportunity for you to read about a team leader or team leading scenario. The case study highlights some of the issues discussed. You can use this to reflect on the situation and answer some questions. You do not have to write down your answers unless your tutor or assessor has asked you to do so.

Objective:	To brief the team on new documentation					
To do	**Mon**	**Tues**	**Weds**		**Thur**	**Fri**
Email invites	*			M I L E S T O N E C H E C K		
Read guidance notes		*				
Produce powerpoint slides	*					
Check email replies			*			
Book meeting room	*					
Copy documents			*			
Check equipment					*	
Book tea, coffee, biscuits					*	
Meeting						*
Deadline						*

Figure A1.2: Example of a simple GANTT chart to monitor progress

CASE STUDY 2

Jen and Pip have had very little to do on their first day and as the store is quiet, Michael tells them they can go home at 3 p.m. It is not possible to check this decision with the store manager, who is travelling to another branch for a meeting.

At 3.30 p.m., a large delivery arrives and no one is available to unload it. Michael ends up working late, dealing with the delivery by himself. When he works overtime, he is usually able to take time off in lieu (TOIL) on another day.

No one has explained to Michael that the organisation has some key performance objectives, including:

- to reduce the amount of overtime and TOIL by 10 per cent each month
- to reduce the risk of injury by always having two people to unload deliveries.

If Michael does not perform his job successfully, it will have a negative impact on others in the workplace and ultimately prevent the organisation meeting its key performance objectives.

What do you think?

1. What do you think about Michael's decision to let Jen and Pip go home early?
2. What are the consequences of his decision?
3. Who else will be affected?
4. What would you have done to avoid this situation happening:
   - if you were Michael?
   - if you were Michael's manager?

DEVELOPMENT ACTIVITY 2 with your virtual adviser

I am here to demystify the assessment criteria and help you relate what you have learned to your own job role. We will look at what you are currently doing and how you can develop your skills and have a real impact in your workplace.

Draw up a simple table with three columns. In the first column write **Where am I now?** and, as if you were explaining to me, make a few notes about your strengths and weaknesses when making contributions and acknowledging the contributions of others in a meeting. Be specific and provide some examples. Be honest with yourself – this is not part of your assessment and identifying weaknesses is the first step to making improvements.

The questions below may help you.

Where am I now?
Think about the job you do.

1. What are the objectives that you have been set at your last appraisal or review?
2. Are those objectives SMART? If not, how could they be rewritten to make them SMART?
3. If you do not meet your objectives, what impact will this have on others?
4. If you do meet your objectives, how does this contribute to your organisation's wider aims and objectives?
5. How do you measure achievement in your day-to-day work?
6. What objectives have you set yourself?
7. What milestones have you set to check your progress?

Now, in your second column, write the heading **Improvements** and in the third column **Action**.

Improvements and action
Are there any areas where your skills could be improved?

What action do you need to take to make those improvements?

Some of the changes you have identified might affect the way things are done in your organisation and you may need to discuss them with your line manager. Some changes can be made by you. Remember, small changes can make a big difference.

When you plan to make a change, remember to make your new objectives SMART!

You can discuss the notes you have made with your assessor. They may provide evidence of your competence.

Learning outcome 3 – Be able to identify gaps in your own performance skills and knowledge

In this section we will explore each of the assessment criteria in more detail to develop your knowledge and understanding.

Assessment criterion 3.1 Explain knowledge and skills required for your own work role

In Activity 1 you identified the knowledge and skills required for your job role. The next step is to identify any gaps between these requirements and your own performance.

Changes in your job or the introduction of new products, services or technologies can bring about a development need. When a new piece of technology is introduced, everyone will need some additional training. When legislation changes, everyone needs to be updated. When company procedures change, everyone needs to develop their working practices to meet the new requirements. These changes prompt us to develop our skills and knowledge.

At other times, you may need feedback from others to identify gaps in your skills and knowledge. This can be formal feedback at a review or appraisal. In addition to feedback from your line manager, you may be able to get 360-degree feedback, from colleagues and those who are part of your team. This can provide more accurate feedback from different perspectives.

Feedback is easier to hear if it is given as a 'sandwich' of positive–negative–positive. Remember this when giving feedback to others.

A useful tool to identify gaps in your skills and knowledge is to use a skills scan. This lists all the skills required in your job and allows you to match yourself either by ticking, giving a 1–5 grade, or by saying whether you do the job Frequently/Sometimes/Never.

You could also complete a SWOT analysis. This identifies your strengths and weaknesses as well as any opportunities you can think of that will help you achieve your goals (this could be a training opportunity or the chance to work with someone more experienced), and any threats or things that get in the way of you being able to do your job. Threats may be possible redundancies in your department, other staff off sick, not having access to the equipment or resources to do the job. Once threats or problems have been identified you are closer to finding a solution or overcoming the hurdle. So, for example, a lack of equipment may be overcome by working in partnership with someone who does have the equipment you need.

The idea is to turn any problems or threats into opportunities.

Assessment criterion 3.2 Identify opportunities and resources available for personal development

Once you have identified the skills and knowledge you need to develop, you can discuss with your line manager the opportunities and resources available:

- Are there any courses you could attend?
- How much do they cost?
- Is there someone at work you could shadow?
- Are there training DVDs you could watch?
- Are there books or study aids you could access?
- Are there internet sites that could be useful?
- Is there a mentor who could give you one-to-one guidance?
- Is there is someone at work who is good at their job? Could you ask them how they do it?

There are many different ways of learning and we all have preferred learning styles. Styles include:

- Visual – some learn better when they are shown a new skill
- Audio – some prefer to have things explained
- Reading – others cannot take anything in unless it is written down
- Kinaesthetic – many people like to try things themselves.

In reality, it depends on what is being learned, and we all may use a mixture of learning styles.

You may prefer to be shown how to use a new piece of equipment rather than sit down and read the manual. You may like to ask lots of questions rather than watch a training video. You may like to use it yourself to improve your learning experience. We are all different. It is worth considering your preferred method of learning before you agree a development plan.

Assessment criterion 3.3 Produce a development plan to address your own needs and agree this with your manager

Having a written plan usually ensures that the training will happen. Or at least it is more likely to happen than if discussed in a passing conversation.

A good development plan should have the following features:

- It should be agreed with your line manager.
- It should be in writing.
- It should have really clear SMART objectives.

There is an example of a development plan in Table A1.1.

If your training takes you away from the workplace, you need to ensure your work is delegated or that you can extend your deadlines to complete it.

The case study below provides an opportunity for you to read about a team leader or team leading scenario. It highlights some of the issues discussed. You can use this to reflect on the situation and answer some questions. You do not have to write down your answers unless your tutor or assessor has asked you to do so.

CASE STUDY 3

Michael is due for his six-monthly review with his line manager. He tells his manager that although he is enjoying his new job role as a team leader, he is not always clear about what is expected and not confident he is making the right decisions.

The manager reassures him that it is early days and promises to look into some training for him.

Several days later, Michael receives an email inviting him to attend a course on team work. He is not sure it is exactly what he is looking for, but signs up anyway, hoping to get something out of it.

It turns out that the course was aimed at those entering work for the first time and covers the basic communication skills needed to work as a team in the workplace. Although Michael found it interesting, it did not address any of the issues he faces in his new job role.

What do you think?

1. Why do you think Michael was sent on this course?

2. Why do you think he agreed to go?

3. What other opportunities for development could Michael and his manager have considered?

4. Which do you think would have been most effective in meeting Michael's development needs?

DEVELOPMENT ACTIVITY 3 with your virtual adviser

I am here to demystify the assessment criteria and help you relate what you have learned to your own job role. We will look at what you are doing and how you can develop your skills and have a real impact in your workplace.

Draw up a simple table with three columns. In the first column write **Where am I now?** and, as if you were explaining to me, make a few notes about your strengths and weaknesses when improving your own performance. Be specific and provide some examples. Be honest with yourself – this is not part of your assessment and identifying weaknesses is the first step to making improvements.

The questions below may help you.

Where am I now?
Think about the way you carry out your job role.

1. Are there any gaps between your performance and your job requirements?

2. Have there been any changes or are changes planned which will need you to retrain?

3. What opportunities and resources are available for personal development?

Now, in your second column, write the heading **Improvements** and in the third column **Action**.

Improvements and action
Are there any areas where your performance could be improved?

What action do you need to take to make those improvements?

Some of the changes you have identified might affect the way things are done in your organisation and you may need to discuss them with your line manager. Some changes can be made by you. Remember, small changes can make a big difference.

When you plan to make a change, remember to make your new objectives SMART!

You can discuss the notes you have made with your assessor. They may provide evidence of your competence.

An example

If you do not have a personal development plan, use the template below to record the best way of filling skills and knowledge gaps.

Table A1.1: Template for a personal development plan

Development need	Activity	Resources	Achieve by (date)	Achieved (Yes/No)

Learning outcome 4 – Be able to carry out and assess planned development activities

In this section we will explore each of the assessment criteria in more detail to develop your knowledge and understanding.

Assessment criterion 4.1 Plan activities in your own development plan and address identified needs

The final step in the process is to carry out the activities that have been set out in your personal development plan. It is worth choosing activities that best suit your preferred learning style, as discussed in section 3 of this unit. If you are not sure which is your personal learning style, you can find many interactive quizzes on the internet.

It is not easy to measure whether a development activity has been successful. One approach might be to show how well you met your performance targets before and after the activity. You may be able to measure some difference in the company's key performance targets. The difficulty is whether the improvement can be directly attributable to the development activity or whether other factors were involved. Either way, this could be a starting point for quantitatively measuring the success of an activity.

Assessment criterion 4.2 Collect feedback from colleagues on the result of these activities on your performance

You asked for feedback in order to identify gaps in your skills and knowledge, don't forget to ask for feedback after you have completed the development activity. This could help qualitatively measure whether the activity was successful.

Assessment criterion 4.3 Assess the success of activities carried out as part of your development plan

Assessing the success of an activity helps you and your line manager judge whether to use this method again or try something different in future.

The case study below provides an opportunity for you to read about a team leader or team leading scenario. The case study highlights some of the issues discussed. You can use this to reflect on the situation and answer some questions. You do not have to write your answers down unless your tutor or assessor has asked you to do so.

CASE STUDY 4

Michael did not benefit from attending the course on team work. He spent half a day away from the workplace, which put extra pressure on his colleagues and left him with work to catch up on when he returned.

He reflected on this experience and decided that attending courses was not for him.

What do you think?

1. Why do you think the course did not benefit Michael?

2. What other development activities would you suggest that might be more effective?

DEVELOPMENT ACTIVITY 4 with your virtual adviser

I am here to demystify the assessment criteria and help you relate what you have learned to your own job role. We will look at what you are currently doing and how you can develop your skills and have a real impact in your workplace.

Draw up a simple table with three columns. In the first column write **Where am I now?** and, as if you were explaining to me, make a few notes about your strengths and weaknesses when carrying out development activities. Be specific and provide some examples. Be honest with yourself – this is not part of your assessment and identifying weaknesses is the first step to making improvements.

The questions below may help you.

Where am I now?

Think about development activities in which you have participated.

Have a look at the personal development plan from Activity 3.

1. What impact will your development activities have on others in the workplace?

2. How can any negative impacts be minimised?

3. Does the activity you have chosen fit in with your preferred learning style?

4. If you do not know your preferred learning style, you could complete the quiz at http://www.businessballs.com/vaklearningstylestest.htm

5. On refection, is there an activity that would better suit your learning style?

6. Once you have carried out the activity and applied your new skills to your work, do you ask your colleagues for feedback?

7. Did you ask for a feedback sandwich 'positive–negative–positive'?

8. Have your colleagues noticed a difference in the way you work?

9. Have you undertaken other activities previously which you feel have made a difference?

Now, in your second column, write the heading **Improvements** and in the third column **Action**.

Improvements and action

Are there any areas where your skills could be improved?

What action do you need to take to make those improvements?

Some of the changes you have identified might affect the way things are done in your organisation and you may need to discuss them with your line manager. Some changes can be made by you. Remember, small changes can make a big difference.

When you plan to make a change, remember to make your new objectives SMART!

You can discuss the notes you have made with your assessor. They may provide evidence of your competence.

TEST YOUR KNOWLEDGE

Here are some questions to test your knowledge and understanding of the issues explored in this unit. You can write down the answers or discuss them with your assessor. They could provide good evidence for your NVQ.

1. What are you required to do in your job role? AC 1.1

2. What qualifications, knowledge and skills do you need to do your job successfully? AC 3.1

3. Who allocates this work to you? AC 1.1

4. What are the agreed deadlines for your work? AC 1.1

5. What do you do if you cannot meet a deadline? AC 1.1

6. How do you ensure the work is done on time? AC 2.1

7. Explain how each of these can be used to measure performance:

   – an agreed deadline AC 2.1

   – a key performance objective AC 2.1

   – a milestone AC 2.1

8. What is a SMART objective? AC 2.1

9. What does SMART stand for? AC 2.1

10. Give an example of each of the following development opportunities in relation to your job: AC 3.2

    Training courses: ....

    Self-study: ....

    Job shadowing...

    One-to-one guidance/mentoring: ....

    Other: ....

11. Given the choice, which of the above is your preferred learning activity? AC 4.1

12. What impact might each of the learning activities from question 10 have on others in the work area? AC 4.1

13. What are the different ways of getting feedback from colleagues about your performance? AC 4.2

14. What can you do to encourage constructive feedback? AC 4.2

Pulling it all together and gathering evidence

You and your assessor will need to agree the most appropriate sources of evidence. Here are some suggestions:

- An electronic portfolio: you could upload your evidence to an e-portfolio package or simply store the evidence in electronic format.
- A paper-based portfolio: you could build a folder with hard copies of your evidence.

Types of evidence:

- Observation: a record by your assessor when observing you discussing your work role or development plan with your line manager.
- Work product: copies of work produced by you that demonstrate your competence, for example your skills scan, SWOT analysis, personal development plan.
- Discussion: a record of you and your assessor discussing how you learn best, what development activities you have undertaken, how successful they were.
- Questioning: a record of your assessor asking questions to test your knowledge.
- Personal statement, reflective account or case study based on the activities in this unit: this should have sentences which start with 'I ...' and should tell a story giving real-life examples.
- Witness testimony from your line manager confirming your competence, in writing or recorded as a discussion with your assessor.

It is a good idea to include a range of evidence from different sources. Your evidence should cover a period of time and not be a 'one-off'. However, try to keep the evidence to a minimum. Your assessor can make a note of product evidence they have seen so it can be left in the workplace.

Remember:

Less is more – quality not quantity!

Be holistic – can you use this evidence again for other units?

EVALUATION

What have you learned from completing this unit?

What new skills and techniques are you using?

How has this affected the people you work with?

How has your organisation benefited? How might it benefit in the future?

SET OBJECTIVES AND PROVIDE SUPPORT FOR TEAM MEMBERS

Introduction and learning outcomes

Learning outcomes for Unit B5:

1. Be able to communicate a team's purpose and objectives to the team members.
2. Be able to develop a plan with team members showing how team objectives will be met.
3. Be able to support team members identifying opportunities and providing support.
4. Be able to monitor and evaluate progress and recognise individual and team achievement.

These learning outcomes say what you will have learned by the end of this unit. Each learning outcome is further broken down into assessment criteria, which we will look at in detail in the following sections of this unit.

This Unit Guide is a resource to help you gather the evidence you require to achieve Unit B5. It can be used as a learning resource if you are new to the role, are studying team leading in preparation for work or as a refresher if you are already an experienced team leader.

You will choose **either** Unit D5 **or** Unit B5 to achieve your qualification. Both units are similar but are adapted for different working environments. D5 involves a greater degree of planning the work, then allocating it to the team, assessing their performance and improving their performance. This unit would work well in an environment where the team members are required to do a job in a particular way, for example a call centre or a production line, or where work has an element of continuity. B5 involves planning with the team, generating their ideas, and would be more appropriate in flexible, creative settings where there are many different ways of meeting the targets or the work project changes regularly. Environments that involve selling, advertising, coaching, training, people skills would be better suited to this unit. Team members may need more input into the planning stages and more close support and supervision during the project.

You and your assessor will agree what you need to do to meet the assessment criteria and show you are competent. This Unit Guide provides some theory to develop your understanding of planning, allocating and monitoring the work of a team, gives some case studies for you to examine and then an opportunity for you to reflect, with a virtual adviser, on how you can develop your skills and gather evidence of competence. Some ideas are provided in the 'Pulling it all together' section at the end of this unit.

So, the purpose of this unit is to develop the skills and knowledge you need to set objectives and provide support for team members.

Learning outcome 1 – Be able to communicate a team's purpose and objectives to the team members

In this section we will explore each of the assessment criteria in more detail to develop your knowledge and understanding.

Assessment criterion 1.1 Describe the purpose of a team

A team can be a group of two or more people who are working towards a common goal. The purpose of a team is to achieve that common and collective goal more effectively than one individual working alone.

Imagine a scenario where a team is in charge of entry to a large charity event. A team of people could have several gates open at once, making queues shorter. One team member could deal with enquiries while others take tickets; one team member may have first-aid experience, another may speak a second language, one could support someone with a disability and another could make everyone a cup of tea! An individual working alone could not achieve this.

A team has many advantages over an individual in the way its members share out the work. They:

- can be in several places at any one time
- can do different tasks at the same time
- have a wider range of skills
- have a wider range of qualities and attributes
- can think in different ways.

Imagine another scenario where a retail supervisor manages 12 individual cashiers. She deals with them on a one-to-one basis and they come in, work their shift and go home. After a time, these cashiers may become bored and uninterested in their job and, as a result, leave. If the supervisor builds a team that has meetings, is aware of common goals, communicates well, shares skills and knowledge, and supports other team members, then generally the cashiers will be more committed and motivated and feel their job is more rewarding.

The benefits to the organisation and the individual of working as a team are:

- better communication
- more support
- learning from each other
- drawing on specialist skills and knowledge
- greater interaction and sociability
- enhanced identification with the team and the organisation
- greater commitment and motivation
- increased sense of well-being.

The main purpose of a team may be to meet organisational objectives more effectively, but as you can see from the list of benefits, there are many reasons why building a strong team is a good idea.

Assessment criterion 1.2 Set team objectives with its members which are SMART (Specific, Measurable, Achievable, Realistic, Time-bound)

At the beginning of a project or piece of work the team members need to know what the objectives are. They need to know exactly what is required, what standard of work is expected and how their work will be measured, whether they have the skills and resources to achieve the job realistically and on time. In other words, they need SMART objectives. You are probably familiar now with these words:

- Specific
- Measurable
- Achievable
- Realistic
- Time bound.

So, we will give a brief example to illustrate the importance of SMART objectives.

Imagine you work for an office removals company. You and a fellow team member have been given an address and instructions to move the office to a new building on the outskirts of town. You pack everything carefully, load it all into the removals van and deliver it safely, the same day, to the new building. You both feel very pleased with the day's work.

Then you get a phone call asking why only one floor was cleared, why the furniture was not unpacked and put in place at the other end, and why it was delivered before the carpet cleaners had done their work.

Clearly the team leader had not given SMART objectives. The instructions did not specify exactly which offices on how many floors had to be cleared. If the team had known there were other floors to clear, the task may not have been achievable with just two people. The team were unaware they had to unpack and arrange the office furniture. They thought they had completed the job well, but the customer had a different measure of success. They completed the job but didn't realise they should have waited until the carpet had been cleaned before delivering the furniture; it may not have been realistic to have the carpet cleaned on the same day. The timing was all wrong.

If only all these details had been communicated clearly and agreed at the beginning.

Assessment criterion 1.3 Communicate the team's purpose and objectives to its members

So, we know it is important to communicate the team's objectives to the team before the work begins. But what about the team's *purpose*? This is something that often gets overlooked. Maybe it is an assumption we all make – that everyone knows why they are there, they just need to know what to do, not *why* it needs to be done.

Figure B5.1

It may seem obvious, especially if you have already told the team of their purpose on several occasions. This is not new information you are giving to the team – they probably know it already. You are repeating this message to remind the team of the bigger picture, to put the work they are doing in some context, to give it meaning and to emphasise the fact that you are all working towards a common goal.

Imagine the scenario where you are introducing new paperwork that has to be completed. This is never popular. You explain the objectives to the team, but they do not look happy and you sense their grumbling resentment.

It is not always guaranteed to work, but imagine how much easier the additional paperwork would be to accept if you explained the bigger picture, that as a team you are there to offer the best possible service to customers and this new paperwork asks for customer feedback, which can then be used to improve the customer service and make the team's work more effective. The team may still groan, but not so loudly.

You need to give some thought to the best way of communicating the team's purpose and objectives. An email does not give you the opportunity to inspire your team or gauge their response or answer immediate questions. At the end of an afternoon meeting, the team members may be more tired and less receptive.

There is a range of ways to communicate that ensure the team are:

● together

● at their most receptive

● able to ask questions.

You may need to choose the method that best suits your organisational needs and the needs of your team. It could be:

● a team talk or meeting

● individual or team progress review.

And it could be reinforced by putting it in a visual format:

● on the notice board

● on a wall chart of targets and results

● in a newsletter.

A visual reminder of targets acts as a way of focusing the team and as they see their progress, it can motivate them to make an extra effort to meet their targets. Later we will discuss how we recognise and celebrate successful achievement.

The case study below provides an opportunity for you to read about a team leader or team leading scenario. It highlights some of the issues discussed. You can use this to reflect on the situation and answer some questions. You do not have to write down your answers unless your tutor or assessor has asked you to do so.

CASE STUDY 1

> Marlon runs his own cake-making business. He makes beautiful cakes to order for weddings, birthdays, parties and other special occasions. This summer he has decided to run a quality cake stall at various festivals and he has taken on a young and enthusiastic team of four who will help run the stalls in return for a free ticket to the festivals.
>
> Marlon calls a team meeting to explain the work shifts and everyone's roles and responsibilities. He goes through the objectives, explaining specifically how many cakes they will need to sell each day to make a profit. Then he asks for any questions or suggestions.
>
> Everyone wants to know what bands are playing, how they will get there, whether they need their own tent, and they suggest they sell sandwiches as well as cakes. Marlon feels they haven't really understood the point of his business or the festival project.

What do you think?

1. Has Marlon explained the purpose of his business and how the team contribute to the overall aim of his organisation?
2. How SMART are Marlon's objectives?
3. How else could Marlon have got his message across?

DEVELOPMENT ACTIVITY 1 with your virtual adviser

I am here to demystify the assessment criteria and help you relate what you have learned to your own job role. We will look at what you are currently doing and how you can develop your skills in a way that has a real impact on your workplace.

Draw up a simple table with three columns. In the first column write **Where am I now?** and, as if you were explaining to me, make a few notes about your strengths and weaknesses when communicating your team's purpose and objectives to the team. Be specific and provide some examples. Be honest with yourself – this is not part of your assessment and identifying weaknesses is the first step to making improvements.

The questions below may help you.

Where am I now?

Tell me about the way you communicate with your team and how you tell them about their purpose and their team objectives. Give me some specific examples:

1. What was the last project you gave your team?
2. When you explained it to them, did you outline SMART objectives?
3. Did you explain the purpose of the work and how it related to the overall needs of the organisation?
4. How and when did you communicate this information?
5. Did you provide any visual reinforcement of the targets?

Now, in your second column, write the heading **Improvements** and in the third column **Action**.

Improvements and action

Are there any areas where your communication could be improved?

What action do you think you could take to make those improvements happen?

Some of the changes you have identified might affect the way things are done in your organisation and you may need to discuss them with your line manager. Some changes can be made by you. Remember, small changes can make a big difference.

When you plan to make a change, remember to make your new objectives SMART!

You can discuss the notes you have made with your assessor. They may provide evidence of your competence.

Learning outcome 2 – Be able to develop a plan with team members showing how team objectives will be met

In this section we will explore each of the assessment criteria in more detail to develop your knowledge and understanding.

Assessment criterion 2.1 Discuss with team members how team objectives will be met

You have communicated the purpose and the objectives to the team so they know what needs to be done and why. Now it is time to develop a more detailed plan to ensure nothing is left to chance.

To ensure all team members will have a chance to contribute their ideas, ask questions and to allow each to take ownership of their particular role it is essential to have a team meeting where everyone is present. It is important to capture all the planning decisions in writing so that there is no confusion later about who agreed to do what.

One method of breaking down the overall objectives into smaller tasks is to use a critical path analysis. This sounds technical but is in fact a very simple and useful tool.

Let's take an example of organising a meeting.

1. First ask the team to brainstorm all the jobs that need to be done, including sending out invites, booking a room and preparing an agenda, and write each task on a separate piece of paper approximately A6 or the size of a large Post-it.

2. Arrange the pieces of paper in the order they need to be done. The agenda has to be prepared before the invites are sent out.

3. Next add the length of time it takes to do each job. You may have to allow several weeks for delegates to confirm their attendance, especially if they are from outside the organisation or are on holiday.

4. At this stage, you could add the name of the person who will do the task.

5. Finally, working back from the date of the meeting, write on each piece of paper the date the task must be carried out. Catering may insist on one week's notice to provide refreshments, so this task must have a due date of one week prior to the meeting.

At the end of this exercise you will have designed a detailed plan of the tasks to be done, allocated a person to do each task and agreed a deadline for each task within the overall timeframe needed to organise the meeting.

This is just one possible tool. You will find many more available in books and on the internet.

Assessment criterion 2.2 Ensure team members participate in the planning process and think creatively

Team members who participate in the planning process tend to be more committed to the successful outcome of the project. They often have greater ownership of the process, having been involved right from the start.

There are few pieces of work that can be done in exactly the same way year in year out. Things change: technology changes, the make-up of the team changes, and often we are having to think of smarter ways of working so that the same objectives can be achieved in less time, for less money, with better customer service.

In order to do things differently, it is important that all the team generate ideas. New team members may have a different approach. Team members with different backgrounds, ages, values, beliefs can all bring a fresh perspective and new ways of solving problems. As team leader, you need to create an environment where each member can participate, think creatively and generate ideas.

Brainstorming is one of the most common ways of getting a team to suggest a range of ideas. It encourages people to think laterally rather than being stuck in the usual way of doing things. You have probably taken part in brainstorming sessions, but if you are running one, this list of dos and don'ts may be useful.

Do:

- have a flip chart, white board or equivalent to capture the ideas
- appoint someone to take notes
- prepare the room so it is comfortable and relaxed
- do an ice-breaker exercise if people don't know each other
- set the tone by being enthusiastic and get a group agreement to be uncritical
- give people time to think of some ideas first, either individually or in groups
- make it fun
- write down the ideas as they are suggested
- welcome all ideas, however quirky
- keep the ideas short – they can be developed later
- keep the ideas coming fast so they trigger other ideas – you can divide people into small groups and then prompt groups for suggestions
- if it's a long session, have a break.

Don't:

- be judgemental or filter the ideas as they come in
- criticise
- analyse.

There are some variations to brainstorming that might work in different circumstances. If you have quiet members of the team who rarely contribute, you could get everyone to suggest something in turn. This ensures everyone has a say. You could reverse the question, so instead of asking 'What would delight our customers?' you could ask 'What would really annoy our customers?'. This can be heaps of fun and get ideas flowing where the original question may have produced very little. You then need to reverse all the solutions at the end of the session.

Assessment criterion 2.3 Develop plans to meet team objectives

Once your ideas have been generated, you can begin to analyse and explore them. Following a brainstorming session, the ideas are likely to be mixed up and scattered around. They need organising and the first step is to group together all the similar ideas so that a theme or a trend emerges. Each theme can then be explored to see if it is the best idea or solution and should be adopted. Remember, the idea or solution must contribute to meeting the team objective.

One very useful tool for exploring different solutions or ideas is a Fishbone diagram (see Figure B5.2). This simply involves drawing a line that represents your idea and some other lines coming off it like fish bones. Each fish bone represents an area that could be affected by the idea or solution. For example, if the idea of delighting customers is to have comfortable seating outside changing rooms, the fish bones could be cost, customers, space, staff, health and safety. You would then write down next to each fish bone how your solution might affect each area. Along the space line you might put 'less space for other clothing', 'comfy chairs too large', 'no room for a sofa', 'walkway restricted'. By analysing each idea you will be able to eliminate those which are not viable.

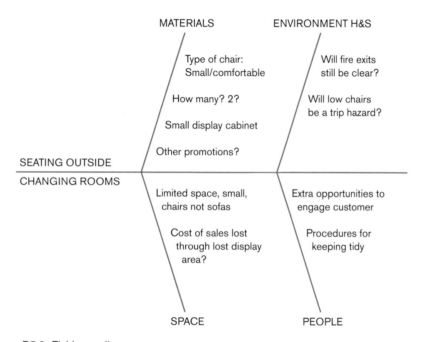

Figure B5.2: Fishbone diagram

Once you have decided on an idea, you can use the critical path analysis (outlined in section 2.1) or record the detailed plan on a Gantt Chart (see example below). The Gantt Chart simply lists all the tasks in the left-hand column and the timeline from now to project completion across the top. This allows you to plan which tasks need to be completed by when. You can build in checks or **milestones** to monitor whether your plan is on course.

There are many tools you can use with your team to shape your ideas into a detailed plan. The more detail you capture, the less likely it is that things will be forgotten or go wrong. Success is all in the preparation.

Assessment criterion 2.4 Set SMART work objectives with team members

When your plan is developed you can allocate tasks to individual team members. There is a danger, if the tasks are allocated verbally, that people will forget some aspect of the job. So make sure that whatever you agree is written down and all parties have a copy.

An example of a record of SMART work objectives is included in Table B5.1. The case study provides an opportunity for you to read about a team leader or team leading scenario. It highlights some of the issues discussed. You can use this to reflect on the situation and answer some questions. You do not have to write down your answers unless your tutor or assessor has asked you to do so.

CASE STUDY 2

Marlon gets his team together for a second time. He clearly outlines the purpose of their roles and explains how they can contribute to the overall objectives of his specialist cake-making business. He answers all their questions about the various festivals. The team are very excited.

Marlon wants to make a real impression at each festival by having a theme for the decoration of the cakes and the stall and having the team dress up as well. He is full of ideas that he can't wait to share with the team. He draws lots of pictures to show them exactly what he thinks they should do at each festival. The team nod in agreement but don't seem quite as excited as he is. No matter how amazing his ideas, Marlon cannot seem to get the team buzzing with enthusiasm.

They pick one idea and Marlon asks for two volunteers to be in charge of stall decoration and two to work on costumes, while he concentrates on cakes. He gives them each a budget. They agree to meet up two weeks before the first festival to see how the work is progressing.

Marlon really can't understand why these young people are not more enthusiastic about this fantastic opportunity. He wonders whether he has chosen the wrong team.

What do you think?

1. The team seemed very enthusiastic at the start of the meeting. What do you think happened to their enthusiasm?

2. Marlon explained his ideas to the team. How else could he have managed this?

3. What would have been the benefits to him and the team if he had brainstormed everyone's ideas?

4. Did Marlon develop the ideas into a plan with the team? How well did he do this?

5. What could go wrong with the plans Marlon has made?

6. How would you have run this meeting differently?

DEVELOPMENT ACTIVITY 2 with your virtual adviser

I am here to demystify the assessment criteria and help you relate what you have learned to your own job role. We will look at what you are currently doing and how you can develop your skills and have a real impact in your workplace.

Draw up a simple table with three columns. In the first column write **Where am I now?** and, as if you were explaining to me, make a few notes about your strengths and weaknesses when developing plans with team members. Be specific and provide some examples. Be honest with yourself – this is not part of your assessment, and identifying weaknesses is the first step to making improvements.

The questions below may help you.

Where am I now?
Think about plans you have developed with your team.

1. What sort of planning meetings/opportunities did you organise?
2. How did you ensure all team members participated?
3. What techniques did you use to encourage creative thinking?
4. How did you develop ideas into plans to meet the team objectives?
5. Did you use any particular tools/exercises?
6. Did you set SMART objectives for each team member?

Now, in your second column, write the heading **Improvements** and in the third column **Action**.

Improvements and action
Are there any areas where your skills could be improved?

What action do you need to take to make those improvements?

Some of the changes you have identified might affect the way things are done in your organisation and you may need to discuss them with your line manager. Some changes can be made by you. Remember, small changes can make a big difference.

When you plan to make a change, remember to make your new objectives SMART!

You can discuss the notes you have made with your assessor. They may provide evidence of your competence.

Example

If you do not have a way of measuring your day-to-day progress, see Figure B5.3 for a simple Gantt Chart* to help you.

* Originally developed by HL Gantt in 1917

Objective:	To brief the team on new documentation						
To do	**Mon**	**Tues**	**Wed**			**Thur**	**Fri**
Email invites	*			M			
Read guidance notes		*		I			
Produce PowerPoint slides		*		L			
Check email replies			*	E			
Book meeting room	*			S T			
Copy documents			*	O			
Check equipment				N		*	
Book tea, coffee,				E			
biscuits				C		*	
Meeting				H E C K			*
Deadline							*

Figure B5.3: Simple GANTT Chart to monitor progress

Table B5.1: SMART objectives

Development plan: Maria Wilson			
Aim: To build confidence and improve telephone technique			
Development objective	**Activity**	**By when**	**Achieved**
To refresh knowledge and basic telephone skills	Attend in-house training course	17 Oct	
To learn a new technique from an experienced employee	Shadow Fiona for half a day	10 Sep	

Learning outcome 3 – Be able to support team members identifying opportunities and providing support

In this section we will explore each of the assessment criteria in more detail to develop your knowledge and understanding.

Assessment criterion 3.1 Identify opportunities and difficulties faced by team members

In order to meet the team objectives, you want to take advantage of every opportunity that moves the work forward and overcome all difficulties that get in the way of your team's progress. But how do we identify these opportunities and difficulties?

The difficulties are easy to spot when they actually happen. If your line manager calls a company-wide half-day meeting and then two of your team are off sick, you know your plan will be behind schedule. In this case you will be reacting to difficulties when or after they have happened. This is like fighting a fire. It is much better to anticipate the difficulties, to be proactive and make contingency plans. Prevention is better than cure, as they say.

It is even more important to be proactive in identifying opportunities as you often need to make these happen.

Let's look at some examples of typical difficulties and opportunities and then look at some techniques for being proactive in their identification.

Even if the difficulties in meeting team objectives are caused by external factors or factors beyond your control, it is better to have identified them and thought about an alternative plan. Difficulties could include:

- External factors
  - customer (needs may change)
  - transport (delays, strikes)
  - weather (if project outdoors)
  - legislation (new requirements)
  - politics/economics (change of direction)
- Organisation factors
  - equipment (failure, availability)
  - time, money (changing levels of availability)
  - technology (new, training needed)
  - targets (change in response to other factors)
  - procedures (change in working methods)
- Team issues
  - sickness
  - holidays
  - conflict
  - personal problems
  - skills shortage.

Being proactive means that, if you are running an outdoor event, you have contingency plans for both good and bad weather. If you know new technology is being introduced, you build in time in your plan for training.

Opportunities can be wide ranging and should answer the question: 'What will help the team meet their objectives?' It could be:

- training (an opportunity to up-skill members of the team)
- networking (opportunities to make useful contacts)
- promotional activities (opportunities to advertise your business)
- access to technology or equipment (making the job easier, quicker)
- new procedures (more effective, smarter ways of working).

You can add to these lists from your experience.

Two tools and techniques which may help you identify the opportunities and difficulties that are relevant to your work are **What if?** and **SWOT analysis**.

You have produced a detailed plan for your work project. You now go through each task and ask:

- What if that does not happen?
- What else can I do to meet the team objectives?

So if your plan to leaflet 2,000 local residences includes these two tasks:

1. Collect 2,000 leaflets from the printers.

2. Employ two people to deliver.

your plan B might be:

1. Get quote from alternative printer.

2. Check availability of other team members in case of sickness.

This will help you identify some of the potential difficulties and make sure you have contingency plans in place.

The SWOT analysis can be used with the team as a whole or can be completed by individual team members. It identifies an individual's or team's strengths, weaknesses and any opportunities that help meet objectives or threats that might prevent achievement. A completed SWOT analysis might look like the one shown in Figure B5.4.

Strengths	**Weaknesses**
Staff: good product knowledge	Staff: missing opportunities to engage customer
Opportunities	**Threats**
A local competitor is closing down	New legislation
New technology	Competitor advantage
New markets	Less demand
Events, opportunities for marketing	Economic downturn
	Seasonal variations

Figure B5.4: Completed SWOT analysis

Assessment criterion 3.2 Discuss identified opportunities and difficulties with team members

One advantage of getting each team member to complete their own SWOT analysis is that it gives you an opportunity to discuss it with the individual.

If there are issues that need to be addressed it is better to discuss them privately rather than at a team meeting. So when you start your project, make sure you set up opportunities for regular one-to-one supervision reviews, performance reviews or personal development meetings. If these are planned at the beginning they are perceived by the team as routine development rather than remedial or disciplinary in nature.

There are advantages to meeting away from the work station. It gives the team member a feeling of distance and perspective when reflecting on their performance. In some situations, you may need to be at the work station in order to make easy reference to the individual's work. This could be agreed with the team member, taking into account a respect for their privacy. Even if your feedback is positive, they may want to use this opportunity to raise a sensitive or personal issue.

Keep a confidential record of what was discussed and any development needs identified. Ensure you have agreed any training or development activities with the individual concerned.

Assessment criterion 3.3 Provide advice and support to team members to overcome identified difficulties and challenges

It is usually easier to provide advice and support when team members have identified the difficulties themselves and asked for your support.

Figure B5.5

Unasked-for advice can sometimes seem interfering; unasked-for support can sometimes seem patronising. So, wherever possible, try to create the opportunity for your team members to identify their difficulties and discuss them with you. You can do this by setting up meetings, progress reviews and performance reviews. You can ensure team members come prepared by giving them something a copy of their objectives and asking them to complete progress or achievements to date. Alternatively, you can ask them to complete a SWOT analysis or similar exercise, which encourages them to reflect on their performance.

There may still be some standards of performance that you feel are not being met but that the team member is not aware of, for example standards of appearance or personal hygiene. These are difficult issues to tackle. I had to challenge one of my team many years ago and I will always remember the advice my line manager gave me. 'Be direct, be quick, move on to something else.' There are no hard and fast rules about dealing with delicate or sensitive situations. Each person and situation will be different. Each team leader will have their own way of resolving issues. If in doubt, treat someone as you would want to be treated yourself.

When pointing out poor performance or weaknesses, it may be a case of knowing the team member and how they will react and taking account of your personality and style of management. Some managers and team leaders can be very direct, for instance, but by using humour manage to offend no one.

Here is a list of some useful skills that may help in these situations. Don't follow them as if they were rules – use your judgement of the situation.

- Empathy – if anyone is underperforming, they like to know they are not alone, that it happens to everyone from time to time.
- Feedback sandwich – when pointing out weaknesses, remember to start and finish with a positive.
- Be specific – don't be vague and dismiss the problem out of kindness. It helps everyone if the problem is explained clearly.
- Humour – good to lighten the mood but use sparingly. Even if you direct your humour at the situation, someone else may feel you are laughing at them.

So, on to the solutions. Clearly these will depend on the nature of the difficulties and challenges. Just remember, as with all problem solving, look at a range of possibilities and weigh each one before jumping in and opting for a particular solution. You could consider:

- training
- job shadowing
- buddying
- different ways of working
- personal development activities.

Lastly, remember to give your whole team support and encouragement in meeting their objectives. This might be ongoing praise and recognition for making good progress, or generally raising team spirits when things are going slowly. If you sense everyone's energy is low, you may be able to revitalise them with some team-building activity, a social event, a change of pace, a change of scene, a dress-down Friday, a fancy-dress day or a sponsored event for charity. The list is endless, but remember, the aim is to refresh the team so that they are better able to meet their objectives.

Assessment criterion 3.4 Provide advice and support to team members to make the most of identified opportunities

Difficulties present themselves in a way that is often hard to ignore, whereas opportunities can sometimes slip by almost unnoticed. To support the team in making the most of opportunities, you may need to be more proactive in identifying the opportunities. Some opportunities were identified in section 3.1 above.

Some opportunities you can create for your team. For example, if you notice one of your team often shows others how to do a particular job, you might suggest they take a lead at one of the team meetings. If someone has developed a good professional rapport with another department or a customer on the phone, you might suggest they attend the next face-to-face meeting. If someone shows an interest in the new product range, you might invite them to attend a trade exhibition.

Initially, these may seem to cost money or take up valuable work time, but they are one of the most effective ways to develop the team. The developments are personal and based on the individuals' strengths and interests and as such could provide a springboard for further training, development and promotion. A broader range of skills in the team will strengthen not only the motivation of the individual but the team as a whole.

These opportunities can be random and it is important to ensure you are creating or offering them fairly and equally to everyone in the team.

The case study below provides an opportunity for you to read about a team leader or team leading scenario. It highlights some of the issues discussed. You can use this to reflect on the situation and answer some questions. You do not have to write down your answers unless your tutor or assessor has asked you to do so.

CASE STUDY 3

During the preparation for the festivals, Marlon decided to stay in regular contact with his team. Every few days he sent an email or a text message to update them on his preparations. He phoned them every week to ask how they were getting on, whether they had everything they needed and whether they needed any support.

The stall decoration team had managed to gather all the materials they would need but were having difficulties finding a staple gun, their local supplier having run out. Luckily Marlon knew someone who agreed to lend them one.

The costume team were struggling to find time to make the outfits. They had probably been a bit ambitious and now had their work cut out. In addition, one of the team had four days' holiday coming up the next week. Marlon suggested they get the stall decorators involved as they had had less to do so far.

Marlon also noticed that the local park was having a community fair and suggested that this might provide an opportunity to test the cakes, stall and costumes. It would also give the team some experience of dealing with customers and processing payments ahead of the busy festivals.

What do you think?

1. How proactive has Marlon been in identifying difficulties and opportunities?
2. How has he helped his team overcome any difficulties?
3. What effect do you think his actions may have had on his team?
4. Without his advice and support, what might have happened?
5. The fair provides an opportunity for the team. Do you think it is worth them doing the fair?
6. If this was your team, how would you encourage them to take this opportunity?

DEVELOPMENT ACTIVITY 3 with your virtual adviser

I am here to demystify the assessment criteria and help you relate what you have learned to your own job role. We will look at what you are currently doing and how you can develop your skills and have a real impact in your workplace.

Draw up a simple table with three columns. In the first column write **Where am I now?** and, as if you were explaining to me, make a few notes about your strengths and weaknesses when supporting team members. Be specific and provide some examples. Be honest with yourself – this is not part of your assessment, and identifying weaknesses is the first step to making improvements.

The questions below may help you.

Where am I now?
Think about the support you give your team members in helping them overcome difficulties and make the most of opportunities.

1. What are some of the difficulties experienced by your team which could have prevented them from achieving their objectives?
2. When and how did you discuss difficulties and opportunities with team members? Did you plan regular one-to-one meetings or discuss them informally as and when situations arose?
3. What advice and support did you give your team to help them overcome these difficulties?
4. What opportunities were there to help the team achieve their objectives?
5. How did you find out about these opportunities?
6. How did you encourage the team to make the most of these opportunities?

Now, in your second column, write the heading **Improvements** and in the third column **Action**.

> **Improvements and action**
>
> Are there any areas where your advice and support could be improved?
>
> What action do you need to take to make those improvements?
>
> Some of the changes you have identified might affect the way things are done in your organisation and you may need to discuss them with your line manager. Some changes can be made by you. Remember, small changes can make a big difference.
>
> When you plan to make a change, remember to make your new objectives SMART!
>
> You can discuss the notes you have made with your assessor. They may provide evidence of your competence.

Learning outcome 4 – Be able to monitor and evaluate progress and recognise individual and team achievement

In this section we will explore each of the assessment criteria in more detail to develop your knowledge and understanding.

Assessment criterion 4.1 Monitor and evaluate individual and team activities and progress

There are opportunities during a project and on completion for you to monitor progress and evaluate the success of both individual performance and the overall success of the team in meeting its objectives.

It is important to **monitor** progress during the project so that you can:

- support and encourage team members
- identify problems or conflict within the team
- get the project back on track if standards or deadlines are slipping.

On completion you can evaluate the success of an individual's performance and the team's success so they:

- can be rewarded for their success
- make plans for future developments
- demonstrate suitability for future projects.

Monitoring progress during a project can be done in many ways, from a very informal question of 'How's it going?' to a formal review. Monitoring can be done by assessing results, for example how many sales have been achieved, or in discussion with the team member. This discussion can be face to face, by phone/text or email. You need to look at the advantages and disadvantages of each method and work out what will work best for you.

Assessing performance by looking at the figures works well in some environments. In a call centre you can see at a glance how many calls per hour an individual is handling. In a retail environment, you can check the till readings and see how many customers have been served and whether the till balances at the end of the shift. These checks provide reliable information. They are also unobtrusive and allow the team member to get on with their job without interruption. But they show only part of the picture and do not assess whether the team member needs support in order to improve their performance.

It is important to make direct contact with individuals to discuss performance. If things are not going well, they can explain the reason why. You have the opportunity to agree remedial action.

If the contact with team members is informal it can create a relaxed working environment: asking how people are getting on, telling them to talk to you any time. However, relying on this method has its disadvantages. You need some boundaries, some time when you are not available so that you can do other work. Often those team members who are not performing well or have problems are the last people to come to see you voluntarily. Your team may be spread out geographically and those furthest away will not have the same access as those who work in the same building as you.

So it is wise to schedule formal team meetings or one-to-one supervision where everyone gets an equal chance to update you on progress and access any support they need. In this way, the monitoring of performance is a joint activity and not a case of a team leader chasing, or nagging the team to do better. These sessions can be arranged in a way that gives each team member responsibility for achieving their objectives. Individuals who are treated like adults will tend to respond like adults; treated like children they will respond like children.

Once you've assessed someone's performance, don't forget to give them feedback. Everyone needs feedback on their performance. Ideally, we all want that feedback to be 100 per cent positive to make us feel good. However, it is even more valuable to receive good constructive feedback on our areas of weakness because this is what will help us improve.

Recognising positive performance is explored in section 4.2 below. If a team member's performance is poor and you need to give negative feedback, you can still do this in a constructive way by:

- starting with a positive
- sandwiching the negative in the middle
- ending with another positive.

For example: 'You've managed to make contact with a good number of customers on the shop floor this week. I'd like to see more converted to sales, how do you think you could achieve that? (Maybe suggests more listening and questioning around customer needs.) Yes, try that this week. You are very good at listening, I think that will work well.'

Acknowledging what the team member has done well relaxes them and makes them less defensive when you want to discuss other issues. And it is important to finish with a positive so they go away motivated rather than devastated. This is often referred to as the feedback sandwich.

It is said that we all hear the negatives about ourselves more than the positives, so when giving feedback remember to find genuine positive feedback and make sure it is heard.

Feedback can be given on any number of occasions, but remember to build it in as an essential feature of appraisals, one-to-one discussions/reviews and in team meetings.

Assessment criterion 4.2 Provide recognition when individual and team objectives have been achieved

Some organisations reward achievement of objectives and targets with bonuses and prizes. There are certain environments where these rewards are a major incentive and it is usually where targets are high and a team member would have to work extremely hard to meet them.

Other working environments are less stressful and the objectives more achievable. Individuals still need some form of recognition when objectives have been met, otherwise work becomes one long thankless task and individuals become demotivated.

If we just consider how you give verbal feedback to an individual who has met their targets, there are many ways this can be done. It won't have a great effect if you mention it casually at the end of a conversation, starting with the words 'By the way …'. You could say this kind of recognition is given grudgingly. Much better to plan what you are going to say and be as positive as possible.

It will usually have more impact if the recognition is given in front of others. So it is worth adding an item to the agenda of the next meeting so the achievement of the individual and the team is acknowledged more widely.

To have a more senior manager within the organisation recognise achievements can reinforce the link between the team's targets and the overall company performance indicators. This builds a greater sense of achievement and strengthens identification with and commitment to the organisation. And then there are other rewards that may motivate teams: prizes for high achievers (often used in sales environments), employee of the month, which brings status and recognition, articles in company newsletters, meals out to celebrate, and so on.

Any rewards offered must be equally motivating for all the team. It is no good offering bottles of champagne if half the team do not drink alcohol. The rewards should also be in keeping with the values of the organisation, so a health and fitness team are unlikely to offer boxes of cigars to top performers.

Whatever way you choose to reward your team and its members, whether it is a physical or verbal reward, the golden rule is:

Never let good performance go unrecognised!

The case study below provides an opportunity for you to read about a team leader or team leading scenario. It highlights some of the issues discussed. You can use this to reflect on the situation and answer some questions. You do not have to write down your answers unless your tutor or assessor has asked you to do so.

The team set up the stall at the first festival. They worked out their shifts, dressed up and the work began. Marlon had agreed to work in the background, making sure they had enough change, banking money and topping up supplies of cakes as they ran out. When they were busy Marlon was useful and worked alongside the team as an extra pair of hands, but during quiet moments he fussed around, endlessly checking on sales and supplies. The team wished he would relax or leave them alone.

At the end of three days, Marlon was able to give the team some feedback on their performance. They had sold more than double the number in the original target. He praised their contribution in decorating the stall so well and for producing amazing costumes. He also acknowledged how individual team members had improved, becoming more confident with the customers, working longer hours, supporting other members who were tired or flagging. He finished by giving them the dates for the next festival where they would be doing it all over again in two weeks' time.

What do you think?

1. How did Marlon monitor progress during the festival?
2. What effect did this have on the team?
3. Do you think he was justified? How else could he have monitored them?
4. How did Marlon evaluate their overall performance?
5. What feedback did he give? Was it all positive?
6. How could he have created an opportunity for improvements?
7. What recognition did he give for a job well done? In your opinion, was it enough?
8. What else might you have planned to say in this debriefing meeting if you were Marlon?

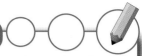

DEVELOPMENT ACTIVITY 4 with your virtual adviser

I am here to demystify the assessment criteria and help you relate what you have learned to your own job role. We will look at what you are currently doing and how you can develop your skills and have a real impact in your workplace.

Draw up a simple table with three columns. In the first column write **Where am I now?** and, as if you were explaining to me, make a few notes about your strengths and weaknesses when monitoring individual and team progress and recognising achievement. Be specific and provide some examples. Be honest with yourself – this is not part of your assessment, and identifying weaknesses is the first step to making improvements.

The following questions may help you.

Where am I now?

Think about how you monitor the progress of your team, how you evaluate their achievements, how you give feedback and how you recognise their success.

1. When monitoring your team's progress, how would you describe your management style? Are you hands-on, intervening, do you stand back and let them get on with it, or somewhere in between?

2. What opportunities do you create for the team to discuss their progress with you?

3. How do you evaluate achievements? What do you use as a measure when judging an individual's or team's success?

4. How do you provide recognition when an individual or team meet their objectives?

Now, in your second column, write the heading **Improvements** and in the third column **Action**.

Improvements and action

Are there any areas where your skills could be improved?

What action do you need to take to make those improvements?

Some of the changes you have identified might affect the way things are done in your organisation and you may need to discuss them with your line manager. Some changes can be made by you. Remember, small changes can make a big difference.

When you plan to make a change, remember to make your new objectives SMART!

You can discuss the notes you have made with your assessor. They may provide evidence of your competence.

TEST YOUR KNOWLEDGE

Here are some questions to test your knowledge and understanding of the issues explored in this unit. You can write down the answers or discuss them with your assessor. They could provide good evidence for your NVQ.

1. What is the purpose of a team? AC 1.1

2. Why should team objectives be SMART? AC 1.2

3. Give three examples of when and where you can communicate the team's purpose and objectives to its members. AC 1.3

4. How do you involve team members in planning how to meet objectives? AC 2.1

5. What activities encourage team members to participate and think creatively? AC 2.2

6. Describe how you record team plans and what details you include in this plan. AC 2.3

7. Give examples of the SMART work objectives you have set and agreed with team members. AC 2.4

8. Identify two difficulties your team members have faced. How and when did you discuss these with the person involved? AC 3.1/3.2

9. What advice and support have you given to help overcome other difficulties or challenges the team has faced? AC 3.3

10. Identify two opportunities to meet targets that presented themselves to your team. How were these discussed? AC 3.1/3.2

11. How have you encouraged team members to make the most of identified opportunities? AC 3.4

12. How do you monitor individual progress? AC 4.1

13. How do you evaluate the success of team activities? AC 4.1

14. How do you reward individuals/the team when objectives have been met? AC 4.2

Pulling it all together and gathering evidence

You and your assessor will need to agree the most appropriate sources of evidence. Here are some suggestions:

- An electronic portfolio: you could upload your evidence to an e-portfolio package or simply store the evidence in electronic format.

- A paper-based portfolio: you could build a folder with hard copies of your evidence.

Types of evidence:

- Observation: a record by your assessor when observing you in a team meeting planning how you will meet your objectives.

- Work product: copies of work produced by you that demonstrate your competence, for example a copy of your plan of work, individual objectives you have set, records of progress reviews, minutes of meetings.

- Discussion: a record of you and your assessor discussing examples of how you overcame difficulties and how you encouraged your team.

- Questioning: a record of your assessor asking questions to test your knowledge.

- Personal statement, reflective account or case study based on the activities in this unit – this should have sentences which start with 'I …' and should tell a story giving real-life examples.

- Witness testimony from your line manager confirming your competence, in writing or recorded as a discussion with your assessor.

It is a good idea to include a range of evidence from different sources. Your evidence should cover a period of time and not be a 'one-off'. However, try to keep the evidence to a minimum. Your assessor can make a note of product evidence they have seen so it can be left in the workplace.

Remember:

Less is more – quality not quantity!

Be holistic – can you use this evidence again for other units?

EVALUATION

What have you learned from completing this unit?

What new skills and techniques are you using?

How has this affected the people you work with?

How has your organisation benefited? How might it benefit in the future?

B11 MANAGING EQUALITY AND DIVERSITY

Introduction and learning outcomes

Learning outcomes for Unit B11:

1. Be able to understand your own responsibilities under equality legislation, relevant codes of practice and own organisational policies.

2. Be able to communicate an organisation's written equality, diversity and inclusion policy and procedures within your own area of responsibility.

3. Be able to monitor equality, diversity and inclusion within your own area of responsibility.

These learning outcomes say what you will have learned by the end of this unit. Each learning outcome is further broken down into assessment criteria, which we will look at in detail in the following sections of this unit.

This Unit Guide is a resource to help you gather the evidence you require to achieve Unit B11. It can be used as a learning resource if you are new to the role, are studying team leading in preparation for work or as a refresher if you are already an experienced team leader.

You and your assessor will agree what you need to do to meet the assessment criteria and show you are competent. This Unit Guide provides some theory to develop your understanding of managing equality and diversity, gives some case studies for you to examine and then an opportunity for you to reflect, with a virtual adviser, on how you can develop your own skills and gather evidence of competence. Some ideas are provided in the 'Pulling it all together' section at the end of this unit.

So, the purpose of this unit is to develop the skills and knowledge you need to manage equality and diversity.

What do we mean by equality, diversity and inclusion?

Equality is about making sure everyone is treated fairly. It does not mean everyone has to be treated in exactly the same way. It recognises that even though people's needs are different, they should all be offered a fair opportunity. **Diversity** is about valuing the differences between people. It is not just another word for equality. By valuing the differences between people, and recognising the varied contributions that people can make, all employees are encouraged to realise their full potential. **Inclusion** is about making sure no one is left out. This could mean ensuring all employees, from cleaners to the board of directors, have a say in the planning and decision-making processes.

To embrace equality, diversity and inclusion creates a positive working environment, motivated employees, and a wider pool of ideas and experience to better serve the needs of customers with different backgrounds. It makes good business sense.

Learning outcome 1 – Be able to understand your own responsibilities under equality legislation, relevant codes of practice and own organisational policies

In this section we will explore each of the assessment criteria in more detail to develop your knowledge and understanding.

Assessment criterion 1.1 Explain how equality of opportunity, diversity and inclusion relate to legal, industry requirements and organisational policies

So if it makes such good sense, why isn't everyone adopting best practice? Why do we need legislation?

Figure B11.1

When resources are in short supply, it is easier to spend whatever time, energy and money you have on things that produce immediate results. Imagine having a piece of cake but not being able to taste it for several months – you wouldn't bother, would you? When a job vacancy comes up, sometimes it seems quicker and easier to advertise it in the usual place or just offer it to a temp, rather than advertise as widely as possible across various local communities to encourage a diverse range of applicants. But who measures the cost to the business of that missed opportunity? One of the strategies used by London Underground to increase the number of women tube train drivers (there were only 100 women out of the 3,000 workforce) was to place an ad in 'Cosmopolitan' magazine. A single ad was placed in January 2001 and London Transport was inundated with 1,400 responses.

The other barrier is awareness. Not every manager is aware of the diverse needs of the existing customer base, let alone that of potential customers. Not every manager knows the diverse make-up of customers or even of the organisation's employees. Not every manager could say whether the organisation's policies and procedures made everyone feel included or not. So, where good practice is not happening, legislation is in place to protect those who experience discrimination.

The Equality Act 2010 updates, simplifies and strengthens the previous legislation. It:

- protects individuals from unfair treatment and
- promotes a fair and more equal society.

It is worth noting that there will be further consultation on aspects of equality legislation and its implementation will be affected by the outcome of various cases tried in court. There are some website addresses at the end of this section so that you can look at the legislation in more detail and check the most up-to-date information.

Before October 2010, there were many different acts which made it unlawful to discriminate. For example:

- Equal Pay Act 1970
- Sex Discrimination Act 1975
- Race Relations Act 1976 and Amended Act 2000
- Disability Discrimination Act 1995 and Disability Equality Duty 2005
- Equality Act 2006.

These acts were growing in number as new characteristics, for example age, sexual orientation, religion or belief, were added to the original protected characteristics of sex, race and disability. As society and its values change, so new legislation is needed to reflect those changes.

The Equality Act 2010 covers a wider range of people, protecting those with the following **protected characteristics**:

- age
- disability
- gender reassignment

- marriage and civil partnership
- pregnancy and maternity
- race (including ethnic or national origins, colour and nationality)
- religion or belief (including lack of belief)
- sex
- sexual orientation.

The Act makes it unlawful to:

- discriminate directly against anyone because they have (or are perceived to have) a protected characteristic
- discriminate indirectly by imposing a policy or practice covering everyone in the same way but that disadvantages one particular group
- harass someone by unwanted conduct which intimidates, humiliates or offends them in relation to a protected characteristic (includes unwanted conduct that is sexual in nature)
- victimise a person because they have made a complaint about any of the above.

The Act obliges employers to:

- make reasonable adjustments to the workplace or to policies and practice to accommodate diverse needs of customers and employees.

The Act allows employers to:

- use positive action where a particular group is under-represented.

To understand how the Act might apply to everyday situations, let's have a look at the following situations. Do you think these are lawful? Compare with the guidance to find out what is and what is not lawful under the Equality Act.

Figure B11.2: **A team**

CASE STUDY 1

Martin applies for a job in a call centre. As the organisation currently employs ten women, the employer decides not to interview Martin because, as the only male employee, he probably would not fit in.

Would this be lawful?

This is direct discrimination because someone has been treated less favourably than another person because of a protected characteristic. This is *not* lawful.

CASE STUDY 2

Jim phones his local garage to enquire about a job he has seen advertised in the paper. The garage owner refuses to consider Jim, making an assumption from his voice that he is gay.

Would this be lawful?

This is direct discrimination. Jim would be protected by the law whether or not he is gay. The law also covers people who have been wrongly thought to have a protected characteristic or have been treated as if they do.

CASE STUDY 3

A cleaning company decides to change its working practice so that all employees have to work some evening and weekend shifts. One employee, Jonathan, can work weekdays only when the local day centre is open as in the evenings and at weekends he looks after his partner who is in a wheelchair.

Would this be lawful?

Unless the company can justify its policy, for example a major new contract for out-of-hours cleaning, this would be indirect discrimination. It is *not* lawful to impose a rule on everyone which particularly disadvantages people who share a protected characteristic.

CASE STUDY 4

The board of directors of a large finance company are interviewing two internal candidates, Phillip and Jane, for promotion to the board. Both candidates are equally qualified and suitable for the job. They decide to take positive action and employ Jane because women are under-represented at this level of senior management.

LEARNING OUTCOME 1

Would this be lawful?

Yes, this example of positive action is lawful. Employers have always been able to encourage applications from under-represented groups or provide training, but now, as long as the candidates are of equal merit, they can appoint an individual because their group is under-represented.

CASE STUDY 5

A busy restaurant is recruiting additional kitchen staff and looking for people who will be reliable. William applies and at the interview is asked whether he had any absences due to sickness in his previous job.

Would this be lawful?

No, it is *not* lawful for an employee to ask questions about a person's health or disability until the applicant has been offered the job. The applicant can be asked questions that assess suitability for the job, for example a roofing company can ask about an employee's ability to climb ladders and work safely at heights, as this is intrinsic to the job. Once a job offer has been made, an employer can ask whether the successful applicant needs any reasonable adjustments to be made in order for them to carry out the work.

CASE STUDY 6

Simone has organised a conference where a woman decides to breastfeed her baby during one of the speeches. Simone feels this will distract other delegates and asks the woman to find somewhere else to breastfeed.

Would this be lawful?

No, this is *not* lawful as it discriminates against a woman because she is breastfeeding a child.

CASE STUDY 7

Ranjit is shopping in her local grocery store and overhears two shop assistants discussing immigration in a derogatory and racially abusive way. Ranjit feels humiliated and degraded although she is British and knows the comments are not directed at her.

Would this be lawful?

No, this is *not* lawful and Ranjit can make a claim of harassment.

Harassment can be:

- unwanted conduct related to a protected characteristic
- unwanted conduct that is sexual in nature.

Harassment has to be unwanted. It is unlawful, whether it is intended or not. A claim will take into account the customer's perception of the unwanted conduct. It does not have to be directed at the customer for it to be harassment. The customer does not have to have the protected characteristic for it to amount to harassment.

Assessment criterion 1.2 Describe how equality of opportunity, diversity and inclusion are considered in planning own area of responsibility

Careful planning is needed to build in opportunities for equality wherever your job affects people. This could be colleagues, team members or customers. You need to break down your job into all the various tasks you carry out and identify who contributes to that process and who benefits from that process. At each stage, ask yourself whether any aspect of your work:

- treats one group less favourably than another, either directly or indirectly
- fails to use the diversity of the workforce in a positive way
- fails to include all groups and all individuals.

An example might be when you call a meeting. If you are using a venue that does not have nearby disabled parking, you are making it more difficult for some individuals to attend that meeting. Your action could be a case of indirect discrimination and would make those who were unable to attend feel excluded. By considering the needs of everyone when planning the meeting, this situation could be avoided. You would then benefit by having the diverse views of any disabled attendees expressed at the meeting.

Complete the development activity below to look at the way you currently plan your work.

DEVELOPMENT ACTIVITY 1 with your virtual adviser

I am here to demystify the assessment criteria and help you relate what you have learned to your own job role. We will look at what you are currently doing and how you can develop your skills and have a real impact in your workplace.

Draw up a simple table with three columns. In the first column write **Where am I now?** and, as if you were explaining to me, make a few notes about your strengths and weaknesses when planning work for your team. Be specific and provide some examples. Be honest with yourself – this is not part of your assessment, and identifying weaknesses is the first step to making improvements.

The following questions may help you.

Where am I now?

Tell me about how you currently consider equality, diversity and inclusion in the planning of your work. You may have different responsibilities depending on the sector you work in:

1. Do you work for a public-sector organisation?

2. Does your company sell goods and/or services?

3. Outside of your paid employment, do you play a role in a voluntary or community organisation?

4. Do you help run a club with 25 or more members with rules about the selection of members?

5. Have you consulted the relevant Equality Act Guides?

6. How do you identify every aspect of your job that involves other people?

7. How do you ensure everyone you deal with is treated equally and fairly?

8. How does the diversity in your team contribute positively to your organisation's objectives?

9. How do you know all your team feel included in all the various work activities?

Now, in your second column, write the heading **Improvements** and in the third column **Action**.

Improvements and action

Are there any areas where your planning could be improved?

What action do you think you could take to make those improvements happen?

Some of the changes you have identified might affect the way things are done in your organisation and you may need to discuss them with your line manager. Some changes can be made by you. Remember, small changes can make a big difference.

When you plan to make a change, remember to make your new objectives SMART!

You can discuss the notes you have made with your assessor. They may provide evidence of your competence.

Learning outcome 2 – Be able to communicate an organisation's written equality, diversity and inclusion policy and procedures within own area of responsibility

In this section we will explore each of the assessment criteria in more detail to develop your knowledge and understanding.

Assessment criterion 2.1 Outline the organisation's equality, diversity and inclusion policy and procedures

Organisations may have written equality, diversity and inclusion policies and procedures in place but they are of little value if they are not communicated to, and understood by, all employees.

First, we can review how best to communicate policy and procedures by looking at the communication channels available. Then let's look at what can be communicated without sending everyone in your team to sleep.

Figure B11.3

There are many ways to communicate policies and procedures to employees, for example:

- training days
- mentoring
- meetings/team briefings
- issuing hard copy
- intranet access
- email
- changing procedures.

They each have advantages and disadvantages.

Training days can bring in trainers with particular expertise and can allow employees to focus on an issue away from the distractions of the workplace. However, it can be an expensive option and sometimes difficult to release everyone from their work at the same time.

Mentoring is about using a role model, someone with experience, to guide and develop employees. Ken Mortimer, an employee at HMRC, introduced a reverse mentoring scheme to raise awareness and combat assumptions made about gay people in the workplace. A gay employee would mentor one of the directors or senior managers, who in turn would use what they had learned to influence change in the organisation. The scheme was introduced in 2007 and HMRC subsequently won an equality award (*Sunday Times'* 'Best Company To Work For' Awards). Following the success of this scheme, HMRC introduced a similar Race Equality Scheme for 2008–2011.

Meetings/team briefings can be arranged locally and may be a regular part of the working week. They can vary in length. This makes them easy and convenient ways of conveying information. However, there are often so many items to be discussed – more than the ideal of three agenda items per meeting – that an important piece of training can be dealt with quickly and superficially.

Issuing hard copy or providing intranet access does not ensure that everyone has read key documents. If the information is important legislation, a company may ask the employee to sign to confirm they have read and understood it. Most people will sign, but there is no way to really check understanding.

Email provides electronic proof that a document has been sent to an individual but is no guarantee that the document has been read or understood. Most employees receive a large number of emails – some have to be dealt with immediately, others can be put aside and skimmed at a later date. Providing an electronic questionnaire that has to be returned by a specific date is a form of e-training which will ensure the document is read and the basics understood. However, this method gives no opportunities to ask questions.

The final one on our list, changing procedures, is not really a communication channel but is one of the most powerful unspoken rules in an organisation.

Figure B11.4

If there is a company procedure that says:

- on the delegate's invite to a meeting, ask whether we need to accommodate any particular physical or dietary needs

then anyone who needs a hearing loop, large print on handouts, wheelchair access, gluten-free lunch will feel included.

If there is a company procedure that says:

- prizes for best sales team must be beneficial to all, i.e. no alcohol, no chocolate, no vouchers for Top Man then those who do not drink alcohol for religious or health reasons, those who cannot eat sugar and anyone who does not shop in Top Man will feel included.

If there is a company procedure that says:

- every job vacancy will be advertised widely and especially targeted at groups that are under-represented

then those under-represented groups will feel included.

Embedding equality, diversity and inclusion in all your policies will give a clear message to your team.

- Treat people as individuals – everyone is different, get to know your team, your colleagues, your customers.
- Avoid stereotypes and don't make assumptions based on people's characteristics (remember to ASSUME makes an ASS out of U and ME).
- Treat everyone fairly, as you would like to be treated.
- Remember that a one-rule-for-everyone policy won't always work as it will disadvantage some more than others.
- Enjoy the diversity – appreciate the benefits it brings rather than seeing it as a hurdle to be crossed.

The case study below provides an opportunity for you to read about a team leader or team leading scenario. The case study highlights some of the issues discussed. You can use this to reflect on the situation and answer some questions. You do not have to write down your answers unless your tutor or assessor has asked you to do so.

CASE STUDY 8

Anya is from Poland and feels her English is not as good as everyone else's in the finance team. She worries that everyone will laugh at her mistakes. Once a month the team meet up on a Sunday morning for a bike ride or a walk. Anya is invited but cannot go as she goes to church on Sunday mornings. Anya likes her job, she has many years' experience in finance and has ideas about how to improve the systems, but says nothing. She finds her co-workers very polite but she does not feel included.

What do you think?

1. In what ways do you think Anya is missing out by not being included?
2. What assumptions do you think the team might have made about her?

3. In what ways do you think the team and the organisation are missing out?

4. If you were the team leader, what steps would you take to turn this situation around?

5. How might you change procedures so that this situation would not arise in future?

DEVELOPMENT ACTIVITY 2 with your virtual adviser

I am here to demystify the assessment criteria and help you relate what you have learned to your own job role. We will look at what you are currently doing and how you can develop your skills and have a real impact in your workplace.

Draw up a simple table with three columns. In the first column write **Where am I now?** and, as if you were explaining to me, make a few notes about your strengths and weaknesses when making contributions and acknowledging the contributions of others in a meeting. Be specific and provide some examples. Be honest with yourself – this is not part of your assessment, and identifying weaknesses is the first step to making improvements.

The questions below may help you.

Where am I now?
Think about the organisation you work for:

- How would you summarise your organisation's equality, diversity and inclusion policy?
- How up to date is it and how often is it reviewed?
- What are the channels in your organisation for influencing policies and procedures?

Think about your area of responsibility:

- What are the key messages about equality, diversity and inclusion that you want to communicate to your team?
- How can you embed these into day-to-day procedures?
- How can you best communicate these messages to your team?

Now, in your second column, write the heading **Improvements** and in the third column **Action**.

Improvements and action
Are there any areas where your contribution to meetings could be improved?

What action do you need to take to make those improvements?

Some of the changes you have identified might affect the way things are done in your organisation and you may need to discuss them with your line manager. Some changes can be made by you. Remember, small changes can make a big difference.

When you plan to make a change, remember to make your new objectives SMART!

You can discuss the notes you have made with your assessor. They may provide evidence of your competence.

Learning outcome 3 – Be able to monitor equality, diversity and inclusion within own area of responsibility

In this section we will explore each of the assessment criteria in more detail to develop your knowledge and understanding.

Assessment criterion 3.1 Monitor how equality, diversity and inclusion activities in own area of responsibility are in line with own responsibility

To monitor means to check or give warning of a situation.

We monitor a whole range of activities, from babies crying to the condition of a failing heart, to the possibility of an earthquake. Monitor lizards were supposedly named because they would listen and give warning that crocodiles were approaching. So monitoring is not simply about gathering data and ticking boxes; it implies that if we don't do it the results could be disastrous. Monitoring can mean we avoid disaster, it can mean survival.

By monitoring equality, diversity and inclusion in your own area of responsibility, you can ensure that your team and your customers are treated fairly. The motivation and loyalty that this brings will, in turn, contribute to the success of your organisation. Organisations that do not monitor and improve the way they treat employees and customers may not survive in an increasingly diverse society.

There are many models for monitoring an activity or a process and they all encompass the following stages:

1. Design and plan.

2. Agree.

3. Collect data.

4. Analyse and interpret.

5. Make recommendations.

We will now look at each of these stages in more detail, identify the skills needed and suggest some tools that may help you.

1 Design and plan

Monitoring cannot be a one-off observation or an assumption based on anecdotal evidence. This type of information is not reliable. Monitoring has to be carried out routinely and systematically. It needs to be planned. You can start by identifying the who? what? why? where? how? and when? of monitoring.

First, identify why the organisation should monitor equality, diversity and inclusion:

- There are legal requirements to be met.
- There may be industry requirements, for example if you are working in the care sector your customers will have a range of diverse abilities. If you work in catering, your customers will have a range of diverse dietary requirements.

- Your organisation should have a policy which states the overall aims and intentions. And maybe a mission statement.
- Your organisation may have made promises to customers about the way they will be treated in a customer service charter.
- Although not always in writing, every organisation has a set of underpinning values which is a basic agreement of how you collectively believe the job should be done.

Before we can say whether we are meeting the overall aims, we need to know and understand what those aims are. Before any monitoring can start, we need to clarify what we want to measure. The activities that directly affect employees and customers were considered in section 2. We now need to identify what data can be collected to measure each of these activities.

At this point it is important to remember the Data Protection Act, which states that personal data must be:

- processed fairly and used accurately only for the stated purpose
- stored safely, especially if in transit, and for no longer than needed
- gathered with the person's consent and right of access.

Once the measurable data has been identified it is easy to see how it is collected, who collects it and when it is collected. It makes sense to follow the natural sequence of events and build your plan around everyday activities. A simple table like the one below could help you design your monitoring plan or schedule.

Table B11.1: Designing a schedule

Who? Team members	What? Training activity	Why? Chosen because:	Why not? No training because:	When? Review training
Bill	Management training July 2011	Identified at annual appraisal		August and February
Marta			No training – investigate	August and February
Paolo	Management training July 2011	Requested training		August and February

2 Agreeing the monitoring plan

At the mention of monitoring, some employees' reactions can be negative:

- Why are they checking up on me?
- What a waste of time!

- Why bother? Nothing's going to change.
- I don't have time for this.
- This is nothing to do with me and my job.

It is essential to communicate the purpose of monitoring, convince employees of the benefit and gain their trust and cooperation. Some useful skills to have here would be:

- preparing the points you want to make
- communicating the purpose clearly at an appropriate time
- allowing people to ask questions
- listening to their ideas and objections
- negotiating, where possible
- giving feedback on the monitoring
- celebrating success and improvements.

3 Data collection

In order for the results to be useful, the data collected must be valid and reliable. By valid, we mean that the data measures what it is supposed to measure. Using a clock or stopwatch is a valid method of measuring the length of a phone call; it is not a valid tool for gauging temperature. Counting the number of complaints is possibly a valid measure of overall customer satisfaction; it does not tell us anything about the nature of the complaints. A more valid way of collecting this information might be to keep a written log of complaints. By reliable, we expect the data to give a true picture of the situation, not on one occasion but over a period of time. Collecting data routinely and systematically at set intervals will provide more reliable results than a one-off collection which may not be representative.

As mentioned earlier, in relation to the Data Protection Act, it is important to be clear about the purpose of gathering data. In this case, the aim is to use individual data to check on the effectiveness of systems and highlight where procedures could be improved. The purpose is not to monitor individuals and therefore data, once gathered, can be anonymised.

Much of the data gathered will be statistical, for example the number of employees who are under 25, or over 55 years old, the number of customers who are male or female, the number of employees who have English as a second language.

There may be issues of equality, diversity and inclusion that do not appear in any written record and therefore cannot be gathered from existing documentation. For example, the religion of employees, or any beliefs that affect the drinking of alcohol or eating of meat, dairy etc. This information may have to be gathered in some kind of survey or questionnaire. Evidence of this kind of diversity in the workplace could highlight practices that need to change, for example:

- team-building activities on a day of religious significance
- bottles of champagne for achievement of team targets
- lack of dietary choice in working lunches.

Remember, all data should be gathered with sensitivity and anonymised and you should always be very clear about the purpose and the benefits of collecting the data.

4 Analysis and interpretation

Gathering data is a meaningless activity unless it is analysed. To analyse the data is to break it down into categories. To give it meaning it is useful to compare it to other data. This could be an internal measure, for example comparing the gender of senior managers with the gender mix five years ago or ten years ago. This would help measure progress. Alternatively, you could choose an external benchmark such as a national average or an average across different countries.

Spreadsheet packages allow both analysis of data and an easy conversion into graphs or charts to ensure that presentation of your findings is attractive and accessible.

5 Reporting your findings

Finally, when your data has been analysed and interpreted, you are ready to report your findings. Consider who your report is for and agree with them how you will present it. Would a presentation at a meeting have a greater and wider impact? Is it being seen or heard by those with the authority to make changes?

- Keep it short.
- Show the main trends.
- Make clear comparisons.
- Show data as visually interesting.
- Make clear recommendations.
- Be factual, avoid opinions.
- Back up your points with evidence.
- Be positive, sell the benefits.
- Celebrate improvements.

There may be more benefits to the organisation if employees are involved in discussions, can contribute their ideas and come up with recommendations for improvements. This would reflect a culture of inclusion.

Managing equality, diversity and inclusion is not a specific task which you can put on a 'to do' list and tick it off by 11 a.m. on a Wednesday. As with all the people skills needed by a team leader, it affects the way you do nearly every single aspect of your job. There are some very simple steps you can take to improve equality, diversity and inclusion in your area of responsibility. You can also boost the awareness of your team and develop in them a more positive, inclusive approach. Small steps can begin a process of change that could revolutionise the culture of your organisation.

Case study 9 provides an opportunity for you to read about a team leader or team leading scenario. The case study highlights some of the issues discussed. You can use this to reflect on the situation and answer some questions. You do not have to write down your answers unless your tutor or assessor has asked you to do so.

CASE STUDY 9

Maxine is asked to monitor the way that customer complaints are handled by the call centre. The call centre receives approximately ten complaints a month and follows this procedure:

- To refer all complaints to a team leader
- who would respond within 24 hours and
- investigate the complaint and
- resolve the issue within five working days.

Maxine talks to the staff and spends several hours listening in to their conversations with customers. She notices that not all complaints are referred to a team leader; some are dealt with effectively by the member of staff; some are not dealt with at all. Staff explain that complaints are not referred if, for example:

- the customer is elderly and has 'just phoned up to have a moan'
- the customer's accent is too difficult to understand
- the person is asking for a service that they don't provide, for example contact by text rather than phone for a hearing-impaired customer.

Maxine talks to the team about the need to treat all customers' needs as equally important and always follow the company procedure, which they agree to do. The following month the number of complaints has doubled to 20.

What do you think?

1. Why do you think staff have filtered out some of the complaints?
2. What are the effects of this filtering on the customer? And on the organisation?
3. How would you interpret the increased number of complaints? Is this a sign that monitoring is making things worse?
4. If a procedure is not followed and everyone deals with situations in their own way, what impact could this have on equality?
5. How else can Maxine monitor the effectiveness of the customer complaints procedure in relation to equality and diversity?

DEVELOPMENT ACTIVITY 3 with your virtual adviser

I am here to demystify the assessment criteria and help you relate what you have learned to your own job role. We will look at what you are currently doing and how you can develop your skills and have a real impact in your workplace.

Draw up a simple table with three columns. In the first column write **Where am I now?** and, as if you were explaining to me, make a few notes about your strengths and weaknesses when monitoring equality and diversity. Be specific and provide some examples. Be honest with yourself – this is not part of your assessment and identifying weaknesses is the first step to making improvements.

The questions below may help you.

Where am I now?
Think about your area of responsibility.

1. What does your organisation's policy say about equality? What is its mission statement? What are the values of the organisation?

2. How do you monitor activities that directly affect employees?

3. How do you monitor activities that directly affect customers?

4. How do you convince your team and your colleagues that monitoring is essential?

Now, in your second column, write the heading **Improvements** and in the third column **Action**.

Improvements and action
Are there any areas where your skills could be improved?

What action do you need to take to make those improvements?

Some of the changes you have identified might affect the way things are done in your organisation and you may need to discuss them with your line manager. Some changes can be made by you. Remember, small changes can make a big difference.

When you plan to make a change, remember to make your new objectives SMART!

You can discuss the notes you have made with your assessor. They may provide evidence of your competence.

An example

If you do not have a schedule for monitoring, you could use or adapt the template in Table B11.2.

Table B11.2: Template for a schedule for monitoring

Activity	Data collectable	How	Who	When
Recruitment	Number of applicants	Equality data on application form	HR	Each post advertised
Selection				
Induction				
Development				
Promotion				
Retention				
Redundancy				
Dismissal				
Pay				

TEST YOUR KNOWLEDGE

Here are some questions to test your knowledge and understanding of the issues explored in this unit. You can write the answers down or discuss them with your assessor. They could provide good evidence for your NVQ.

1. What is the legal requirement covering equality of opportunity and diversity? AC 1.1

2. When did this Act of Parliament come into force? AC 1.1

3. Why was this new Act introduced and what other equality legislation has it replaced? AC 1.1

4. What other equality and diversity requirements (if any) relate to your industry? AC 1.1

5. What does your organisation's equality and diversity policy say? AC 2.1

6. How do organisational procedures ensure equality, diversity and inclusion in the following areas? AC 2.1

   6.1   Recruitment...

   6.2   Selection ....

   6.3   Induction ....

   6.4   Development ....

   6.5   Promotion ....

   6.6   Retention ....

   6.7   Redundancy ....

   6.8   Dismissal ....

   6.9   Pay ....

   6.10   Other organisational terms and conditions...........................

7. How do you consider equality, diversity and inclusion when planning within your area of responsibility? AC 1.2

8. How do you monitor equality and diversity in your area of responsibility against organisational policies? AC 3.1

Further information

More information about equality legislation can be found at:

Government Equalities Office
www.equalities.gov.uk

The Equality and Human Rights Commission
www.equalityhumanrights.com

ACAS
www.acas.org.uk

Advice UK
www.adviceuk.org.uk

Citizens Advice
www.citizensadvice.org.uk

Employers' Forum on Disability
www.efd.org.uk

Office for Disability Issues
odi.dwp.gov.uk

Stonewall
www.stonewall.org.uk

Pulling it all together and gathering evidence

You and your assessor will need to agree the most appropriate sources of evidence. Here are some suggestions:

- An electronic portfolio: you could upload your evidence to an e-portfolio package or simply store the evidence in electronic format.
- A paper-based portfolio: you could build a folder with hard copies of your evidence.

Types of evidence:

- Observation: a record by your assessor when observing you discussing aspects of equality with your team.
- Work product: copies of work produced by you that demonstrate your competence, for example work plans, records of monitoring.
- Discussion: a record of you and your assessor discussing examples of equality, diversity and inclusion in your workplace.
- Questioning: a record of your assessor asking questions to test your knowledge.
- Personal statement, reflective account or case study based on the activities in this unit: this should have sentences which start with 'I …' and should tell a story giving real-life examples.
- Witness testimony from your line manager confirming your competence, in writing or recorded as a discussion with your assessor.

It is a good idea to include a range of evidence from different sources. Your evidence should cover a period of time and not be a 'one-off'. However, try to keep the evidence to a minimum. Your assessor can make a note of product evidence they have seen so it can be left in the workplace.

Remember:

Less is more – quality not quantity!

Be holistic – can you use this evidence again for other units?

EVALUATION

What have you learned from completing this unit?

What new skills and techniques are you using?

How has this affected the people you work with?

How has your organisation benefited? How might it benefit in the future?

Introduction and learning outcomes

Learning outcomes for Unit C1:

1. Be able to develop team ideas and develop creativity of team members
2. Be able to assess the viability of team members' ideas
3. Be able to support team members to implement ideas
4. Be able to implement team ideas

These learning outcomes say what you will have learned by the end of this unit. Each learning outcome is further broken down into assessment criteria, which will be looked at in detail in the following sections of this unit.

This Unit Guide is a resource to help you gather the evidence you require to achieve Unit C1. It can be used as a learning resource if you are new to the role, are studying team leading in preparation for work or as a refresher if you are already an experienced team leader.

You and your assessor will agree what you need to do to meet the assessment criteria and show you are competent. This Unit Guide provides some theory to help you support team members in identifying, developing and implementing new ideas, gives some case studies for you to examine and then an opportunity for you to reflect, with a virtual adviser, on how you can develop your own skills and gather evidence of competence. Some ideas are provided in the 'Pulling it all together' section at the end of this unit.

So, the purpose of this unit is to develop the skills and knowledge you need to support team members in identifying, developing and implementing new ideas.

Why do we need to identify, develop and implement new ideas?

Different people have differing views – that's the world we live in and the way we like to behave in a democratic society. Some people have ideas that they would like to develop and implement. Small changes can offer something new and different

– by thinking of something that works and carrying the idea forward to the end the person who proposed the idea gets a feeling of well-being. To be able to stand back and state, 'I did that, it was my idea and I am happy with the results' offers the incentive.

We are all different and some people do not like major changes; they are not comfortable with the process of change either. They would rather be left alone with something they are comfortable with; their viewpoints are static and they prefer others not to move around the working environment too much. They say things like, 'If it isn't broke, why fix it?' and that's fine as long as the object they refer to is not outdated, unsuitable, not fit for purpose or unsafe. Other people may say, 'Why should I come up with an idea? I am not paid as an ideas person. I come to work, do my best and leave when my work is done.'

That may be the case, payment may not be forthcoming, but if an idea assists your work and saves time, why not consider it and use it if it makes life easier overall? When Henry Ford developed his production line, the Ford T car was then produced quickly, making it affordable for the masses.

Working with a team involves challenges, not least having a number of individuals working together with different views. However, the idea that we can make things easier for each other must be desirable and thought provoking. Once again the mix of the team and the way the individuals work together provides the scope for team members to come up with ideas. They then need the support to sell their ideas to others and develop them as normal practice.

Let's look once again at the model concept of an emerging team (B. Tuckman, 1965):

- forming
- storming
- norming
- performing.

During the norming stage the team manages to have one goal and come to a mutual plan. Some members may have to give up their ideas and agree with others in order to make the team function. In this stage, all team members take the responsibility and have the ambition to work for the success of the team's goals. So by progressing through this model of team development the ideas need to be shared and agreed.

Learning outcome 1 – Be able to develop team ideas and develop creativity of team members

In this section we will explore each of the assessment criteria in more detail to develop your knowledge and understanding.

Assessment criterion 1.1 Encourage team members to identify ideas

As mentioned earlier, teams are made up of a group of individuals with differing opinions and viewpoints. They may come from different backgrounds and have differing social needs at home. Teams may also be challenged by the demographics of the group – remote sales teams for example, may not come together frequently. Also, some teams are not together at all times to develop and encourage ideas.

Nevertheless, these constraints can be removed or worked upon when a project or initiative needs to be developed. Work-based teams can take time to develop their interactions with each other, so the team leader needs to offer a number of options when considering how to encourage team members to identify ideas.

Let us consider some of the options available. They may be in use in your workplace already or they may have been tried before. Some concepts do fail, depending on the team, the timing, the conditions and the demographics in place. Don't be afraid to try again or to use another approach – you need to be seen to move things along. The idea is to encourage participation and develop creativity, even with those who adopt the entrenched 'static' stance.

Identify ideas using:

- one to ones
- ideas box
- task change
- improvement groups
- team talks
- team or individual incentives.

One to ones

When reviewing a team member's performance or just in having a chat, some ideas 'bubble to the surface'. The discussion should allow the team member to bring out any ideas they may have, but remember, the worst thing that can happen is for the idea to be ignored. Try asking for ideas at the mid point when you are talking about the actual work done. In a development discussion a section should be added for this. Normally, at the end, the 'anything else' section is used. However, this may not be the best point as the team member will probably be wanting to draw the meeting to a close.

Ideas box

This is not the best method for ideas, as they can easily be ignored. The ideas box concept tends to be or can become lip service to an ideas initiative. They are often referred to during meetings and discussions, then they are not used to the best effect. The overarching belief is that if all staff have been presented with the opportunity to place ideas in the box, 'if they don't use them it is not our fault'. The ideas box works well if attached to incentives.

Task change

If a job or task is about to change, perhaps with the installation of equipment, this is an ideal point to ask for any ideas. The review may bring about new duties or the development or change in a role, so the inclusion of ideas will benefit the team. Ask the question: 'How will this task change alter other areas?' Then follow up with the punchline: 'Ideas, anyone?'

Improvement groups

These are used in a number of team-building areas and have connections with Japanese methods such as Kaizen, Kanban, just-in-time and 5s.

Groups are requested to look at their work areas and then discuss how improvements can be made. Generally, the ideas fall out of these groups and are broken down into smaller sections so the team can have an input from maybe a specialist, or crossover teams outside the direct involvement are used to bring in ideas.

Team talks

Through communication methods that the team is comfortable with, an ideas section can be added. Team talks offer this opportunity. However, they can create a point where ideas can be slated as the full team offer counter opinions and do not give an idea a chance to get off the ground. So they are a good time to state 'I have an idea', but follow-up discussions on the full content will need to be requested and carried out.

Team incentives

Some organisations offer incentives to staff and team members, in some cases linked to the success of an idea and progressing it to an actual change. Incentives can be wide ranging and can include cash-based offers, such as a meal out with the family, or, in some areas, promotion if the idea offers a real progressive change. Incentives have their critics: 'Why should the team be rewarded for actually doing part of their role?' But they can be very successful as a buy-in to the concept of offering ideas and information.

A lot of the above can be used together as a project plan moves from one approach to another to capture a wide range of views and ideas. Once again, other methods are available – these are examples only.

Assessment criterion 1.2 Record team member ideas

By recording team members' ideas you begin the process of 'buy-in' for the team. This act of acknowledging a potential idea assists team bonding as it shows that you do listen and are willing to record and log an idea ready for review. Of course, this is an early stage – the idea has just been suggested – but the move forward is immense and as a team leader it is an invaluable breakthrough.

Just a point: carry a notebook or diary with you. For this and other requirements for your role, it makes sense.

Let's look at this process and take the list from earlier to look at the recording mechanisms that you may consider:

- one to ones
- ideas box
- task change
- improvement groups
- team talks
- shared spreadsheet access.

Team incentives are not on this list as they are linked to the methods you employ to encourage.

During one to ones the chat may be in any area of your workplace as a one to one can be formal or informal. So if you are away from the desk or office, ask the team member to recap or actually come back to your work area if possible. Record the detail, in the team member's words, as you may misinterpret their idea and that may become problematic later when the idea is reviewed. Form a log of the idea: write down the date and ensure the team member is actively part of the recording or logging process.

If an ideas box is in place, ensure you access it at the same time each week – it is good practice to review the contents regularly. The process for using the ideas box needs to be defined – documents for recording need to be left near the box together with a simple users' guide. 'Please record your idea on the document provided, ensure you have signed and dated the log and provide enough detail to explain your idea. Your team leader will get back to you to advise that the idea is logged within one week.'

The ideas box sheet may be simple and look something like Table C1.1.

Table C1.1

NAME –	TEAM –
My idea is as follows:	
DATE –	Signature

Once you have collected the sheets, record the idea on your log or spreadsheet and retain the sheet for future reference.

When changing a task it is important to involve those who carry out the work, so team involvement and ideas need to be captured. Generally at work a protocol or procedure is in place when changing a task. Manufacturing operations, for instance, tend to have standard operating procedures that are formal and prescriptive.

When recording ideas for a task change, a particular point in the operating procedure will be identified and the idea for the change will be documented, with a new review number and date being issued. An example is shown below.

Table C1.2: Example of Standard Operating Procedure

1	**Purpose**
1.1	To fill a kettle with cold water
2	**Scope**
2.1	The filling of the kettle is a manual task
3	**Health and safety and environmental protection**
3.1	Correct PPE must be worn
3.2	Only trained personnel to carry out this task
4	**Responsibilities**
4.1	The team leader is responsible for ensuring that:
4.2	● the procedure is current and any changes meet best practices and are implemented as required
4.3	● all team members are trained to carry out the operation detailed in the procedure
4.4	The team member is responsible for ensuring that:
4.5	● they carry out the procedure in the correct manner
4.6	● any problems are logged with the team leader
4.7	● the operator is responsible for wearing correct PPE
5	**Procedure**
5.1	Unplug kettle from power supply
5.2	Carry kettle to water supply
5.3	Remove kettle lid, open with care – could be hot
5.4	Put kettle under tap, ensuring tap is in open area of kettle
5.5	Turn on tap, allowing cold water to free flow into kettle
5.6	Check level and when filled to the desired level turn off tap
5.7	Replace lid on kettle
5.8	Return to power supply and reconnect
6	Review number 6 – Date 120911 Named reviewer – A. Nother

So new ideas will be altered on the operating procedure once they have been reviewed and considered by the team and others involved. The detail of the changes will be outlined and the 'step number' will be used to locate the change. For example, 'alter step 5.7 from Replace lid on kettle to Replace lid on kettle and ensure it is secure'. Once the review is agreed, the document will be issued with a new review number and date. Existing documents will be withdrawn.

Improvement groups are generally asked to look at a specific area; it may be that the organisation has a problem with a particular area of work. The team will be asked to gather and come up with some ideas for improvement. Defined techniques are generally used to gather and record the information, for example Fishbone analysis and brainstorming sessions. Team members are asked to offer their ideas and the group discusses the methods and reviews the potential of the idea.

A number of recording methods can be used, from flip charts to display boards, and the findings are documented. They are then placed on view on notice boards and other prominent places for others to view, consider and offer feedback.

Team talks are a regular communication opportunity to offer ideas, although in some instances presenting an initial idea to the team 'cold' can cause problems. The group may respond by offering counter arguments and this can present a problem for the instigator of the idea, so it is probably wise to circulate the idea prior to the meeting and then discuss in a controlled manner with reasonable and responsive debate. The content of the talk should be captured and the ideas formally presented and documented in the agreed record log.

Spreadsheets offer an ideal log for overall recording of ideas. By opening up access to an ideas spreadsheet on a shared drive, the team can consider their ideas and post them for all to see. This concept works best if the protocol is to state that all ideas will be considered no matter how small or radical.

Also this gives the opportunity for the ideas to be debated further by using some of the other methods mentioned above.

The case study below provides an opportunity for you to read about a team leader or team-leading scenario. The case study highlights some of the issues discussed. You can use this to reflect on the situation and answer some questions. You do not have to write down your answers unless your tutor or assessor has asked you to do so.

CASE STUDY 1

Douglas works in a factory that manufactures chemicals. The factory has a mix of manual and computer controls in place. The team leader, Brian, has recently had to report an accident that occurred last week and he mentioned this during a team talk. Michael was lifting some drums of chemicals to pour them into a vessel when he hurt his back and was now off work. The task is recorded as hazardous and all team members are aware of the health and safety issues; they are all trained in manual handling.

Douglas responded to Brian's report: 'I have come up with an idea to sort this, but why should I tell management? They never listen to us.'

Brian's response was to advise Douglas that there were good methods to follow up ideas and if his idea helped stop another accident then he should really put his idea forward.

Douglas considered this response for a moment and then stated that he would put the idea in the shared spreadsheet and wait for it to be ignored.

What do you think?

1. What should Brian do to further encourage Douglas to detail his idea?
2. Where else should Brian record the proposed idea?
3. Does Brian have enough information?

DEVELOPMENT ACTIVITY 1 with your virtual adviser

I am here to demystify the assessment criteria and help you relate what you have learned to your own job role. We will look at what you are currently doing and how you can develop your skills and have a real impact in your workplace.

Draw up a simple table with five columns. In the first column, list the methods or practices you use to encourage team members to offer ideas. The heading should be **Where am I now?** In the second column, put the heading **Strengths**, in the third column put the heading **Weaknesses**. Make a few notes about your successes and failures when encouraging team members to identify ideas. Remember to include in your table the manner in which you record the ideas presented by your team. Be specific and provide some examples. Be honest with yourself – this is not part of your assessment, and identifying weaknesses is the first step to making improvements.

The questions below may help you.

Where am I now?
Tell me about the methods you use to encourage team members to develop ideas.

1. Do you hold regular meetings or one to ones to discuss team ideas?
2. How do you record ideas raised by team members?
3. Do you have regular reviews on ideas presented?
4. Do these reviews offer responses back to team members?

Now, in your table, in the fourth column write the heading **Improvements** and in the fifth and last column write **Action**.

Improvements and action
Are there any areas where you gather or process team ideas that could be improved?

What action do you think you could take to make those improvements happen?

Some of the changes you have identified might affect the way things are done in your organisation and you may need to discuss them with your line manager. Some changes can be made by you. Remember, small changes can make a big difference.

When you plan to make a change, remember to make your new objectives SMART!

You can discuss the notes you have made with your assessor. They may provide evidence of your competence.

Learning outcome 2 – Be able to assess the viability of team members' ideas

In this section we will explore each of the assessment criteria in more detail to develop your knowledge and understanding.

Assessment criterion 2.1 Assess with team members the potential benefits and risks associated with an idea and the resources required

When dealing with the potential implementation of new ideas, response times are beneficial. Speedy responses provide the team and the individual who thought of the idea with the view that 'it was worth it' – we (or I) put a proposal forward and already my team leader has acknowledged the fact. However, that acknowledgement takes you to another stage, that of assessing the idea for potential. That debate must start as soon as possible, generally with a meeting or review with the full team.

The meeting should look at the idea and consider it using agreed methods. When team members offer up ideas it is important to respond as quickly as possible to the individual. The team also need to be aware of the proposal as soon as possible. You could start with a simple review during which it is important to identify:

- What are the risks and resources involved?
- Who will benefit from the idea or change?
- Why use the idea and develop the concept?

The consequences of not knowing this information may mean you will not be able to convince others of the idea's potential.

So where do we start with these three 'Ws'? Ask the originator of the idea to supply a little more detail – this can be done when the idea is acknowledged. Organisational and local procedures and guidelines then need to be followed.

To debate and discuss the idea correctly, all parties who may benefit or may be affected in some way need to be aware of the concept and background.

So what methods would you employ to ensure this communication was carried out? Your ideas log should be discussed with your team and others as the ideas are recorded. So that most parties will have a little piece of information, the use of a shared accessible file in spreadsheet form comes into its own for giving members in your organisation a 'heads up' on ideas tabled. Also the notice board mentioned earlier will provide other accessible information on the ideas as they progress.

A simple progress chart could be used in both cases. Headings could be as shown in Table C1.3.

Table C1.3: Example of progress chart

Date idea logged	Originator name (dept.)	The idea or concept	Meeting planned	Idea accepted	Idea on hold	Follow up detail and progress

The ideas will be at various stages and obviously the example shown needs more space in certain columns.

The meeting, team talk or presentation should then follow. The originator of the idea is a key attendee so that they can put forward their reasoning. Your selected group to determine the validity and basic application of the concept can then use a number of methods. They may start by debating, with perhaps a brainstorming session, and they will provide a number of responses either for or against the idea. Moving on, the group could consider the responses using a force field analysis technique. This looks at the driving forces – the positives – and then the restraining forces – the negatives.

In each case, and no matter what measurement or technique is used, it needs to be consistent and applicable to the idea. These conditions will be set in your place of work and may include some of the following:

- health and safety
- cost
- time
- energy
- environmental
- resources required to implement
- resources required later
- how the change impacts on other practices.

This is not a definitive list as other considerations may apply, but each should have a measure – perhaps a grade or score for each condition.

Simple ideas that have a real impact on the required work for a team sometimes fall out of the scope of assessment. They may have no negatives and fully meet your pre-set conditions. Nevertheless, still use your measures for consistency, even if the process takes five minutes.

The case study below provides an opportunity for you to read about a team leader or team-leading scenario. The case study highlights some of the issues discussed. You can use this to reflect on the situation and answer some questions. You do not have to write down your answers unless your tutor or assessor has asked you to do so.

Figure C1.1: Sharing ideas with the team

CASE STUDY 2

Douglas has recorded his idea on the shared spreadsheet. Brian has acknowledged the idea and today is the team meeting to propose the idea. Engineering staff and other managers have been invited, along with team members from the other shifts (the process is continuous and the teams work a 12-hour shift pattern).

Douglas advises the group of the idea: he proposes to remove the drum-handling task and replace it with a semi-automatic pumped system. The 20kg drums could be replaced with large 1,000kg tanks, the tanks would be attached to an air-activated pump and the supply would be transferred into the large vessel without the need to handle the drums. The potential contact with the chemical inside the drums would thus be reduced.

The engineering representative responds quickly by saying that the change would offer a number of restrictions and a direct cost would be involved. Douglas replies with the view that he thought that would be the reaction to any ideas from the shop floor.

What do you think?

1. What should Brian do as the chair of the review meeting? How should he respond to the comments?
2. What should be the next step for the meeting?
3. What measures do you think the team should use to assess this idea?
4. What technique should the group use to assess the idea?

DEVELOPMENT ACTIVITY 2 with your virtual adviser

I am here to demystify the assessment criteria and help you relate what you have learned to your own job role. We will look at what you are currently doing and how you can develop your skills and have a real impact in your workplace.

Using the list of potential measures and methods mentioned in this section, prepare a list that you have either used or participated in when assessing ideas presented in your workplace. Mark each measure to indicate whether you felt the technique was successful. Also indicate whether your organisation uses any other methods that you have not yet experienced or used in your role.

Write as if you were explaining to me. Make a few notes about your strengths and weaknesses when reviewing or assessing ideas presented. Be specific and provide some examples. Be honest with yourself – this is not part of your assessment, and identifying weaknesses is the first step to making improvements.

The questions below may help you.

Where am I now?
Think about the various assessment methods and techniques you use or that are in use in your organisation.

1. When did you use an ideas assessment method?
2. What was the idea presented?
3. Who were the originators of the idea at this time?

Now, alongside your list, write the heading **Improvements** and then in the next column **Action**.

Improvements and action
Are there any areas where your assessment of ideas methods could be improved?

What action do you need to take to make those improvements?

Some of the changes you have identified might affect the way things are done in your organisation and you may need to discuss them with your line manager. Some changes can be made by you. Remember, small changes can make a big difference.

When you plan to make a change, remember to make your new objectives SMART!

You can discuss the notes you have made with your assessor. They may provide evidence of your competence.

Learning outcome 3 – Be able to support team members to implement ideas

In this section we will explore each of the assessment criteria in more detail to develop your knowledge and understanding.

Assessment criterion 3.1 Explain how to support team members in submitting formal proposals for approval

The decision to progress with an idea needs to be made with all factors considered. An idea may be the best option but due to the lack of background information supported by sound recording methods it is moved to 'on hold or rejected'. That is very demotivating for the idea originator and also sends the wrong messages about future idea proposals. It is also a potential missed opportunity for your organisation.

The need to support your team through the process of providing enough information is therefore highly desirable and in fact vital. Organisations have a protocol for presenting information or proposals: they may be formal or informal. But reaching the correct individuals and asserting your intentions in the correct manner pays dividends. Let's look at the types of methods and requirements to prepare and submit proposals for approval.

Formal proposals carry more weight – they show to others that the originator of the idea means business and has thought through their concept and wants to be considered seriously. Start with a list of potential activities that you may use or consider with your team member as actions for proposal preparation:

- objectives of the proposal
- how to present the idea or improvement
- how to document the potential change
- how to cost the proposal and offer payback information.

Objectives should be clear and concise: if they move away from the idea-specific content, they lose impact.

1. My objective is to switch off all of the lights when I leave an area.

2. My objective is to switch off the lights when I leave an area not in use by others.

Objective 2 offers more information – the challenges to the objective are therefore reduced as you don't want others kept in the dark!

The objective needs to be SMART, a phrase well used throughout this book and in business generally:

Specific: ask the team member to offer information regarding the idea that clearly sets out what they are seeking to achieve. It may be appropriate to prepare an outline of the idea and how it fits, replaces or improves a task or work-based issue. The team leader should actively endorse the idea by ensuring the information provided is credible and is the team member's own work.

Measurable: review the idea with information on what, could or can be saved. Measures could be different in each case, for example cost, time, safety or environmental. Existing information on these points will be valuable – look at accident records, budgets, environmental records or logs. Set the existing measures against the desired outcomes of the idea or concept.

Achievable: an idea needs to be achievable and the proposal will require information on how it may be achieved. Information on the interaction of the team, who carries out what tasks and the resources required will help promote the idea. Potential targets and plans to suit the change will assist.

Realistic: ideas that are based on a 'would like to have condition' tend to be put at the bottom of a list, but those that offer sound alternatives to existing problems or issues are brought forward. Opportunities that require extra staff or high expense will fall foul of the assessment process.

Time-bound: objectives need to have a completion date. In some cases this may fit in with any potential savings as the implementation of the idea needs to be carried out to achieve results early.

Some team members are not used to meetings and their interaction with others in the organisation may be limited, so this hurdle needs to be negotiated. To progress their idea a meeting is a means to an end, but also they could adopt different approaches or methods to deliver their message rather than the structure of a PowerPoint presentation.

The methods that can be used vary, once again depending on the team's work. The presentation needs to offer as much information as possible but not to over-emphasise the idea or concept. Overselling or offering false claims will result in problems later.

Meetings are generally considered the best means for putting forward ideas, but the approach to presentation needs to link into the idea. Perhaps if the work is external to the office environment a visit to the proposed site of the change or idea would assist – to actually see the physical aspect that the team member wants to promote as their idea could present better explanations. If the idea is a change in a procedure, the original procedure may be used with the insertions and comments relating to the idea for change attached. So ask the team member to use the methods they are familiar with to get the message over to the idea's review team.

Already we have identified one potential method for documenting a change through the use of a procedure. However, you need to remind the team member not to use jargon or technical information that they use in team situations as people attending the meeting could be from various operational backgrounds. Clear examples of the idea should be readable and expressed in terms that everyone will be familiar with.

The point is to document the potential of the idea or change: this is where we are now and this is where we could be. The idea is almost like a new bypass in a road – people need to be aware of it to see the benefits, the document needs to guide them and offer the alternatives.

Costs and payback proposals will need to be examined in some of the ideas presented. Financial savings are a major factor in all change in business and if an idea can affect overheads or benefit the budget, then it will be given a keen review.

Although not all savings present immediate results, the idea may require some expenditure that will not be paid back for some time. These financial savings may be dependent on larger investment now with a payback in two to three years perhaps. That is something that the accountants involved in the review may balk at and they may reject the idea. But in this approach the team member may require help in reviewing the prices of the items in current use, as they may not be involved in the costing of these items in their normal duties, so may need direct assistance to assess how their idea measures up financially. Remember, though, that access to information of this nature can be sensitive, particularly if an agreed contract is in place for materials over a period of time yet to expire.

Assessment criterion 3.2 Explain to team members how to identify and overcome barriers to implementing an idea

Barriers to ideas are common, especially from parties who wish they had thought of it first! In work we have set functions and generally people like stability and consistency; they come into work and know exactly what they have to do and when to do it. Ideas generally mean some form of change and with that change comes learning and doing something either new or additional.

Also, some ideas do not benefit everyone – let's be honest, automation reduces the need for people and can affect team presence. So bear that in mind when attempting to sell an idea that means a change in duties which unsettles and frightens those involved.

Barriers are firmly in place if job roles are perhaps threatened or even considered to be threatened. These types of ideas are generally discussed and debated at a strategic level; the implementation of such is generally carried out on a higher management pathway. But some simple task changes can be viewed as a potential move to undermine the stability of the team make-up, so these at team level need to be considered carefully.

Generally, team members understand the operational needs of the mixed functions they carry out and identification of an idea to change a task for the better may be welcomed. It may be that the measures used in assessing an idea present a result for one part of the function that outweighs another. Cost versus health and safety is generally considered a well-matched bout. For example, the use of statistics on the number of accidents in an area may override additional expenditure as the time lost by team members is high due to the accident numbers. This may be due to the functionality of a piece of equipment or the condition of a slippery floor that needs replacing.

Once again meetings or discussions prior to an idea review will help consider the factors that offer barriers to an idea.

Team members should be prompted to hold discussions with affected parties so the feel for the change through the idea is considered. Preparation prior to the review should be encouraged, with all benefits possible checked and documented: health and safety, cost, time, energy savings, environmental impact and team interaction.

The case study below provides an opportunity for you to read about a team leader or team-leading scenario. The case study highlights some of the issues discussed. You can use this to reflect on the situation and answer some questions. You do not have to write down your answers unless your tutor or assessor has asked you to do so.

CASE STUDY 3

Douglas continues to present his idea to the group. He welcomes comments but requests everyone to wait until he has finished. He thanks his team leader, Brian, for assisting him in some of the aspects of his proposal and idea. Douglas lists his findings against the measures.

Health and safety: by removing the drums, injuries would be reduced, and the aspect of chemical handling and potential splash-back would be removed. The large tanks are on pallets and can be located with ease in an accessible area in the chemical bund (an area sealed from the general drains for environmental requirements); the smaller drums need to be carried to the storage location.

Cost: currently the company pays for transit, supply and removal of the existing drums. Also an extra charge is applied as the supplier needs to charge for high packaging costs. The large tanks have 10 per cent reduction on the actual contents due to lower handling charges. Some equipment would be required to transfer the liquid (pipes). Cost details on that are not available until the process is reviewed.

Equipment: some redundant equipment has been identified that may be fit for purpose for the task, for example a weighing device is available suitable for weighing pallets and contents. The chemical can be dosed into the system using the weighing device as a measure; this would be similar to that used in a car to record fuel tank contents. A pump has been located that is also in the stores, removed from another application. Douglas has indicated he needs the engineers to ascertain whether its function would be suitable for chemical handling.

Environmental: by using reusable tanks rather than disposable drums the environmental impact is decreased.

What do you think?

1. How has Douglas performed in relation to the proposal of his idea?
2. What other information would be useful for the team?
3. What other considerations would help to support the idea?

DEVELOPMENT ACTIVITY 3 with your virtual adviser

I am here to demystify the assessment criteria and help you relate what you have learned to your own job role. We will look at what you are currently doing and how you can develop your skills and have a real impact in your workplace.

Prepare a short statement detailing your process for supporting teams to implement new ideas. This reflective account should consider the aspects of your involvement and consider: **Where am I now?** In the content, consider your strengths and weaknesses when supporting your team to develop ideas. Be specific and provide some examples. Be honest with yourself – this is not part of your assessment and identifying weaknesses is the first step to making improvements.

The questions below may help you.

Where am I now?

Think about a situation when you have supported team members to implement ideas.

1. How did you ensure the team member understood the ideas process?

2. How did the team indicate they had been supported?

3. Have you ever had to review ideas presented by others?

Progress your statement by considering **improvements** and your possible **actions**.

Improvements and action

Are there any areas where your support of team members while progressing ideas could be improved?

What action do you need to take to make those improvements?

Some of the changes you have identified might affect the way things are done in your organisation and you may need to discuss them with your line manager. Some changes can be made by you. Remember, small changes can make a big difference.

When you plan to make a change, remember to make your new objectives SMART!

You can discuss the notes you have made with your assessor. They may provide evidence of your competence.

Learning outcome 4 – Be able to implement team member ideas

In this section we will explore each of the assessment criteria in more detail to develop your knowledge and understanding.

Assessment criterion 4.1 Monitor the implementation of ideas by own team

Once an idea is considered as a viable 'going concern' the team leader must ensure the idea and the concept are managed and delivered by the team offering the benefits they presented. The idea now really becomes a project to develop and move on. It needs to be progressed and monitored through to the implementation stages using team members and parties who were involved in the review stages.

In some organisations an official process is used, with a sponsor or lead coordinator selected from the review and group stages. This concept of using sponsors comes from methods used in improvement groups. These are normally linked to team developments similar to those used in Japan. Nissan and Toyota, for instance, use these methods to great effect.

The sponsor's role is to ensure that the barriers to implementation are removed or dealt with and the resources required for implementation are available. The sponsor is generally a manager, and that manager can be the team leader. It makes sense that the team leader supports and drives the idea forward.

The factors that may be considered during implementation are:

- funds and implementation costs
- operational requirements
- physical resources
- team involvement
- impact of change.

The sponsor in our case is the team leader, who needs to set ground rules for the implementation and these need to be stressed as essential. A plan with target dates needs to be prepared, which should consider the final implementation date and then apply the factors above to reviews that will occur along the way. Meetings for these reviews can be proposed; however, the best option is to have reviews in your normal team meetings or talks. The implementation progress will be communicated as an extra section or topic. In that the team can contribute on how they feel the idea is progressing into an actual event and moreover how it has affected them as individuals within the team.

Funds for an idea need to be measured and generally a budget is applied. The payback conditions will be reviewed during the lead meetings prior to moving the idea forward. Most ideas need some kind of implementation cost; they all need to be managed. An outline of the proposed costs will generally be supplied and any deviations need to be recorded to see whether the payback conditions are affected. Simple spreadsheets to develop the monitoring process should be used, or an expenditure log. Financial experts may need to be contacted as the funds required will have to come out of an overarching section of the main budget. If the idea is a totally new concept then sometimes the budget source needs to be considered in advance. The team needs to be made aware of the budget constraints as they may want to extend their initial plan and get carried away with the developments.

Operational requirements need to be 'spelled out' with the originator of the idea involved. The specific points of the initial idea should be captured and turned into a plan. The plan should consider as many of the factors associated with the success of the idea as possible. Specialists may need to be called in or enlisted onto the team to provide extra support. Ideas can have a number of options, so each of these needs to be reviewed for potential.

Moving on to the physical resources, the team needs to review current practices and associated equipment or methods employed. If new 'kit' is required it must have a budget allocation as per the original specification.

In some cases an idea may involve moving something; obviously equipment or people may be required to assist the move.

All of these considerations need to be applied to the plan so the implementation can be as seamless as possible. Team involvement is therefore highly desirable, as mentioned earlier, with good communication the key. Team discussion on the progression needs to also give detail and pinch points in the plan. These areas could be the date for a significant change or alteration that came from the idea. A team member would be very disgruntled to suddenly find their desk had moved to accommodate the plan!

Active ongoing involvement from the team is also crucial – any planned change brought on from a fellow team member's idea needs to be supported and assistance provided.

As the idea moves forward from the drawing board to implementation, the impact of the change will start to manifest itself. At this point the impact should be positive; if not, a full review should take place, backtracking the stages to see whether anything has altered due to the change. If this occurs, the team leader should endeavour to keep the team positive and progress with clear roles to check and double check the conditions.

When the impact of the change is a positive improvement and the idea has shown good results, other associated areas may be affected, so interlinked services or conditions need to be reported upon. For example, an idea to process orders and invoices quickly may have an impact on the accounts department or the stores when they order material.

Assessment criterion 4.2 Communicate the progress of implementation to relevant others in organisation

The communication of the progress of an idea is very important. We mentioned team communication in the previous section. However, people can miss meetings due to holidays and sickness, so updates need to be available around the workplace.

The updates are not just for the team, of course, they also provide information for others. Consideration needs to be given to those involved on the peripheral of the team, such as other managers and accounts. Progress reviews can be placed on notice boards, the intranet, in-house publications, and in notes or minutes from meetings. Email updates are also suitable to keep information circulating.

How much detail is really down to the recipient's knowledge of the idea and how it affects them. And do not forget the protocol in place in your working environment – perhaps everyone may need an update, for example.

Other more detailed information needs to be prepared by you and your team to maybe expand on the existing idea. It could well be a prototype that your team has developed and the next stage may be to run with the idea on a larger scale. So written evaluation reports on the implementation and progress would assist. It is good practice to keep a diary or log of the events leading to and developing from the initial idea to full implementation. (Remember the point made in AC 1.2!)

The case study below provides an opportunity for you to read about a team leader or team-leading scenario. The case study highlights some of the issues discussed. You can use this to reflect on the situation and answer some questions. You do not have to write down your answers unless your tutor or assessor has asked you to do so.

CASE STUDY 4

The idea for improvement from Douglas was accepted, the budget was agreed and the installation has just been completed. Brian has held a commissioning meeting with those involved from his team, and a test on the system using water was planned to ensure it works. At that time the team would prepare a standard operating procedure with consideration to the new task and how it links in with other procedures.

An invitation to attend the trial run was quickly sent out to the other teams involved the day before, but sadly no other team members attended. Brian challenged this with the other team leaders, who indicated that as the project was completed early and no information was posted on the timings of the final installation stage, no one was aware of the commissioning date and therefore they were not released to attend.

Also a rumour had spread that due to the installation, team members would be removed from each team, so some of the other team members were aggrieved by the speed and now impending implementation of the equipment. Brian's team were now concerned over this feedback.

What do you think?

1. What is missing from the implementation process?
2. List any activities that would have helped with the implementation.
3. What might the outcome be?
4. What are the good and bad points in this case study?

DEVELOPMENT ACTIVITY 4 with your virtual adviser

I am here to demystify the assessment criteria and help you relate what you have learned to your own job role. We will look at what you are currently doing and how you can develop your skills and have a real impact in your workplace.

Draw up a simple table with three columns. In the first column write **Where am I now?** and, as if you were explaining to me, make a few notes about your strengths and weaknesses when implementing team ideas. Be specific and provide some examples. Be honest with yourself – this is not part of your assessment, and identifying weaknesses is the first step to making improvements.

The questions below may help you.

Where am I now?
Think about a time when you have implemented team ideas. Did you review or reflect on the implementation process?

1. Consider your actions during implementation. What was your input?
2. What types of monitoring did you use? How long did you monitor the approach?
3. Did you prepare any records on the developments?

Now, in your second column, write the heading **Improvements** and in the third column **Action**.

Improvements and action

Are there any areas where your implementation approach could be improved or modified?

What action do you need to take to make those improvements?

Some of the changes you have identified might affect the way things are done in your organisation and you may need to discuss them with your line manager. Some changes can be made by you. Remember, small changes can make a big difference.

When you plan to make a change, remember to make your new objectives SMART!

You can discuss the notes you have made with your assessor. They may provide evidence of your competence.

TEST YOUR KNOWLEDGE

Here are some questions to test your knowledge and understanding of the issues explored in this unit. You can write the answers down or discuss them with your assessor. They could provide good evidence for your NVQ.

1. What encouragement methods or approaches have you used with your team to present ideas? AC 1.1

2. How do you record team members' ideas? AC 1.2

3. How do you assess team members' potential ideas? AC 2.1

4. Describe the support offered to team members when submitting proposals for approval. AC 3.1

5. How do you overcome barriers to implement ideas with the team? AC 3.2

6. What is the organisation's approved process for monitoring implementation of ideas from your team? AC 4.1

7. What is the normal communication process regarding the implementation of ideas or projects in your organisation? AC 4.2

Pulling it all together and gathering evidence

You and your assessor will need to agree the most appropriate sources of evidence. Here are some suggestions:

- An electronic portfolio: you could upload your evidence to an e-portfolio package or simply store the evidence in electronic format.
- A paper-based portfolio: you could build a folder with hard copies of your evidence.

Types of evidence:

- Observation: a record by your assessor when observing you during a team discussion on idea development and implementation.
- Work product: copies of work produced by you that demonstrate your competence, for example emails, presentations, briefing notices and team talk minutes.
- Discussion: a record of you and your assessor discussing examples of things that happened during the development and implementation of ideas from the team and how you dealt with them.
- Questioning: a record of your assessor asking questions to test your knowledge.
- Personal statement, reflective account or case study based on the activities in this unit: this should have sentences which start with 'I …' and should tell a story giving real-life examples.
- Witness testimony from your line manager confirming your competence, in writing or recorded as a discussion with your assessor.

It is a good idea to include a range of evidence from different sources. Your evidence should cover a period of time and not be a 'one-off'. However, try to keep the evidence to a minimum. Your assessor can make a note of product evidence they have seen so it can be left in the workplace.

Remember:

Less is more – quality not quantity!

Be holistic – can you use this evidence again for other units?

EVALUATION

What have you learned from completing this unit?

What new skills and techniques are you using?

How has this affected the people you work with?

How has your organisation benefited? How might it benefit in the future?

DEVELOP WORKING RELATIONSHIPS WITH COLLEAGUES

Introduction and learning outcomes

Learning outcomes for Unit D1:

1. Understand the benefits of working with colleagues.
2. Be able to take establish working relationships with colleagues.
3. Be able to act in a professional and respectful manner when working with colleagues.
4. Be able to communicate with colleagues.
5. Be able to identify potential work-related difficulties and explore solutions.

These learning outcomes say what you will have learned by the end of this unit. Each learning outcome is further broken down into assessment criteria, which we will look at in detail in the following sections of this unit.

This Unit Guide is a resource to help you gather the evidence you require to achieve Unit D1. It can be used as a learning resource if you are new to the role, are studying team leading in preparation for work or as a refresher if you are already an experienced team leader.

You and your assessor will agree what you need to do to meet the assessment criteria and show you are competent. This Unit Guide provides some theory to develop your understanding of the need to develop working relationships with colleagues. It also gives some case studies for you to examine and then an opportunity for you to reflect, with a virtual adviser, on how you can develop your skills and gather evidence of competence. Some ideas are provided in the 'Pulling it all together' section at the end of this unit.

So, the purpose of this unit is to develop the skills and knowledge you need for working relationships in a team.

Why should we develop working relationships with colleagues?

Relationships at work involve the same principles as in everyday life – respect for others, integrity, honesty, compassion – the general principles we all hold as high human qualities. By understanding each other's personalities we are able to develop and progress in a team that is comfortable with each other and identifies each other's strengths and weaknesses.

As the enabler in a team you also need to be aware of these traits and offer help by developing your people, which involves more than behaviour, relationships, skills, knowledge and processes. At work the team need to feel happy and fulfilled. A good leader can facilitate this.

Working on mutual objectives pulls people together by balancing what they put into a job or task and what they get out of it. In fact, team relationships are like any relationship – give and take is required, and you as the team leader need to aware of that and provide a good response to any situation when relationships teeter on the verge of breaking down.

There may be a clash of personalities, perhaps, a difference of opinion over work-related issues or a problem from some personal contact outside of work.

Teams can be quite complex and often there is a subtle balance between work-related issues and personalities. As a team leader, maintaining this balance can be quite challenging.

In the 1960s Dr Bruce Tuckman, an American psychologist, described his popular model on the way groups behave. He identified four distinct phases of team development:

- Forming: the team is uncertain how to proceed and behaviour is often reserved.

- Storming: the team often argues about who should do what and how.

- Norming: the team agrees its core tasks and individual roles within the team.

- Performing: the team operates along the agreed 'norms'.

As teams develop, the forming phase is the point during which relationships are developed. Team members are individuals and as such have varying values regarding how they perceive fairness. So how the team leader behaves towards each team member needs to be consistent as this contributes to the development of good working relationships.

Learning outcome 1 – Understand the benefits of working with colleagues

In this section we will explore each of the assessment criteria in more detail to develop your knowledge and understanding. You need to communicate and explain the required standards of behaviour expected of your team with regard to relationships.

Figure D1.1: What standards are required?

Assessment criterion 1.1 Describe the benefits of productive working relationships

The effectiveness of productive working relationships at any level in a business can have a direct impact on the overall success of your work.

Within a team this importance is perhaps higher as the effectiveness of a team is reliant on interrelated work. So relationships do not exist just between a company and its customers or suppliers but also internally between team leaders, their teams and between colleagues.

When you develop a good relationship with a team member or colleague, you have probably secured yourself someone you can call upon should any problems arise. They will probably expect you to provide them with any support or assistance they may require in return. So the success of a good working relationship means it can help to boost confidence and morale and ensure continuing support between team members.

Positive relationships can also help to build trust within a team and can ensure that people feel comfortable with airing their concerns or issues within the team environment. The general consensus is that if there are positive working relationships within a team, they tend to be happier and therefore more productive.

A good team works together towards the achievement of both individual and shared objectives while a team built on poor relationships can have a serious impact on the overall performance of the business.

During team development is probably the best time to communicate to the team the expected working relationships required. A number of communication approaches can be adopted and may include:

● team talks

● presentations

● supervisions

● one-to-ones.

Each of these approaches would be suitable, but generally as you want the message to reach all team members at the same time, a group communication method is best. Remember, by discussing something you open up communication channels that are highly important within a team.

The impact of good working relationships cannot be ignored and as the team leader you more than anyone else need to promote the value at all given opportunities.

The case study below provides an opportunity for you to read about a team leader or team leading scenario. The case study highlights some of the issues discussed. You can use this to reflect on the situation and answer some questions. You do not have to write down your answers unless your tutor or assessor has asked you to do so.

CASE STUDY 1

This is a statement from Kevin, a team leader, to describe his team working relationships:

I have worked at Fruit Juice Enterprises for five years; we package fruit juice, which is brought into our plant on tankers. We have production targets to complete, which are defined by production plans issued by the planning office on a weekly basis.

My team consists of plant operators, six in total. Four of these operate the line for filling the juice cartons or bottles. The other two ensure that the tankers are offloaded and they support the line by moving materials around the plant.

What do you think?

1. How well does the statement describe Kevin's team relationships at work?

2. Do you understand how the factory exchanges information?

3. Is this the full team? How do they interrelate? Are others involved?

DEVELOPMENT ACTIVITY 1 with your virtual adviser

I am here to demystify the assessment criteria and help you relate what you have learned to your own job role. We will look at what you are currently doing and how you can develop your skills and have a real impact in your workplace.

Write up a personal statement describing what you feel are the benefits you and your team get out of productive working relationships. Consider your organisation's guidelines on this. Do they consider working relationships?

The questions below may help you.

Where am I now?
Tell me about your working relationships.

1. How effective are team members in communicating with each other?
2. Are all of your team aware of the need to exchange information?
3. Can your team explain how they work and support each other?
4. Do you have any team members who work alone as they do not work well with others?
5. What do you do to prepare for a team talk? Do you have a section regarding working together?

Now, write the heading **Improvements and action**.

Improvements and action
Are there any areas in your personal statement where you did not understand the benefits of working relationships?

What action do you think you could take to ensure the team understands the benefits of productive relationships?

Write these improvements and actions in your personal statement to reflect on your findings.

Some of the changes you have identified might affect the way things are done in your organisation and you may need to discuss them with your line manager. Some changes can be made by you. Remember, small changes can make a big difference.

When you plan to make a change, remember to make your new objectives SMART!

You can discuss the notes you have made with your assessor. They may provide evidence of your competence.

Learning outcome 2 – Be able to establish working relationships with colleagues

In this section we will explore each of the assessment criteria in more detail to develop your knowledge and understanding.

Assessment criterion 2.1 Identify colleagues within own and other organisations

Team structure is obviously important – who links up with who for job role cover or for interlinked team actions. Your working structure should give you the general reporting levels internally and externally within the team and through this an overview of your team's expected working relationships. This, the requirement to understand how your team's overall role links into the system for exchanging information, is an important part of your work.

- The team may be working on mutual objectives.
- They will need to offer effective communication.
- They will need to understand the importance of exchanging information.
- There may be times when they require or need feedback on work carried out.

It is important to identify:

- What the benefits are of productive working relationships.
- Who colleagues are, internal and external.
- When the deadline is for the work of the team.
- Who they can refer to if they have a problem.

List your colleagues. Consider team members as well, then add others in a simple grid, as in Table D1.1, when you meet and what you talk about in relation to work. Example: 'My name is Kevin. I am a Team Leader working in a fruit juice bottling plant. John is another Team Leader. We meet daily to discuss handovers and targets for our team.'

Provide some examples from your workplace.

Table D1.1

Colleague	When and why do you meet?

Once you have identified your internal and external colleagues you need to agree or understand the roles and responsibilities they carry out to develop working relationships.

Internal colleagues:

- team members
- planning

- fellow line managers
- sales
- customer relations
- human resources
- finance
- service managers
- project partners.

External colleagues:

- project partners
- suppliers
- logistics
- sector-specific contacts.

In order to understand the roles and responsibilities you need to discover the line responsibilities and the relevance to the work being carried out – who actually makes a decision that affects your role?

Assessment criterion 2.2 Agree the roles and responsibilities for colleagues

Your colleagues in your organisation may have different titles and responsibilities. However, as you progress with your work you will soon realise who does what and how it affects your role. These line responsibilities will detail the work required for participating in a team as a leader and as part of a wider team of the management group.

Organisations will require project teams from all sectors from time to time. This contribution and participation of the teams is generally desirable by those in overall charge. These decision makers may be perhaps the owner of the company or the core team of senior management. Normally the roles within these extra teams will be decided after taking into consideration the relevance of the work being carried out. Also, teams that work closely together need the leaders of these teams to have special working relationships to develop the interaction required. In all of these cases the roles and responsibilities will have to be agreed and defined.

The roles within your team need to be considered and how they have clear line responsibilities to your section's targets. Each team member should be able to identify their contribution and its relevance to the work being carried out.

The case study below provides an opportunity for you to read about a team leader or team leading scenario. The case study highlights some of the issues discussed. You can use this to reflect on the situation and answer some questions. You do not have to write down your answers unless your tutor or assessor has asked you to do so.

Here is a statement from Kevin regarding other departments:

Plans are reviewed daily by the site planner, Karen. She checks on stock movements and reports any problems to Mr Shaw – we are then held to account on any issues seen.

We also have hygiene targets for the plant area – as it is a food factory we must comply with industry standards. One such standard is the Hazard Analysis of Critical Control Points (HACCP) system. We must ensure the juices are not contaminated or over pasteurised; we are constantly audited by the laboratory, who check on our procedures. The site auditor is Steven, who puts reports together that he supplies to the site manager direct by email. We are then challenged on our key performance indicators for all points in the process. Also, the documents must be completed at each CCP to show compliance. On shift start we have a team meeting to discuss targets and problems and defend our position.

What do you think?

1. What do you think about the reporting system used by the site planner and the site auditor?
2. What are the consequences of the reports?
3. What would you have done to avoid this situation?
4. Are working relationships in good order?

DEVELOPMENT ACTIVITY 2 with your virtual adviser

I am here to demystify the assessment criteria and help you relate what you have learned to your own job role. We will look at what you are currently doing and how you can develop your skills and have a real impact in your workplace.

Using the example of the colleagues 'grid' you prepared earlier, think about your current working relationship with those named individuals. As if you were explaining to me, make a few notes about your strengths and weaknesses within that relationship. Be specific and provide some examples. Be honest with yourself – this is not part of your assessment and identifying weaknesses is the first step to making improvements.

The questions below may help you.

Where am I now?
Think about situations within your relationships with colleagues at work.

1. Can you think of a time during your work when you felt that you and a colleague were not working together as you should? Had you any prior awareness of this team conflict?
2. Think of a strong relationship you have with a colleague. Why do you think it is so strong?

3. How have you developed your strong relationship? Is it due to joint projects or other contributions? Think of examples.

Now, create two lists: in one write the heading **Improvements** and in the second write **Action**.

Improvements and action
Are there any areas where your working relationships could be improved?

What action do you need to take to make those improvements?

Some of the changes you have identified might affect the way things are done in your organisation and you may need to discuss them with your line manager. Some changes can be made by you. Remember, small changes can make a big difference.

When you plan to make a change, remember to make your new objectives SMART!

You can discuss the notes you have made with your assessor. They may provide evidence of your competence.

Learning outcome 3 – Be able to act in a professional and respectful manner when working with colleagues

In this section we will explore each of the assessment criteria in more detail to develop your knowledge and understanding.

Assessment criterion 3.1 Explain how to display behaviour that shows professionalism

Let us simply put up some headings that support this learning outcome:

- Mutual support
- Respect
- Cooperation and helpfulness
- Honour commitments
- No unreasonable requests.

All of these display behaviours that show professionalism. Also these behaviours are the desired behaviours (I would hope!) you would expect from your team. Required behaviours are actually defined in most company rule books and as such workers at all levels within an organisation should comply with these requirements. However, to establish that the above list is counter to what an individual is actually portraying in their behaviour is difficult.

Professional and respectful characteristics in the workplace may also include some of the following:

- Purpose: members proudly share a sense of why the team exists and are invested in accomplishing its objectives.

- Priorities: members know what needs to be done next, by whom and by when to achieve team goals.
- Roles: members know their roles in getting tasks done and when to allow a more skilful member to do a certain task.
- Decisions: authority and decision-making lines are clearly understood.
- Conflict: this is dealt with openly and honestly.
- Personal traits: members feel their unique traits are accepted.
- Norms: group norms for working together are set and seen as standards for everyone in the group.
- Effectiveness: members find team meetings efficient and productive and look forward to this time together.
- Success: members know clearly when the team has met with success and share in this equally and proudly.
- Training: opportunities for feedback and updating skills are provided and taken advantage of by team members.

The case study below provides an opportunity for you to read about a team leader or team leading scenario. The case study highlights some of the issues discussed. You can use this to reflect on the situation and answer some questions. You do not have to write do you think your answers down unless your tutor or assessor has asked you to do so.

Figure D1.2

CASE STUDY 3

The site manager has advised the teams that the annual audit is due and all records must be presented along with a report on any problems encountered from other sections. In Kevin's case, his team have indicated that the shift handovers are not presented well from the other team. Gaps in records are apparent and this is affecting traceability and auditable processes. In turn, the information when presented reflects on the professionalism of both teams. Kevin has initially discussed these points with John, his counterpart, and the response is similar. John's team have reported inconsistencies in the reports presented during handovers, so in effect both teams are not happy with information on handover.

What do you think?

1. What would you consider the next course of action for the teams?
2. How will they resolve this situation when each team feels the other is to blame?
3. As the team leader involved, how would you manage this situation?

DEVELOPMENT ACTIVITY 3 with your virtual adviser

I am here to demystify the assessment criteria and help you relate what you have learned to your own job role. We will look at what you are currently doing and how you can develop your skills and have a real impact in your workplace.

1. Draw up a simple list. In the list, detail the traits that you consider professional and respectful.
2. If you have had others who have behaved in an unprofessional and disrespectful manner, list them also. Be specific with regard to behaviours you consider professional and respectful, then in some notes provide some examples. Be honest with yourself – this is not part of your assessment and by considering options in this manner will prepare you for any developments that may occur in the future.

The questions below may help you.

Where am I now?
Think about any situations during which someone behaved unprofessionally or disrespectfully.

1. Do you consider mutual support when working with colleagues?
2. Have you ever had to discuss respect with a team member?
3. How and when do you update the team on expected behaviours?

Now, in your list, write how you would make **improvements** and then how you would implement any **action**.

> **Improvements and action**
>
> Are there any areas where you could improve your approach with your team members when developing relationships?
>
> What action do you need to take to make those improvements?
>
> Some of the changes you have identified might affect the way things are done in your organisation and you may need to discuss them with your line manager. Some changes can be made by you. Remember, small changes can make a big difference.
>   When you plan to make a change, remember to make your new objectives SMART!
>   You can discuss the notes you have made with your assessor. They may provide evidence of your competence.

Learning outcome 4 – Be able to communicate with colleagues

In this section we will explore each of the assessment criteria in more detail to develop your knowledge and understanding.

Assessment criterion 4.1 Identify information to others clearly and concisely

Information sharing is vital for all organisations. Effective communication needs to be clear and concise, especially when communicating to groups.

However, we need to consider the audience and use agreed communication methods, remembering that information is best received if it has a direct interest for the tasks in hand.

To establish how information is received during communication, direct feedback is essential, so a review following communication methods is essential. We are not saying your colleagues have hearing difficulties, but they may have been focused on other needs when you met with them! Therefore some questions on how information was received and understood should take place soon after delivery.

Assessment criterion 4.2 Explain how to receive and clarify own understanding of information

Let us look at a direct communication example for this section. This transfer of information is of great importance to all team leaders' work. Those of you who work with continuous processes or production will relate to the 'hot' handover from one team leader to another. Obviously in these situations you are not able to say 'quick, stop everything' to your team as the process or production must continue, so the handover procedure is generally agreed and may include the following:

- agreed communication methods
- progression timings on the process
- reviews of conditions

- feedback
- general discussion on process plans and developments.

This information may be delivered to you and onto your team through early morning meetings or presentations.

All meetings or team leader handovers need to have a structure so that information such as the team's measures on how they are meeting key performance indicators can be passed forward.

Most of what goes awry with communications is the result of people and team members making assumptions, so effective business communication requires us to keep asking questions – 'What do you mean by that?' – rather than just filling in the gaps for ourselves. As a team leader you also need to ask questions and use your trusty notebook to keep a record.

The case study below provides an opportunity for you to read about a team leader or team leading scenario. The case study highlights some of the issues discussed. You can use this to reflect on the situation and answer some questions. You do not have to write down your answers unless your tutor or assessor has asked you to do so.

CASE STUDY 4

Kevin decides to be proactive and discusses the handover issue with John in more detail. Kevin realises that John defends his team's stance well and therefore his discussion needs to involve some diplomacy. So Kevin offers the view that it would appear that both teams have some faults and flaws in the manner in which they exchange information.

By offering this opinion he is then able to open up the debate. John's view seems to be much the same as Kevin's and he is aware of the implications of non-effective handovers. So a meeting is called, with a representative from each team, to discuss the problem.

The content and ultimate focus of the meeting would be an agreement of each team's expectations at handover. The information would be captured on a simple but effective handover log, with all crucial points and headings highlighted to include a history log from the shift data so follow-ups can be effected by the receiving team.

What do you think?

1. Would you include anyone else in the meeting?
2. Do you feel there are any other topics for the teams to discuss?
3. How would you capture any developments from the meeting?
4. How would you review the process?

DEVELOPMENT ACTIVITY 4 with your virtual adviser

I am here to demystify the assessment criteria and help you relate what you have learned to your own job role. We will look at what you are currently doing and how you can develop your skills and have a real impact in your workplace.

1. Draw up one list on which how you identify information from others.

2. On another list indicate how you receive and clarify information.

The questions below may help you.

Where am I now?
Think about how you communicate with colleagues.

1. Do you have records of communication used?

2. Do you keep a diary or a log on communications with colleagues?

3. Have you agreed communication methods?

Now, if you do not keep records or logs, write up a short statement on how you would make **improvements** and then how you would implement any **action**.

Improvements and action
Are there any areas where you could improve your communication methods?

What action do you need to take to make those improvements?

Some of the changes you have identified might affect the way things are done in your organisation and you may need to discuss them with your line manager. Some changes can be made by you. Remember, small changes can make a big difference.

When you plan to make a change, remember to make your new objectives SMART!

You can discuss the notes you have made with your assessor. They may provide evidence of your competence.

Learning outcome 5 – Be able to identify potential work-related difficulties and explore solutions

In this section we will explore each of the assessment criteria in more detail to develop your knowledge and understanding.

Assessment criterion 5.1 Identify potential work-related difficulties and conflicts of interest

As individuals make up a team, disputes often occur, as the motivations of one person may not be the same as those of another. This is true in all areas of an organisation, so on that basis at some point as a team leader you will meet up with someone who has a direct conflict of interest with either your beliefs or the way you do something.

I once worked with a fellow and we shared a desk. He was particularly tidy, I was not. Obviously this did not go down too well with my colleague and he mentioned it each time we came into contact. He was, of course, correct – a tidy desk is the best way to work. We eventually resolved the problem when the organisation introduced a tidy desk policy. So in this instance I was wrong and admitted it. (I still left the occasional item out of place just to gently wind him up!)

Joking apart, work-related difficulties need to be dealt with and my colleague was quite clear in his opinion. Opinions count. So it is important to identify conflicts of interest, whether these arise through someone's opinions or through a situation or act. Here are some of the things to look out for and consider that can create a work-related difficulty:

- conflict of interest
- unreasonable requests
- impact of own actions
- unable to meet agreed expectations.

An unreasonable request, for instance, could be a suggested deadline that is impossible to achieve, particularly if the individual requesting this target is well aware that the target is beyond reach.

Agreeing to a condition and not delivering is possibly the worst thing for everyone in the organisation – never mind untidy desks, this could impact on the full team failing and actually have far-reaching implications.

Assessment criterion 5.2 Explain how to resolve identified potential difficulties

Real responses to a problem or difficulty need to be made as soon as the difficulty is discovered. If the problem cannot be resolved, a plan needs to be progressed to counter the difficulty.

First of all, offer feedback: 'Yes, we have a problem or difficulty and we are working on it.' At the very least the response acknowledges the fact that a plan will soon be in place. Working relationships need to have other systems in place to bind them together. We have discussed points during which guidelines are in place and structures to show reporting relationships. In the case of difficulties or problems we generally have some procedures to follow – 'Who are you going to call?' – to assist with and offset a difficulty. Perhaps there is a code of practice in place. Alternatively, there may be some industry guidelines or procedures. Direct feedback with a supporting agency may be required through some contractual arrangements or agreements.

Most organisations have a system for support when significant difficulties arise. When you are using the procedures all the time is when you realise the difficulty is not going to be resolved early – that is the time a team leader's heart sinks.

The case study below provides an opportunity for you to read about a team leader or team leading scenario. The case study highlights some of the issues discussed. You can use this to reflect on the situation and answer some questions. You do not have to write down your answers unless your tutor or assessor has asked you to do so.

CASE STUDY 5

The meeting between the teams created another dilemma for Kevin and John. Through the handover process the opposing team members had become entrenched in their belief that their point of view on how the system would work was the best for the system. Two individuals were involved, one from each team.

This situation was identified by the team leaders and they decided that the participation of both of these individuals in the decision-making process was the best course of action. On this basis the two team members, who were in fact 'poles apart' from a unified decision on methods and paperwork developments, attended the meeting.

What do you think?

1. Would you include these individuals in the meeting?

2. What other methods should the team leaders use in the development of the handover process?

3. How would you resolve the position the two team members had adopted?

DEVELOPMENT ACTIVITY 5 with your virtual adviser

I am here to demystify the assessment criteria and help you relate what you have learned to your own job role. We will look at what you are currently doing and how you can develop your skills and have a real impact in your workplace.

Draw up one list on which you display your top five potential work-related difficulties and conflicts of interest. On another list indicate how you have resolved these potential difficulties.

The questions below may help you.

Where am I now?
Think about how you identify potential work-related difficulties and have explored solutions.

1. Describe the difficulty and its type.

2. Do you keep a diary or a log on solutions to difficulties?

3. Have you agreed codes of practice or guidelines to follow during a potential difficulty?

Now, if you do not keep records or logs, write up a short statement on how you would make **improvements** and then how you would implement any **action**.

Improvements and action
Are there any areas where you could improve responses to work-related difficulties?

What action do you need to take to make those improvements?

Some of the changes you have identified might affect the way things are done in your organisation and you may need to discuss them with your line manager. Some changes can be made by you. Remember, small changes can make a big difference.

When you plan to make a change, remember to make your new objectives SMART!

You can discuss the notes you have made with your assessor. They may provide evidence of your competence.

TEST YOUR KNOWLEDGE

Here are some questions to test your knowledge and understanding of the issues explored in this unit. You can write down the answers or discuss them with your assessor. They could provide good evidence for your NVQ.

1. Describe the benefits of productive working relationships. AC 1.1

2. Who are your colleagues within your organisation? AC 2.1

3. Who are your colleagues external to your organisation? AC 2.1

4. Do you agree roles and responsibilities for colleagues? AC 2.2

5. How do you display behaviours that show professionalism – do you have a code of conduct, for example? AC 3.1

6. Do you have any identified and agreed communication methods? AC 4.1

7. What action do you take to show your understanding of information? AC 4.2

8. Describe any identifiable work-related difficulties in your operational area. AC 5.1

9. How have you resolved any identified potential difficulties? AC 5.2

10. What agreed support do you call upon to resolve difficulties? AC 5.2

Pulling it all together and gathering evidence

You and your assessor will need to agree the most appropriate sources of evidence. Here are some suggestions:

- An electronic portfolio: you could upload your evidence to an e-portfolio package or simply store the evidence in electronic format.
- A paper-based portfolio: you could build a folder with hard copies of your evidence.

Types of evidence:

- Observation: a record by your assessor when observing you taking part in a work relationship situation.
- Work product: copies of work produced by you that demonstrate your competence, for example: agenda, your notes, minutes.
- Discussion: a record of you and your assessor discussing examples of things that happened in a meeting and how you dealt with them.
- Questioning: a record of your assessor asking questions to test your knowledge.
- Personal statement, reflective account or case study based on the activities in this unit: this should have sentences which start with 'I …' and should tell a story giving real-life examples.
- Witness testimony from your line manager confirming your competence, in writing or recorded as a discussion with your assessor.

It is a good idea to include a range of evidence from different sources. Your evidence should cover a period of time and not be a 'one-off'. However, try to keep the evidence to a minimum. Your assessor can make a note of product evidence they have seen so it can be left in the workplace.

Remember:

Less is more – quality not quantity!

Be holistic – can you use this evidence again for other units?

EVALUATION

What have you learned from completing this unit?

What new skills and techniques are you using?

How has this affected the people you work with?

How has your organisation benefited? How might it benefit in the future?

PLAN, ALLOCATE AND MONITOR WORK OF A TEAM

Introduction and learning outcomes

Learning outcomes for Unit D5:

1. Be able to plan work for a team.
2. Be able to allocate work across a team.
3. Be able to manage team members to achieve objectives.
4. Be able to monitor and evaluate the performance of team members.
5. Be able to improve performance of a team.

These learning outcomes say what you will have learned by the end of this unit. Each learning outcome is further broken down into assessment criteria, which we will look at in detail in the following sections of this unit.

This Unit Guide is a resource to help you gather the evidence you require to achieve Unit D5. It can be used as a learning resource if you are new to the role, are studying team leading in preparation for work or as a refresher if you are already an experienced team leader.

You and your assessor will agree what you need to do to meet the assessment criteria and show you are competent. This Unit Guide provides some theory to develop your understanding of planning, allocating and monitoring the work of a team, gives some case studies for you to examine and then an opportunity for you to reflect, with a virtual adviser, on how you can develop your skills and gather evidence of competence. Some ideas are provided in the 'Pulling it all together' section at the end of this unit.

So, the purpose of this unit is to develop the skills and knowledge you need to plan, allocate and monitor the work of a team.

What is a team and what can it achieve?

A team can be a group of two or more people who are working towards a common goal. Ideally, between them, they should have all the skills needed to complete a task. The pool of knowledge, skills and characteristics will be much greater than that of any one individual. And the energy created by different people working together, learning from each other and bouncing ideas off each other, results in the overall team performance being greater than the sum of all the individual members of that team.

There are many things that would not happen without a team, sports for instance. There would be no football or netball without a team of players, each with their own skills. Each member has their role to play and contribution to make. Without a team, there is no one to pass the ball to. Think of a rowing team. Each individual may be able to row a boat from the start to the finish line of a race, but eight rowers in a boat harness much more power and speed. However, each member of that team needs a common goal, they need to pull together in the same direction, in harmony, otherwise there is chaos. It is the same with teams in the workplace.

Learning outcome 1 – Be able to plan work for a team

In this section we will explore each of the assessment criteria in more detail to develop your knowledge and understanding.

Assessment criterion 1.1 Agree team objectives with own manager

There are many reasons why an organisation exists. Some are there to make a profit for shareholders, others to carry out essential public services, some are voluntary organisations supporting a particular cause. Each one has its own set of values for how it will operate. These values can be seen in the various mission statements, charters and promises, policies and procedures, and key performance indicators, which in turn are passed down through the organisation as individual or team objectives and targets.

Your individual objectives must contribute to the success of your team objectives. And the team objectives must in turn contribute to departmental or organisational objectives. So it is essential that your team objectives are agreed with your line manager.

You may have heard about the need for objectives to be SMART, that is:

- specific
- measurable
- achievable
- realistic
- time-bound.

If the brief given to you by your line manager is not in the form of SMART objectives, you may need to ask a few questions to make sure you have all the information you need for your team to succeed.

Let's say you work for a company providing cleaning services to large public spaces and you have just got a new contract for the local shopping mall. You manage a team of ten cleaners. If your manager informs you of the new contract and tells you the team should be ready to start on Monday, let's consider the questions you need to ask.

1. **Specific** details: when, where, what is expected, who is the contact. This list could go on until all the details have been established.

2. How will this be **measured**? Is there a probationary period? Will there be agreed standards and who will inspect them? How will the company judge whether the team has been successful?

3. Is this **achievable** with a team of ten cleaners or might you need to consider taking on more people?

4. Can you **realistically** commit your team to working early mornings and late evenings?

5. What is the length of the contract? How much **time** can be allocated to this work?

All projects come with budget limitations. You may like to use 12 people full time on this job but your line manager may decide it is feasible only to pay the equivalent of ten half-time workers. It is important to agree the boundaries of time and cost at the beginning of the project. It is harder to ask for more time or money or people halfway through.

As a team leader, you also have the role of representing the needs of your team. You know your team and what they are capable of doing. You know their skills and levels of knowledge. You also know what they cannot do. You know how much overtime they are willing or not willing to do. You know when they have booked holidays. You need to make sure your manager is aware of these factors when you agree to take on work. Then success is achievable and realistic.

Assessment criterion 1.2 Develop a plan for a team to meet agreed objectives, taking into account capacity and capabilities of the team

Once you have established exactly what is required of your team, you can begin to make a plan. You have agreed the overall objectives for your team and now your job is to break that down into a more detailed plan.

It is useful to map this out in some form of development plan. An example has been provided in Table D5.1, but you can adapt this to your own needs.

Table D5.1: Example of a development plan

Overall team objective:		To provide cleaning service for shopping mall		
What	**When**	**Who**	**Capabilities**	**Capacity**
Clearing litter	Shop hours 9 a.m. – 6 p.m.	2 people on a.m. shift, 2 people on p.m. shift	Not Marsha: prefers not to work with public	Jane a.m. M, T, W only Mika on holiday 21/7 1 week
Cleaning windows	Early morning 6 a.m. – 9 a.m.	2 experienced window cleaners	Not Bill: no ladder work	Only 1 at present, may need to recruit
Cleaning floors	Early morning 6 a.m. – 9 a.m.	6 trained in use of equipment	Trained: KN, ML, RT, PO, DF, DH	All OK for early shift
Toilets and washrooms	Early morning and during day	Extra 2 people to cover p.m.	Not Marsha: prefers not to work with public	Confirm availability for p.m. shift

This example shows that the overall objective has been broken down into smaller job roles. The particular type of work involved has dictated the working hours and shift patterns. You have decided the number of people and the number of hours needed to get the job done.

When deciding who will take on the various roles in the team, you need to know the capabilities of your team members. Some roles will require a minimum level of training or experience. Some roles will require certain attributes. You need to know your team well to make best use of their skills.

In addition, you need to be aware of their capacities, that is, how much time and energy they can put into this project. In the example of our team of cleaners, you would need to establish who is willing to work an early shift. In other situations where your team may be made up of employees from different departments, you need to establish what their workloads are like and how much time they and their line managers are realistically able to contribute.

Some of the key skills you will need are:

- a good rapport with your line manager
- listening, questioning and negotiation skills
- a good knowledge of the job so that you can break it down and develop realistic plans
- a good knowledge of your team and their strengths and weaknesses
- a good knowledge of team members' availability.

The case study below provides an opportunity for you to read about a team leader or team leading scenario. The case study highlights some of the issues discussed. You can use this to reflect on the situation and answer some questions. You do not have to write down your answers unless your tutor or assessor has asked you to do so.

CASE STUDY 1

In a busy call centre, Daljeet has just been promoted to team leader. She is keen to make a good impression in her first meeting with the manager and the three other team leaders.

The manager announces that they have a new contract with a national car dealership and will be training all employees to take the customer details and filter calls before transferring them to a local branch. The manager says the teams can have a two-hour training session and then the aim is for each person to process ten calls an hour.

Daljeet agrees and goes back to brief her team. The agents in Daljeet's team are not happy with the target calls per hour because of the time they need to process after-call work. All the calls have to be rushed and when Daljeet monitors some of the calls, she finds her agents do not sound relaxed and the customer service is suffering.

What do you think?

1. Things are not going well at the call centre. How do you think this might affect:
   - the customer
   - the team
   - the team leader, Daljeet
   - the manager?
2. What do you see as the cause of these problems?
3. What would you have done differently if you were Daljeet?

DEVELOPMENT ACTIVITY 1 with your virtual adviser

I am here to demystify the assessment criteria and help you relate what you have learned to your own job role. We will look at what you are currently doing and how you can develop your skills and have a real impact in your workplace.

Draw up a simple table with three columns. In the first column write **Where am I now?** and, as if you were explaining to me, make a few notes about your strengths and weaknesses when planning the work of your team. Be specific and provide some examples. Be honest with yourself – this is not part of your assessment, and identifying weaknesses is the first step to making improvements.

The questions below may help you.

Where am I now?

Tell me about the work your team does.

1. How do you establish the team's objectives? Who do you discuss this with? Are the objectives SMART? Do you have enough information early on in the process to enable you to plan?

2. What is the overall mission statement or aim of your organisation?

3. How does the success of your team contribute to your manager's objectives and the success of the organisation as a whole?

Now, in your second column, write the heading **Improvements** and in the third column **Action**.

Improvements and action

Are there any areas where your planning could be improved?

What action do you think you could take to make those improvements happen?

Some of the changes you have identified might affect the way things are done in your organisation and you may need to discuss them with your line manager. Some changes can be made by you. Remember, small changes can make a big difference.

When you plan to make a change, remember to make your new objectives SMART!

You can discuss the notes you have made with your assessor. They may provide evidence of your competence.

Learning outcome 2 – Be able to allocate work across a team

In this section we will explore each of the assessment criteria in more detail to develop your knowledge and understanding.

Now that you have agreed what work needs to be done and made a plan, you need to think about how to communicate this to your team. There are several ways of doing this, depending on the result you want and the different approaches or styles of leadership have been categorised as:

● autocratic

● democratic

● laissez-faire (a French phrase meaning 'let them do it themselves').

An autocratic leader is one who gives orders. 'This is how I want it done, it has to be done this way, by this date.' This is a useful leadership style to have in an emergency situation where things are not up for negotiation. It may also be used when deadlines are tight and there is no room to change either a customer's specification or a standard working procedure. When a team member is new, it may be helpful to be told exactly what has to be done. However, if used all the time, this style can cause resentment and rebellion in team members.

A democratic leader is one who gets everyone involved in the planning and listens to and adopts their ideas. When a creative approach is required, for example generating ideas to attract new customers, the democratic style of leadership is more productive. It works especially well when the aim is to involve people in the project, for example when setting up a community garden with local residents. It can also have the effect of motivating team members and making them feel their contribution is valued. This can bring enormous longer-term benefits to the team, but it can take time.

The laissez-faire leader has a more hands-off approach. For this to be effective, the leader must know and trust the team well and the team must be competent and able to work with a degree of autonomy. This style is often used when the team has specialists who know their role better than the team leader, maybe production, IT, or health care. It treats the team members as professionals and acknowledges that each person has a preferred way of working. However, if individuals are not working well, this style of leadership may not pick up on it for some time.

You may have a leadership style that works well with your team, but from time to time you may need to use another style to get the best response to a particular situation.

Assessment criterion 2.1 Discuss team plans with a team

First, when discussing plans with the team, it is important to put the work in context. By emphasising how the team's work contributes to the organisational objectives you can help your team realise the importance of their role. Your team may be sterilising the equipment that doctors and nurses use to treat patients in a hospital. Your team should know that the hospital has key performance objectives to achieve high levels of recovery after treating patients. The team need to see how their work contributes to the work of the hospital; that they are not just cleaning but helping to save lives.

Second, it is good to outline the objectives for the whole team before allocating individual work. This helps build a strong team who work together towards a common goal. Individuals who see themselves as part of a team are more likely to support each other in achieving the targets or key performance objectives for the whole team.

Assessment criterion 2.2 Agree work allocation and SMART objectives with team members

You may work with a team on a long-term project, for example the finance team in a company will have an ongoing aim to process payments and wages, or a short-term project such as the production of a new advertising brochure.

At the beginning or when reviewing a project, you need to consider the make-up of your team. You need to ask yourself:

- How many people do I need to complete this job?
- What skills and qualities do they need?
- Who is best suited to take on the various roles?

The first question can be answered by breaking down the job into smaller parts and calculating roughly the amount of time it takes to do each task. The newsletter may take (depending on the subject):

- two weeks of interviews and research
- one day for photography
- two days in production
- one day for printing.

Meeting with the team to discuss the plans should have provided you with an idea of individuals' availability. You need to know which members of the team have a flair for photography and printing, who would be best at interviewing people, who is a good researcher and who has e-publication skills. It is unlikely that one person will have all these skills, but a team of maybe four people with complementary skills should come up with a better end product.

You then need to agree the contribution of each team member. You will probably be familiar now with the need for objectives to be SMART, that is:

- specific
- measurable
- achievable
- realistic
- time bound.

Your team need to know specifically what they have to do. Nobody can work with confidence if they have only vague or general instructions. Can you imagine playing a game of chess for the first time without knowing the rules?

Both you and the team need to have an agreed way of measuring success. In chess, it is agreed that the winner has succeeded when the opponent's king is in checkmate. All projects need a way of measuring success and here you can also agree the standard of work expected. Your newsletter will be successful when the finished quality is of a particular standard.

You could ask a beginner to beat a master while playing a game of chess in a Force 9 gale. This would not be achievable or realistic. Make sure you set realistic objectives for your team. They must realistically have the appropriate skills, resources and time to complete the job successfully. And everyone needs to know when time is up. Neither team would win a game of football unless it was agreed that the game would finish after 90 minutes.

Assessment criterion 2.3 Agree standard of work required by team

One of the most common oversights when allocating work to a team is to focus on what needs to be done, when it needs to be done, but not how it needs to be done. There may be an assumption that everyone has the same understanding of the standard of work. This can lead to disappointment.

It is better to agree the standard of work at the start of a project rather than correct someone's work after they have done it. If you ask your catering team to make a roast dinner, it is no good telling them at the end that the meat should have been rare. Criticising your team for something they did not know about and cannot change will be demoralising and demotivating for individuals.

The golden rules are:

Agree the standard of work at the beginning of the project.

And

Ask team members to repeat it back to you so you know they have understood.

The case study below provides an opportunity for you to read about a team leader or team leading scenario. The case study highlights some of the issues discussed. You can use this to reflect on the situation and answer some questions. You do not have to write down your answers unless your tutor or assessor has asked you to do so.

CASE STUDY 2

Daljeet's team will be taking calls for a chain of music venues, answering queries about tour dates and ticket availability, and taking bookings. She sends an email to her team, asking them to undertake the online training session on how to use some new screens.

A week later, when they are due to go live, only half the team have completed the training session and only two people said they understood it all. The others had not realised the work was due to start so soon. One person said they had not received the email.

After a hurried training session to ensure everyone could use the screens, the work began and Daljeet listened in to monitor some of the calls. She was not happy that most of the callers were young and spoke casually, yet her team were responding formally as if dealing with a commercial client. Most of her team had not considered adapting their approach to the customer and Daljeet realised she would have to tell them that this was not the standard of work that was expected.

What do you think?

Clearly, things have not gone as well as they could.

1. How do you think Daljeet's method of communicating the work contributed to the problem?
2. How else could she have allocated this work to her team?
3. Why did the team not perform to the expected standard?
4. How could Daljeet have prevented this?
5. What role could SMART objectives have played?

DEVELOPMENT ACTIVITY 2 with your virtual adviser

I am here to demystify the assessment criteria and help you relate what you have learned to your own job role. We will look at what you are currently doing and how you can develop your skills and have a real impact in your workplace.

Draw up a simple table with three columns. In the first column write **Where am I now?** and, as if you were explaining to me, make a few notes about your strengths and weaknesses when making contributions and acknowledging the contributions of others in a meeting. Be specific and provide some examples. Be honest with yourself – this is not part of your assessment, and identifying weaknesses is the first step to making improvements.

The questions below may help you.

Where am I now?
Think about how you allocated work to your team in the past.

1. Did you involve them in the planning? If not, what was the reason?
2. How did you decide on the make-up of your team?
3. Were you happy that you had chosen the best person for each role?
4. When you agreed the allocations, did you use SMART objectives for each person's contribution?
5. How did you agree the standard of work expected?
6. What problems did you encounter during the project?

Now, in your second column, write the heading **Improvements** and in the third column **Action**.

Improvements and action
Are there any areas where you could have allocated work in a different way?

What action do you need to take to make those improvements?

Some of the changes you have identified might affect the way things are done in your organisation and you may need to discuss them with your line manager. Some changes can be made by you. Remember, small changes can make a big difference.

When you plan to make a change, remember to make your new objectives SMART!

You can discuss the notes you have made with your assessor. They may provide evidence of your competence.

Learning outcome 3 – Be able to manage team members to achieve team objectives

In this section we will explore each of the assessment criteria in more detail to develop your knowledge and understanding.

Assessment criterion 3.1 Support all team members in order to achieve team objectives

In an ideal world you could give work to your team and it would all be done on time, to the required standard, without any problems along the way. But in the real world there are a number of things that can go wrong and it is a key part of your role to support your team to ensure the team objectives are met.

Before we look at the problems and how they can be solved, we need to find out who needs support. Some individuals will talk to you the minute they are stuck, some will ask questions or ask for your opinion along the way. This allows you to monitor their progress. Others will simply struggle in silence, even when they are not able to do the work. It is good to have an open door and be approachable, but it is essential to be proactive and find the problems before they find you.

You need to plan some checks along the way – these are often called milestones – and let everyone know at the beginning of the project when these will be and what you will be looking at or measuring. If your brochure or newsletter needs to be completed by the end of the month, you may agree that you will check the first draft two weeks before the deadline. On a longer project or for ongoing work, it is useful to build in some one-to-one supervision meetings to check progress and give each person the chance to discuss any problems they are having.

There are many reasons why work does not go to plan:

- individual training needs
- insufficient resources
- time management
- personal issues.

First, members of the team may not have the skills to do the job. Your team may be putting together a brochure or newsletter and one person has agreed to take photographs. However, the camera they have been given is not one they have used before. They need help learning how to operate it. You may be able to pair them up with a more experienced photographer.

Most jobs are dependent on equipment, maybe copiers, computers, having the right personal protective equipment to do the job. We are all slowed down if we run out of supplies of paper, stamps or petrol in the car. It is part of your role as team leader to ensure there are sufficient resources to enable everyone to do their job. This is where you can anticipate needs rather than wait until supplies run out.

Time is a key resource and one that always runs out. Your team will have other things that compete for their time: other work, personal life, absence through sickness or holidays. Some of these are foreseeable and some are not. You need to support each person through a range of issues if you want them to have enough time and energy to focus on achieving the team objectives.

Some of the support you give to individuals in your team may be work related. They may not get on with another member of the team and you may need to resolve conflict between team members. Or the issue may be unrelated to work. They may come to you with personal issues that are affecting their ability to concentrate at work. You cannot solve all problems, but you can listen and maybe refer them to another organisation. As a people manager, it is useful to have a list of local contacts, whether it is the company's human resources (HR) department or local counselling, housing, drugs and alcohol advisers.

The key skills you need to support your team are:

● anticipate needs where possible

● arrange regular checks

● have an open door

● listen

● arrange additional training

● provide the necessary resources

● refer to another agency, if necessary.

The case study below provides an opportunity for you to read about a team leader or team leading scenario. The case study highlights some of the issues discussed. You can use this to reflect on the situation and answer some questions. You do not have to write down your answers unless your tutor or assessor has asked you to do so.

CASE STUDY 3

Daljeet's team has taken on six new recruits. These new agents are all students, who will be working part-time evenings and weekends while they are studying. Daljeet has carried out an induction and drawn up a rota so each new recruit can work next to a 'buddy' who will show them how to do the job.

She has also told them to come and see her at any time if they have a problem and has arranged a one-to-one meeting with each person every week to talk to them about their progress.

She notices that one of the new recruits is very quiet and tends to arrive late for his shifts. He hasn't come to speak to her about it, so she plans to bring it up in his weekly supervision.

What do you think?

1. If you were a new recruit at the call centre, how well supported would you feel by your team leader, Daljeet?

2. What has Daljeet done to ensure all her team feel equally supported?

3. How does Daljeet benefit from these measures?

4. Is there anything else she could do?

5. What do you think could be the new recruit's problem?

6. What questions might you ask him during supervision?

7. What remedial action might you agree?

DEVELOPMENT ACTIVITY 3 with your virtual adviser

I am here to demystify the assessment criteria and help you relate what you have learned to your own job role. We will look at what you are currently doing and how you can develop your skills and have a real impact in your workplace.

Draw up a simple table with three columns. In the first column write **Where am I now?** and, as if you were explaining to me, make a few notes about your strengths and weaknesses when managing team members. Be specific and provide some examples. Be honest with yourself – this is not part of your assessment, and identifying weaknesses is the first step to making improvements.

The questions below may help you.

Where am I now?
Think about the support you give your team.

1. Do you provide the team with opportunities to ask for support?

2. Are these informal (open door) or formal (supervision)?

3. What are the benefits and drawbacks of each?

4. What type of support has your team needed?

5. How have you provided this?

Now, in your second column, write the heading **Improvements** and in the third column **Action**.

Improvements and action
Are there any areas where the support you offer your team could be improved?

What action do you need to take to make those improvements?

Some of the changes you have identified might affect the way things are done in your organisation and you may need to discuss them with your line manager. Some changes can be made by you. Remember, small changes can make a big difference.

When you plan to make a change, remember to make your new objectives SMART!

You can discuss the notes you have made with your assessor. They may provide evidence of your competence.

Learning outcome 4 – Be able to monitor and evaluate the performance of team members

In this section we will explore each of the assessment criteria in more detail to develop your knowledge and understanding.

Assessment criterion 4.1 Assess team member's work against agreed standards and objectives

There are opportunities during a project and on completion for you to monitor progress and assess an individual's contribution to the overall success. It is important to **monitor** progress during the project so that you can:

● support and encourage team members

● identify problems or conflict within the team

● get the project back on track if standards or deadlines are slipping.

On completion you can evaluate the success of an individual's performance so they can:

● be rewarded for their success

● make plans for personal development

● demonstrate their suitability for future projects.

Monitoring progress during a project can be done in many ways, from a very informal question of 'How's it going?' to a formal review. Monitoring can be done by assessing results, for example how many sales have been achieved, or in discussion with the team member. This discussion can be face to face, by phone/text or email. You need to look at the advantages and disadvantages of each method and work out what will work best for you.

Assessing performance by looking at the figures works well in some environments. In a call centre, you can see at a glance how many calls per hour an individual is handling. In a retail environment, you can check the till readings and see how many customers have been served and whether the till balances at the end of the shift. These checks provide reliable information. They are also unobtrusive and allow the team member to get on with their job without interruption. But they show only part of the picture and do not assess whether the team member needs support in order to improve their performance.

It is important to make direct contact with individuals to discuss performance. If things are not going well, they can explain the reason why. You have the opportunity to agree remedial action.

If the contact with team members is informal it can create a relaxed working environment: asking how people are getting on, telling them to talk to you any time. However, relying on this method has its disadvantages. You need some boundaries, some time when you are not available so that you can do other work.

Often the team members who are not performing well or have problems are the last people to come to see you voluntarily. Your team may be spread out geographically and those furthest away will not have the same access as those who work in the same building as you.

So it is wise to schedule formal team meetings or one-to-one supervision where everyone gets an equal chance to update you on progress and access any support they need. In this way, the monitoring of performance is a joint activity and not a case of a team leader chasing, or nagging the team to do better. These sessions can be arranged in a way that gives each team member responsibility for achieving their objectives. Individuals who are treated like adults will tend to respond like adults; treated like children they will respond like children.

Once you've assessed someone's performance, don't forget to give them feedback. This is covered in section 5.2 of this unit.

Assessment criterion 4.2 Identify and monitor conflict within a team

It is not surprising that there is occasionally conflict in the workplace when you consider that teams are made up of different personalities, with different values, different interests and different ways of working. People spend long hours together in the workplace. Sometimes communication is poor and resources are scarce. Every now and again there will be an office romance. Someone may have personal problems and their performance may be poor.

When you look at the list of variables it's surprising there isn't more conflict.

So what do we mean by conflict and is it always a bad thing? Conflict can be defined as 'a perceived incompatibility between two parties'. It can be a one-off or recurring, it can be trivial or quite serious. It does not have to be a bad thing for an organisation. If a manager or team leader can avoid blaming the individuals involved, it can be an opportunity to improve the organisation's systems and procedures.

However, if not handled appropriately, conflict can lead to stress for those involved and those around them who may be forced to take sides and join split camps. It can be the start of gossip. It can lead to non-cooperation and missed deadlines. So let's look at the skills a team leader needs to identify and monitor conflict in a team and some techniques which may be helpful to manage or resolve the conflict.

It's worth checking the procedure in your organisation for dealing with conflict. There may be an HR department, a more senior manager or union representative who has specialist skills in conflict resolution. If you are in a position to deal with it yourself it is worth seeing both parties together so you appear open and unbiased. It is also reassuring to know there is no best way to deal with a conflict.

There are some listening skills you need to have and several techniques you can use depending on the situation. When listening in a conflict situation it is good just to listen without interrupting; let the person have their say, get everything off their chest. It is best to avoid passing judgement or being directive, so avoid saying what you think they should do. Sometimes stating their needs out loud and listening to the other party do the same is enough to move things on and resolve the situation. So remember:

- listen without passing judgement
- ask questions to clarify the situation
- acknowledge how the person is feeling
- paraphrase what they have said
- help both parties hear each other
- ask both parties to say what they want from each other.

When the issue is not resolved by the parties themselves you may have to decide the outcome. There is no best way of managing conflict, but there are some different approaches, as suggested by Dr Rahim in a study in *The International Journal of Conflict Management* (2001). Each of these may be used depending on the situation:

- Avoidance: you can ignore conflict altogether. If it is trivial and has occurred just the once, this may be the best course of action.
- Integration: if both parties disagree about the way a job should be done but basically they are both committed to the success of the project, you might try to use both working styles.
- Obliging: if one party has a strong desire to have their needs accommodated, you may decide to oblige them as long as the success of the project is not in danger.
- Dominating: on occasions you may just have to lay down the law and tell team members how it has to be. If you are short of time, the needs of the project have to come before the different needs of the individuals.
- Compromise: this aims to find a win–win situation where both parties have been heard and find a solution that benefits them both.

To resolve the conflict, both parties need to reach some agreement. Where this is not possible, the situation has to be managed as well as you can by agreeing to differ but perhaps spend less time in the same office or work on different parts of the project where paths don't cross. Hopefully this will lead to some form of damage limitation.

Assessment criterion 4.3 Identify causes for team members not meeting team objectives

While you are monitoring and evaluating the performance of team members you need to be able to identify the causes for team members not meeting their team objectives. There may be many reasons for this and it is worth checking that the targets that were set were realistic. It may be that circumstances have changed, making them no longer achievable. For instance, it is not possible to deliver goods to overseas customers if there are disruptions, maybe strikes, maybe weather conditions, that affect the transport systems. Targets may need to be reviewed in the light of changing outside influences or alternatives found.

A team member may not be achieving targets because they have insufficient resources – perhaps more supplies have been ordered but not yet delivered. Or they may have less time due to other changing priorities, a holiday or sickness. They may have personal problems that are affecting their ability to concentrate at work and you may need to find others who can compensate by working extra hours. They may not be the best person for the job role and some reallocation of work may be necessary. Or they may lack the skills and need additional training. We will look at ways of improving the team performance in learning objective 5 of this unit.

By noticing a change in behaviour or work rate, or by speaking to team members, you will be able to identify the cause of the problem and look for alternative ways of achieving the overall team objective. The earlier you identify the problem, the more time you have to make changes and still hit your targets.

The case study below provides an opportunity for you to read about a team leader or team leading scenario. The case study highlights some of the issues discussed. You can use this to reflect on the situation and answer some questions. You do not have to write down your answers unless your tutor or assessor has asked you to do so.

CASE STUDY 4

Daljeet is monitoring the performance of the team by checking the number of calls received each hour and listening in on the quality of the call. She notices that Bill is working slower than usual and Marcia's usual bubbly voice is sounding flat and tired. She asks each of them if they are OK and discovers they had a brief romantic fling which is now over. They were trying to avoid spending any time together and both went out during breaks rather than use the restroom. The restroom has a TV and a pool table and is a sociable place where agents get to know each other and stronger teams are built. Everyone jokes about callers they have spoken to on that shift and it helps to relieve some of the work stress.

Daljeet is uncertain whether to speak to the team members involved before their behaviour further affects not only their work but that of the team, or simply ignore it because the issue is personal.

What do you think?

1. What would you do in Daljeet's position?
2. Why do you think that would be the best course of action?
3. What effect would your solution have on the team members?
4. And on others in the team?
5. Would it help the team achieve their team objectives?

DEVELOPMENT ACTIVITY 4 with your virtual adviser

I am here to demystify the assessment criteria and help you relate what you have learned to your own job role. We will look at what you are currently doing and how you can develop your skills and have a real impact in your workplace.

Draw up a simple table with three columns. In the first column write **Where am I now?** and, as if you were explaining to me, make a few notes about your strengths and weaknesses when assessing your team's performance. Be specific and provide some examples. Be honest with yourself – this is not part of your assessment, and identifying weaknesses is the first step to making improvements.

The questions below may help you.

Where am I now?
Think about how you assess the performance of your team:

1. What criteria are you using to assess team members?
2. Are you measuring their performance against their agreed objectives?
3. Are you comparing one member with another?
4. What are the factors that prevent your team from achieving their objectives?
5. What alternatives have you suggested?
6. Has there been any conflict between members of the team?
7. If so, how did you deal with it?

Now, in your second column, write the heading **Improvements** and in the third column **Action**.

Improvements and action
Are there any areas where your monitoring of the team could be improved?

What action do you need to take to make those improvements?

Some of the changes you have identified might affect the way things are done in your organisation and you may need to discuss them with your line manager. Some changes can be made by you. Remember, small changes can make a big difference.

When you plan to make a change, remember to make your new objectives SMART!

You can discuss the notes you have made with your assessor. They may provide evidence of your competence.

Learning outcome 5 – Be able to improve the performance of a team

In this section we will explore each of the assessment criteria in more detail to develop your knowledge and understanding.

Assessment criterion 5.1 Identify ways of improving team performance

Having monitored and evaluated the team's performance, you will now have a good idea of the strengths and weaknesses of individuals and the team as a whole. Here we will look at a range of ways of improving team performance.

Depending on the development issue and whether it affects the whole team or an individual, you could consider:

- putting on a training session for the whole team
- running a workshop as part of a team-building event
- giving a training presentation at a team meeting
- giving feedback to the team
- giving feedback to an individual.

Factors such as time and budget will no doubt influence the type of development activity you choose. Be as flexible and creative as possible and remember there are good training materials online, some good DVDs and many resources which can be adapted for your own situation.

Assessment criterion 5.2 Provide constructive feedback to team members to improve their performance

Everyone needs feedback on their performance. Ideally, we all want that feedback to be 100 per cent positive to make us feel good. However, it is even more valuable to receive good constructive feedback on our areas of weakness because this is what will help us improve.

If someone has achieved their objectives or performed well, it is important to give them some positive feedback. Without it, team members, especially if they are new, may feel unappreciated and undervalued. They can become demoralised and their motivation will sink. Some organisations recognise this and have incentive schemes and rewards for its high achievers. Being acknowledged as Employee of the Month, featured in a newsletter, winning a prize, a handshake and a few kind words from a manager, all this helps to boost self-esteem, build company and team loyalty and motivate employees. As team leader, you can do this with 'thank yous', 'well dones' and some general positive praise when it is deserved. Some say be careful not to overdo it or it could lose all its value, others say you can never have enough.

If a team member's performance is poor and you need to give negative feedback, you can still give the feedback in a constructive way by:

- starting with a positive
- sandwiching the negative in the middle
- ending with another positive.

For example: 'You've managed to make contact with a good number of customers on the shop floor this week. I'd like to see more converted to sales, how do you think you could achieve that? (Maybe suggests more listening and questioning around customer needs.) Yes, try that this week. You are very good at listening, I think that will work well.'

Acknowledging what the team member has done well relaxes them and makes them less defensive when you want to discuss other issues. It is important to finish with a positive so they go away motivated rather than devastated. This is often referred to as the feedback sandwich.

It is said that we all hear the negatives about ourselves more than the positives, so when giving feedback remember to find genuine positive feedback and make sure it is heard. Feedback can be given on any number of occasions, but remember to build it in as an essential feature of appraisals, one-to-one discussions/reviews and in team meetings.

Assessment criterion 5.3 Implement identified ways of improving team performance

In section 5.1 we looked at some possible ways of improving team performance. So the final part of this unit will just emphasise the ongoing nature of development, sometimes call continuous professional development. Once you have identified training needs and have implemented a suitable way of improving the performance of your team, so another development need will present itself and round we go again.

It is good to establish a culture of continuous development in your team. Emphasise the importance of moving forward, always learning new skills, always developing knowledge. Then assessing performance, giving constructive feedback and improving performance, becomes part of everyday workplace activities and is seen as a benefit rather than a criticism.

There are some ways to involve the team in this development culture, including:

- improvement groups within the team
- team champions for particular aspects of the team's work
- 360-degree feedback
- peer training and review.

Improvement groups might consist of a number of volunteers who meet to discuss areas for improvement and generate new ideas on improving systems, procedures or performance. A champion, for example a customer service champion, would attend meetings, training and generally read up on new customer service developments and promote these within the team.

360-degree feedback encourages individuals to seek feedback, not just from their line manager but from peers and customers and anyone else to whom they provide a service. A wider picture of their competence emerges and is often used during appraisals. Team members can review each other's performance and also be involved in training each other, thereby recognising an individual's skills or knowledge and sharing best practice. Team members may cascade training that they have received to the rest of the team.

These methods are excellent for building a strong and committed team and embedding the whole idea of continuous development.

The case study below provides an opportunity for you to read about a team leader or team leading scenario. The case study highlights some of the issues discussed. You can use this to reflect on the situation and answer some questions. You do not have to write down your answers unless your tutor or assessor has asked you to do so.

Daljeet has now been a team leader for a year and has dealt with many situations along the way. She has watched her team take on new accounts and develop into good agents. She has carried out their appraisals and has given them all positive feedback.

She knows the call centre environment never stands still and wants to provide training for her team to take their customer service skills to the next level. She has heard about an excellent training course, but there is no budget to send the whole team away or even to book the presenter to deliver the training in the call centre. She decides to leave it and see whether there is more money available for training next year. She runs a brief session herself at the next team meeting.

What do you think?

1. What other training options could Daljeet have implemented?
2. What would be the advantages of the options you suggested?

DEVELOPMENT ACTIVITY 5 with your virtual adviser

I am here to demystify the assessment criteria and help you relate what you have learned to your own job role. We will look at what you are currently doing and how you can develop your skills and have a real impact in your workplace.

Draw up a simple table with three columns. In the first column write **Where am I now?** and, as if you were explaining to me, make a few notes about your strengths and weaknesses when improving the performance of your team. Be specific and provide some examples. Be honest with yourself – this is not part of your assessment, and identifying weaknesses is the first step to making improvements.

The questions below may help you.

Where am I now?
Think about how you improve the performance of your team.

1. How did you identify the team's needs?
2. How do you give feedback to your team on their strengths and weaknesses?
3. What training options were available and which did you choose?
4. What were the advantages and disadvantages of this training?
5. Did it achieve what you hoped?

Now, in your second column, write the heading **Improvements** and in the third column **Action**.

Improvements and action

Are there any areas where your team improvement skills could be improved?

What action do you need to take to make those improvements?

Some of the changes you have identified might affect the way things are done in your organisation and you may need to discuss them with your line manager. Some changes can be made by you. Remember, small changes can make a big difference.

When you plan to make a change, remember to make your new objectives SMART!

You can discuss the notes you have made with your assessor. They may provide evidence of your competence.

TEST YOUR KNOWLEDGE

Here are some questions to test your knowledge and understanding of the issues explored in this unit. You can write down the answers or discuss them with your assessor. They could provide good evidence for your NVQ.

1. Why do you need to agree team objectives with your own manager? AC 1.1

2. How do you take into account the capacity and capabilities of the team when developing the overall team plan? AC 1.2

3. Give two benefits to be gained by discussing the plans with the team. AC 2.1

4. Explain why individual team members' objectives should be SMART. AC 2.2

   Specific because: ....

   Achievable because: ....

   Measurable because: ....

   Realistic because: ....

   Time-bound because: ....

5. What might happen if you did not agree the standard of work at the beginning of the project? AC 2.3

6. Give two examples of the type of support a team member may need in order to achieve team objectives. AC 3.1

7. What is the reason for assessing team members' work against agreed standards and objectives? AC 4.1

8. Give three possible causes of conflict within a team. AC 4.2

9. Give three reasons why team members might not meet targets. AC 4.3

10. Identify three ways of improving team performance. AC 5.1

11. When providing constructive feedback to team members on improving their performance it is good practice to: AC 5.2

Start with ....

Then ....

And finish with ....

12. Why is this feedback technique considered to be the most effective? AC 5.2

13. Give an example of a new method (something you have not tried before) of improving the performance of your team. AC 5.3

Further information

Rahim, M.A., Antonioni, D. and Psenicks, C. (2001) A structural equations model of leader power, subordinates' styles of handling conflict, and job performance. *International Journal of Conflict Management, 12* (3), 191–211.

Unit D10 of this book is about conflict within teams.

Pulling it all together and gathering evidence

You and your assessor will need to agree the most appropriate sources of evidence. Here are some suggestions:

- An electronic portfolio: you could upload your evidence to an e-portfolio package or simply store the evidence in electronic format.

- A paper-based portfolio: you could build a folder with hard copies of your evidence.

Types of evidence:

- Observation: a record by your assessor when observing you:
  - talking to your team about goals, plans and objectives
  - supporting your team
  - giving feedback to your team on their performance.
- Work product: copies of work produced by you that demonstrate your competence, for example project plans, team objectives, notes/agendas for meetings, minutes of meetings, team or individual development plans.

- Discussion: a record of you and your assessor discussing reasons for choosing team members, capacity and capability of the team, how you have supported your team, areas of conflict within the team, reasons for non-achievement of objectives, ways of improving performance.
- Questioning: a record of your assessor asking questions to test your knowledge.
- Personal statement, reflective account or case study based on the activities in this unit: this should have sentences which start with 'I ...' and should tell a story giving real-life examples.
- Witness testimony from your line manager confirming your competence, in writing or recorded as a discussion with your assessor.

It is a good idea to include a range of evidence from different sources. Your evidence should cover a period of time and not be a 'one-off'. However, try to keep the evidence to a minimum. Your assessor can make a note of product evidence they have seen so it can be left in the workplace.

Remember:

Less is more – quality not quantity!

Be holistic – can you use this evidence again for other units?

EVALUATION

What have you learned from completing this unit?

What new skills and techniques are you using?

How has this affected the people you work with?

How has your organisation benefited? How might it benefit in the future?

MANAGE CONFLICT IN A TEAM

Introduction and learning outcomes

Learning outcomes for Unit D10:

1. Be able to support team members' understanding of their role and position within a team.

2. Be able to take measures to minimise conflict within a team.

3. Be able to understand how to encourage team members to resolve their own conflicts.

4. Be able to understand legal and organisational requirements concerning conflicts.

These learning outcomes say what you will have learned by the end of this unit. Each learning outcome is further broken down into assessment criteria, which we will look at in detail in the following sections of this unit.

This Unit Guide is a resource to help you gather the evidence you require to achieve Unit D10. It can be used as a learning resource if you are new to the role, are studying team leading in preparation for work or as a refresher if you are already an experienced team leader.

You and your assessor will agree what you need to do to meet the assessment criteria and show you are competent. This Unit Guide provides some theory to develop your understanding of how to manage conflict in a team, gives some case studies for you to examine and then an opportunity for you to reflect, with a virtual adviser, on how you can develop your own skills and gather evidence of competence. Some ideas are provided in the 'Pulling it all together' section at the end of this unit.

So, the purpose of this unit is to develop the skills and knowledge you need to manage conflict in a team.

Why does conflict occur in team work?

As a competitive and highly interactive species, human conflict situations have been recorded throughout history. Sadly, each day, news items detail stories centred on conflicts and how they have escalated. Generally, this escalation and conflict circumstance has begun with some form of dispute, and the manner of the escalation is usually due to how the dispute was handled or managed in the early stages.

Some minor disputes are perhaps inevitable and can be healthy to clear the air and move on, but control of disputes in the workplace is paramount. Conflict should not be encouraged.

All organisations strive to be effective and efficient in achieving their goals. The people in the organisation need to have a shared vision of what they are striving to achieve. Coupled with this is the need for clear objectives for each team, department and individual. So recognising and resolving conflict among your people is paramount. You must not allow conflict to become so serious that cooperation is impossible.

Teams by their very structure are often prone to some form of conflict. Thus it is important for the team leader to be aware of group dynamics. There may be a clash of personalities, a difference of opinion over work-related issues or a problem from some personal contact outside of work. Teams can be complex and often there is a subtle balance between work-related issues and personalities. As a team leader, maintaining this balance can be challenging.

In the 1960s Dr Tuckman described a popular model for the way groups behave. He identified four distinct phases of team development:

- forming: the team is uncertain how to proceed and behaviour is often reserved
- storming: the team often argues about who should do what and how
- norming: the team agrees its core tasks and individual roles within the team
- performing: the team operates along the agreed 'norms'.

As teams develop or change, the 'storming' phase is the obvious point during which potential conflict situations may occur. The way a team works will alter and change as new practices are introduced or new team members are brought in.

Conflict within or between teams can often be viewed in the following traits:

- rivalry – between colleagues or teams
- disagreements – over targets or work-related performance
- resentment – team members perceived not to be contributing.

Particular team concerns leading to conflict could centre on pay rates, changes in working practices, redundancy, health and safety, and general communication requirements. Individuals also have varying values regarding how they perceive fairness when dealing with teams. The manner in which they are managed contributes to conflict as they consider how their manager or team leader deals with them in relation to perhaps another manager's style.

So it is hardly surprising that a clear and active policy, procedure or guidelines in relation to the expected organisational standards relating to conflict is not only desirable but also pertinent for the workplace.

Figure D10.1

Learning outcome 1 – Be able to support team members' understanding of their role and position within a team

In this section we will explore each of the assessment criteria in more detail to develop your knowledge and understanding. You need to communicate and explain the required standards of behaviour expected of your team with regard to conflict.

Assessment criterion 1.1 Communicate to team members the standards of work and behaviour expected of them

As a team leader, at some time you will be involved with a situation or action (no matter how small) involving some form of conflict. The best form of preparation is to ensure that you have set out your stall clearly and that you communicate, act and firmly react in line with your organisational guidelines, policies and procedures. During team development is probably the best time to communicate to the team the standards of work and behaviour expected of them. However, as we have already identified, at times of change in a team it is worthwhile reinforcing these guidelines, policies and procedures.

A number of communication approaches can be adopted and may include:

- team talks
- presentations
- supervisions
- one-to-ones.

Each of these approaches would be suitable, but generally, as you want the message to reach all team members at the same time, a group communication method is best. Remember, though, that there are different types of potential conflict situations and that may mean your approach needs to be flexible.

Support material should be provided. The written documentation in place in your organisation regarding conflict in the workplace, your policies, procedures and guidelines should be presented during your chosen communication method. Copies of these documents should be supplied to the team and/or posted on notice boards or intranet systems. Continued reference to these documents should be made during communication to once again reinforce the message.

Other work-related organisations, such as trade unions and ACAS for example, have their own policies or guidelines on conflict. It is worthwhile using these guidelines to offer alternative viewpoints to the team and to reiterate that conflict behaviours or actions are recognised by established work-related organisations as not acceptable.

Let's review the content of your chosen communication method and consider the issues facing you as a team leader.

Assessment criterion 1.2 Explain how team members can work together and support each other

When a team is brought together, generally they are required to work to expected organisational standards. They will have obvious tasks to perform; they may have procedures to follow in order to carry out their role. As the team members work together, roles and responsibilities are developed. These can be clearly defined or with some crossover of duties. Later the team should move towards an expectation of mutual respect and work-based harmony. However, to find all of these qualities within a team at all times can be difficult, to say the least.

So what are the qualities you would expect in an effective team? Let's look at some and then consider how conflict situations could develop as these qualities are challenged or questioned.

Potential team member qualities:

- reliability
- active participant
- communicates constructively and listens actively
- shares knowledge and information
- cooperates and assists
- flexibility

- commitment
- problem solver
- respectful and supportive.

This list is not definitive but gives a general feel for potential team qualities. The problem we have as team leaders is that when one or some of these qualities are not displayed by one or more of the team, conflict conditions are created. To have team members with all of these qualities (at all times) will require a highly innovative team selection process! So the best we can do is to start by communicating our desired team standards and use procedures, guidelines and policies to assist in identifying and deterring potential team conflict. This will be discussed further under assessment criterion 2.2.

The case study section provides an opportunity for you to read about a team leader or team leading scenario. The case study highlights some of the issues discussed. You can use this to reflect on the situation and answer some questions. You do not have to write down your answers unless your tutor or assessor has asked you to do so.

CASE STUDY 1

Samantha (Sam) works for a soft drinks company. She is the team leader for the laboratory and her team of four (including herself) carry out quality checks on a packaging line bottling carbonated drinks. Recent events have meant that Sam will soon be responsible for another line with three team members. The team of seven will carry out similar roles but have not worked with each other before.

They are due to work together in two weeks, but Sam is concerned that the group may have slightly differing working practices. Some of the new team are quite verbal and have expressed views such as, 'Why should we change? We have always carried out our work in this manner. They should change and use our regimes.'

Sam has requested a full meeting of the new team (team talk) at the end of this week to discuss team work and expected duties.

What do you think?

1. How do you think Sam should prepare for the team talk?
2. On what should Sam base the content of the team talk?
3. If you were Sam, what would you bring along to support the team talk?
4. What would you ask the team members to bring to the meeting?

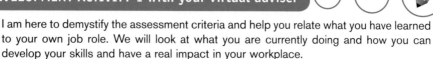

DEVELOPMENT ACTIVITY 1 with your virtual adviser

I am here to demystify the assessment criteria and help you relate what you have learned to your own job role. We will look at what you are currently doing and how you can develop your skills and have a real impact in your workplace.

Write up a personal statement describing your knowledge of your organisation's expected standards of work and behaviour. Consider your organisation's guidelines, procedures and policies regarding roles and responsibilities. Do the documents consider input from the team members?

The questions below may help you.

Where am I now?

Tell me about the expected standards of behaviour.

1. How clear are you about your team's expected standards of work and behaviour?

2. Are all of your team aware of the standards of work and behaviour required?

3. Can your team explain how they work and support each other?

4. Do you have any team members who work alone as they do not work well with others?

5. What do you do to prepare for a team talk? Do you have a section regarding working together?

Now, write the heading **Improvements and action**.

Improvements and action

Are there any areas in your personal statement where you did not understand the need to communicate standards of behaviour?

What action do you think you could take to ensure the team understands and reacts to poor standards of behaviour?

Write these improvements and actions in your personal statement to reflect on your findings; this will assist you in considering your options. Your options could include a change in the way you communicate, the style, method or timing. Some of the changes you have identified might affect the way things are done in your organisation and you may need to discuss them with your line manager. Some changes can be made by you. Remember, small changes can make a big difference.

When you plan to make a change, remember to make your new objectives SMART!

You can discuss the notes you have made with your assessor. They may provide evidence of your competence.

Learning outcome 2 – Be able to take measures to minimise conflict within a team

In this section we will explore each of the assessment criteria in more detail to develop your knowledge and understanding.

Assessment criterion 2.1 Identify issues with organisational structures, systems or procedures that are likely to give rise to conflict

First, let's consider the obvious barriers within a structure. The main reason individuals come to work is for financial reward. So pay and grading differences can and do form a huge gap between individuals, especially if they are working within the same team carrying out similar roles or duties.

Training and skill levels can also offer some negative points when discussing team interaction. The mix of skills in a team may differ and lead to graded payments within the team. Lower grades within a team may create a 'them and us' status, which in turn reduces the chances of team harmonisation. The team ethos approach should be that everyone has an impact on the outputs and efforts of the team, so some other form of incentive may have to be put in place.

Within organisational structures one of the problems may be the options for promotion. If the organisation movement is static, team members may view this as a barrier and offer less in terms of team contribution. Similarly, if promotion is commonplace, we could see movement in a team on a frequent basis. This, too, can be unsettling for a team as members move on quickly and do not have enough time to offer team input.

So we have a number of potential issues that could create unrest in a team and ultimately develop into a conflict situation. If you are aware of the issues then you are able to offer some form of action plan to counter the problems.

Discussion and direct communication will help. Team members are also individuals and some organisational systems or procedures will obviously not suit everyone. However, the process is in place for a reason and you need to reinforce the message at times, no matter how unpalatable that may be. You may be aware of the situations or circumstances but need to work with organisational systems, procedures and policies that are in place until they are changed or altered through debate, discussion and negotiation with those involved.

Take, for example, a team brought together from two organisations carrying out very similar roles and producing similar products. The first group (Team A) has excellent pay scales and good training packages. The second group (Team B) has a reduced pay rate and static training. The two groups have been brought together as one organisation merged with another, so transfer of undertakings arrangements exist. These arrangements are set out in employment law, Transfer of Undertakings (Protection of Employment) Regulations 2006. Basically, this law is in place so that organisations do not alter the affected employees' terms and conditions and 'contracts are not worsened'. Negotiations will then take place over an agreed period of time. All parties must agree before any changes can be made to the terms and conditions of the employees affected.

So imagine the barriers to the team structure in this particular event. The negotiations could be protracted, with real conflict developing as the groups are trying to carry out the same role. The higher paid team will be concerned over a possible reduction in conditions through negotiation, while the lower paid team will need to apply the same input to the role to ensure employment.

Assessment criterion 2.2 Identify potential conflict between team members

Teams are prone to some form of conflict. If you view the Tuckman model from the 1960s, storming is still as evident today as it was then as team members often argue about who should do what and how. Teams go through the phases in the model frequently as team composition or workload alter. Change is something we have to consider all too frequently in today's climate and is evident in all sectors of work.

The team leader needs to be aware of the conditions that could provide a catalyst for conflict. Identifying potential conflict between team members is difficult and is dependent on good communication methods and techniques. Team leaders and members should be alert to signs of conflict between colleagues so that they can action any intervention that may reduce or resolve the conflict by getting to the cause.

Some signs of potential conflict may be team members:

- not speaking to each other or ignoring each other
- contradicting or bad-mouthing one another
- undermining or not cooperating with each other.

All of these issues will lead to the downfall of the team ethos.

Remember the team qualities mentioned previously? If you add 'does not' or 'will not' before any team member's quality statement, you know you will have some form of conflict developing or 'simmering' under the surface.

- does not offer – reliability
- will not – actively participant
- does not – communicate constructively and listen actively
- does not, will not – share knowledge and information
- does not – cooperate and assist
- will not offer – flexibility
- does not offer – commitment
- does not, will not – problem solve
- will not be – respectful and supportive.

Each one of these points will potentially offer a reaction from other team members. Personality clashes are another issue and strong personalities within a team can be difficult to deal with.

Grading and operational respect are potential flash points for conflict. In some cases the fact that someone has been recognised as an achiever could create a claim of preferential treatment from other team members who may feel they have contributed to the same level.

Let's refer back to our scenario of the merger of two factions to create a new 'team'. The groups have developed in their previous organisations on slower pathways. Team A, for example, was used to frequent team talks and direct one-to-one discussion. Team B, meanwhile, held meetings infrequently and a one-to-one would be considered only if a union representative was present. So the team leader would in effect have to work on Team B to develop the required interaction and level of contribution required.

Although they are reliable in terms of attending work and carrying out tasks they have had training upon, the members of Team B are not used to active communication methods and the required sharing of information is thus protracted. The conflict aspects between the two factions are therefore on a number of issues and levels. Team talks at this stage will be lopsided and team development as a whole sketchy, to say the least.

For this group of 'team' workers the potential areas of conflict are all too easy to identify. Actions required to resolve the conflict may take longer to identify.

Assessment criterion 2.3 Explain action required to avoid potential conflict and agree strategies for conflict resolution

Developing and agreeing a strategy for any process involves others. In the case of managing and avoiding conflict, the activities are the same. The relevant parties need to apply the process and be actively involved in the process.

So what type of team involvement should we consider to avoid potential conflict situations? Teams need people who are not afraid to express their thoughts with clarity and brevity. Direct, honest and with respect for others is the way a team should communicate. Based on these points the team members need to devise actions to avoid potential conflict situations.

Possible methods could include the following:

- team training, inclusive and in-house to consider the team qualities as prescribed by the organisation
- team charter, detailing expected mutual respect within the team
- team talks, emphasising the team values.

A mix of these methods could work or the selection of one, ensuring it is reinforced at every opportunity.

Let's go back to our team made up from two previous teams. In terms of their obvious backgrounds the enormity of the work required to build the team is clear. However, as a merged team from two companies they have a common objective: to make the team operate successfully to ensure future employment.

Ignoring the past is difficult and trying to move forward from an entrenched position is also a problem. By separating the problem of terms and conditions and leaving that to the human resources department to deal with, the team can focus on the issues and develop processes that will assist progression.

A team charter linked with training requirements will support the group's development; the charter should be defined by them and be supported by them. Adherence to its guidelines will assist in breaking down barriers and conflict situations will reduce. Not all conflict situations will halt, but in the future the team will stop to consider actions and thus the team is then part of the way to resolution. The term 'drawing a line in the sand' fits in this scenario as the groups move on from a particular entrenched position.

The case study below provides an opportunity for you to read about a team leader or team leading scenario. The case study highlights some of the issues discussed. You can use this to reflect on the situation and answer some questions. You do not have to write down your answers unless your tutor or assessor has asked you to do so.

CASE STUDY 2

The team talk has ended and Sam has ensured she has noted all points made by the newly formed team. She had brought along the procedures for the team as a reference guide. There are differences in the manner that the work is done, which, although there are only minor issues that are not detailed in the standard operational procedure, are enough to slow down the process.

Two of the team, Lisa and Marie, were highly vocal on the working differences and argued quite strongly to support their point of view, so Sam intervened. She tasked them to work together to review the procedures and take the two examples and apply the points they raised as solutions to the problem.

During the team talk it was clear that the obvious personality clash between Lisa and Marie was affecting the other team's contribution to the talk. Sam indicated that she would like everyone to contribute to any future team meetings or team talk; to this end the next monthly meeting would be to form a team charter. The charter would outline expected behaviours within the team and also detail how future team talks would be handled, ensuring everyone had some form of contribution to the tabled topics.

What do you think?

1. Was Sam prepared for this team talk?

2. How do you think the evidence she brought along supported the discussion?

3. How might others have reacted differently if she did not have any back-up evidence?

4. How did things change when she presented the team members with a joint task?

5. Why do you think this technique is effective?

6. How do you think the other team members felt when the two argued over the procedure?

DEVELOPMENT ACTIVITY 2 with your virtual adviser

I am here to demystify the assessment criteria and help you relate what you have learned to your own job role. We will look at what you are currently doing and how you can develop your skills and have a real impact in your workplace.

Draw up a simple table with three columns. In the first column write **Where am I now?** and, as if you were explaining to me, make a few notes about your strengths and weaknesses when handling or managing conflict in your team. Be specific and provide some examples. Be honest with yourself – this is not part of your assessment, and identifying weaknesses is the first step to making improvements.

The questions below may help you.

Where am I now?
Think about team situations where conflict developed.

1. Can you think of a time when working with your team you have had to remind people of their behaviour towards other team members?

2. Did you have any prior awareness of the potential team conflict?

3. Do you have any procedures or structures that could lead to conflict?

4. How have you at any time put together an action or strategy to resolve a conflict situation?

Now, in your second column, write the heading **Improvements** and in the third column **Action**.

Improvements and action
Are there any areas where your skills to manage a conflict could be improved?

What action do you need to take to make those improvements?

Some of the changes you have identified might affect the way things are done in your organisation and you may need to discuss them with your line manager. Some changes can be made by you. Remember, small changes can make a big difference.

When you plan to make a change, remember to make your new objectives SMART!

You can discuss the notes you have made with your assessor. They may provide evidence of your competence.

Learning outcome 3 – Be able to understand how to encourage team members to resolve their own conflicts

In this section we will explore each of the assessment criteria in more detail to develop your knowledge and understanding.

Assessment criterion 3.1 Explain how team members can be encouraged to identify and resolve their own problems and conflicts

In the previous case history, Sam used a technique to encourage team members to work together. In her situation the development of the procedure offered itself up as a solution. Sadly, situations like that are rare. Nevertheless, working together on an initiative to develop something offers a clear response to a potentially negative conflict issue.

Team interaction needs individuals who are actively part of the process within a team; they should treat all team members with respect and support. These qualities are expected and as the team leader you must ensure they are prominent topics in all of your communication methods and techniques.

All team leaders need to be alert to group dynamics that can spill over into conflict. By doing so they will be able to support and assist the team to identify and resolve their own problems, or at least be able to show that some issues may be out of the team's direct control.

Sources of team conflict are many and varied and are linked to the 'forming, storming, norming and performing' model as they will directly affect a team's desire or attitude to work together. They may be as follows:

- the lack of resources (finance, equipment, facilities, etc.)
- different attitudes, values or perceptions
- disagreements about needs, goals, priorities and interests
- poor communication
- inadequate organisational structure
- a lack of clear roles and responsibilities.

So how do we as team leaders encourage the team to identify and resolve their own problems and conflicts?

Team talks provide an opportunity for the team to raise topics that concern them; generally the team talk can be a fairly open forum. With ground rules set in a team charter, the team can debate without prejudice and offer potential solutions. Focus groups on issues raised also help the team understand how certain circumstances can oppose the desire to work together.

Let's take one of the potential sources of conflict and consider how the team can resolve the issue. Roles and responsibilities are generally established at the onset of a team's development or creation, but they do not need to remain fixed as the team develops. The team members themselves can decide or consider who would be best at what activity as they understand the required skills in place and the general desired interaction within the team. The team leader should be party to this group as they are part of the team and therefore part of the process. By developing an 'in build' exercise like this the team has ownership of a 'problem' and by progressing to resolve the issue they work together to challenge some of the normal pre-set perceived roles within a work group.

As the team leader you can also use direct and progressive discussions with individuals within the team; one-to-one supervision can detail any potential or perceived conflict issues. In some cases this method is better than an open forum as issues of conflict can be very personal and different attitudes, values or perceptions can be expanded upon. The need to explore why an individual did not receive any plaudits for good work when another team member did, for example, would be considered 'sour grapes' by the other team members if discussed in a team talk or full meeting.

Assessment criterion 3.2 Explain how respect can be developed and maintained between team members

An ideal team member treats fellow team members with courtesy and consideration, not just some of the time but consistently. Team members should show support and understanding to each other to ensure the team task is completed. No conditions are applied when assistance is provided; they will listen and share information.

Ideal team members show commitment to the full team's targets, not just the task or condition they are focusing on, contributing to the overall success of the team and behaving in a professional manner. But the ideal team member is a rare breed (although you may have a number of your team who show, display and offer some of these qualities). So the promotion of these qualities offers you the opportunity to develop and enhance your team.

Team members need to be coached to learn that it is important to trust and respect each other. They must learn that to get the job done they have to rely on others to do their part and that others are counting on them to do what they have said they would do.

As we are aware, personal and business problems outside the team can affect a team member's ability to accomplish agreed tasks. As soon as it becomes clear that a team member cannot complete their task they must advise the team on the causes and ask for help. This process of offering information will help convince other team members that this person is trustworthy.

Identification of potential conflicts that will affect the team's work also assists the building of trust and respect, without blaming any particular party, team member or otherwise. Trust and respect need to be worked on – as a new team builds, the level of loyalty increases as time goes by. Take, for example, our team formed from two organisations mentioned above. They did not have the opportunity to be acquaintances prior to the team creation as they were from different organisations. So trust and respect will take some time to develop and they will need to work towards an understanding of the way they should interact and assist each other.

However, we can help the team to develop trust and respect. Initial training and induction into the team, generally getting to know each other and sharing views on aspects of the work and general information, is a useful first step. Breaking down some of the perceived barriers and allowing interaction is a positive move. Some team exercises or discussions relating to general group work, together with the development of the team charter, will offer viewpoints on how the team should work. It will also show others how each of the team members views the team's potential development.

The case study section provides an opportunity for you to read about a team leader or team leading scenario. The case study highlights some of the issues discussed. You can use this to reflect on the situation and answer some questions. You do not have to write down your answers unless your tutor or assessor has asked you to do so.

CASE STUDY 3

Marie and Lisa have returned the new operating procedure to Sam, the team leader. They returned the work at different times during the first day at work, Monday, and each had highlighted their own contribution. The pair have offered work that is concise and covers the aspects they had raised during the initial team meeting, but neither of them during the discussion offered any comments on the other's involvement or contribution.

During the discussion with Marie and Lisa, Sam took the opportunity to discuss expected team behaviours. Both acknowledged they had behaved in a manner that was not appropriate and apologised for their actions. Sam accepted the apology and indicated that it would benefit the team if they were to apologise to each other during the next team meeting.

The next monthly meeting would develop the team charter.

What do you think?

1. How would you build on the work that the team members have completed?
2. What will be a gained (if anything) from Sam's request for the team members to apologise to the full team?
3. How would you prepare for the next meeting?
4. If you were Sam, how would you have handled this situation?

DEVELOPMENT ACTIVITY 3 with your virtual adviser

I am here to demystify the assessment criteria and help you relate what you have learned to your own job role. We will look at what you are currently doing and how you can develop your skills and have a real impact in your workplace.

Draw up a simple table for a 'to do' list. In the list detail the methods you have used to help your team to resolve conflict. If you have not had any situations of conflict to deal with, prepare a written statement, as if you were explaining to me, regarding how you would encourage team members to resolve their own conflicts. Be specific with regard to methods you have used and provide some examples. Be honest with yourself this is not part of your assessment, and by considering options in this manner will prepare you for any developments that may occur in the future.

The questions below may help you.

Where am I now?

Think about any conflict situations you have been involved in.

1. Do you discuss potential conflict situations or circumstances with your team?

2. Do you have a team topic detailing how respect, trust and support are handled?

3. How and when do you update the team on expected behaviours?

Now, in your second section, write up a reflective account on how you would make **improvements** and then how you would implement any **action**.

Improvements and action

Are there any areas where you could improve your approach to encouraging team members to resolve their own conflicts?

What action do you need to take to make those improvements?

Some of the changes you have identified might affect the way things are done in your organisation and you may need to discuss them with your line manager. Some changes can be made by you. Remember, small changes can make a big difference.

When you plan to make a change, remember to make your new objectives SMART!

You can discuss the notes you have made with your assessor. They may provide evidence of your competence.

Learning outcome 4 – Be able to understand legal and organisational requirements concerning conflict

In this section we will explore each of the assessment criteria in more detail to develop your knowledge and understanding.

Assessment criterion 4.1 Explain legal and organisational requirements concerning conflict in own team

In most working environments we have legal and organisational requirements that govern our activities in the workplace. These requirements are in place to assist all parties and offer guidance. The content of these documents will detail the required standards of behaviour for that particular workplace; these requirements may be set into contracts, agreements, policies, procedures and job descriptions.

Generally, these documents follow current overarching law – Employment Act 2008 and the ACAS Code of Practice. The aim is to ensure that the role of any manager is to not allow conflict to develop and to maintain an approach of not taking sides. By adhering to the legal and organisational requirements the team leader can then act as a mediator in conflict situations and use official processes as the final solution.

No one likes conflict situations, but ignoring and avoiding the potential confrontation will only add to the problem. The requirement to intervene quickly in cases of conflict will bring a solution; this must be tempered by not stepping in too early without understanding the issues. So the process can be complicated, to say the least!

Let's look at the positive and negative uses of official processes during a conflict situation.

Negative:

- Making the situation 'official' before seeking a resolution with those involved.
- Intervening early and taking up the complaint as official prior to the situation being reported, working on hearsay.
- Not following organisational procedure regarding conflict.

Positive:

- Ensuring you communicate procedures and policies to all team members, then reinforce during your communication sessions.
- Use all procedures in line with organisational guidelines.
- Set examples when required to show you follow procedures and understand them.

Assessment criterion 4.2 Explain how to maintain complete, accurate and confidential records of conflicts and their outcomes

Within the content of the units we have covered one particular aspect of a team leader's work appears in all areas, that of communication. When presented with a conflict situation, communication skills and methods to maintain complete, accurate and confidential records are of great importance. The requirement to communicate organisational procedures and policies needs to be detailed and recorded in a number of ways. But in order to offer a conclusion to any conflict situation the following records should be present in the team member's files:

- signed one-to-one reviews (policies, procedure acceptance and acknowledgement)
- full induction records showing reference points to expected behaviours
- if events develop, the documentation detailing events leading to conflict
- disciplinary actions, detailing all conflict references.

Record keeping generally for all interaction with your team is best practice; documents and accounts of discussions with points raised should be kept for future reference. Use your diary or notepad, and date and note the topics discussed as you would generally. If you believe team members have some form of interaction that looks like friction or disagreement, question it with those concerned and ensure they are aware that you have noted it. Such accounts may be required later if the conflict escalates to a disciplinary review. Also, ensuring records are kept maintains the professionalism required within a team and establishes expectations of team conduct.

Records need to be kept in the same format for all team members. This shows employees that they are equally important and that the values are the same for all.

It also demonstrates that you will use a systematic approach to all issues that may arise within the team.

Depending on the organisation, the files regarding individuals within a team are kept in a safe environment. This may be locked cabinets held by the human resources department, or in some organisations with the line manager or team leader. This maintains the integrity of the documents and keeps employee issues private and confidential.

The case study below provides an opportunity for you to read about a team leader or team leading scenario. The case study highlights some of the issues discussed. You can use this to reflect on the situation and answer some questions. You do not have to write down your answers unless your tutor or assessor has asked you to do so.

Figure D10.2: Keeping accurate records is important

CASE STUDY 4

The meeting to discuss the team charter is due. Sam has decided to prepare for the meeting by ensuring each team member is knowledgeable on the behaviours expected by the team. She has started one-to-ones, during which the team members offer views on how the charter should progress.

However, a disturbing theme emerges. Two of the team indicate that Marie has made reference to the previous argument with Lisa and has stated she will 'take it further' to ensure her methods are established rather than Lisa's.

Sam is due to meet with Lisa and later with Marie for their one-to-one discussions.

What do you think?

1. How should Sam handle this problem?

2. What would you do?

3. Should Sam start discipline procedures with Marie?

4. What types of records should be completed and reviewed in relation to this latest situation?

DEVELOPMENT ACTIVITY 4 with your virtual adviser

I am here to demystify the assessment criteria and help you relate what you have learned to your own job role. We will look at what you are currently doing and how you can develop your skills and have a real impact in your workplace.

Draw up a list. In the list detail your organisational standards of behaviour. How do you record events relating to these standards of behaviour? List the methods in place.

The questions below may help you.

Where am I now?

Think about any conflict situations you have been involved in.

1. Have you documented all discussions regarding conflict in formal records?

2. Do you keep a diary or a log on interaction with the team that you could use to refer to a situation or event?

3. How are records kept and maintained?

Now, if you do not keep records or logs, write up a short statement on how you would make **improvements** and then how you would implement any **action**.

Improvements and action

Are there any areas where you could improve your understanding of your legal and organisational requirements regarding conflict?

What action do you need to take to make those improvements?

Some of the changes you have identified might affect the way things are done in your organisation and you may need to discuss them with your line manager. Some changes can be made by you. Remember, small changes can make a big difference.

When you plan to make a change, remember to make your new objectives SMART!

You can discuss the notes you have made with your assessor. They may provide evidence of your competence.

TEST YOUR KNOWLEDGE

Here are some questions to test your knowledge and understanding of the issues explored in this unit. You can write down the answers or discuss them with your assessor. They could provide good evidence for your NVQ.

1. What is your organisation's preferred communication method to ensure team members are aware of the standards of work and behaviour expected of them? AC 1.1

2. How were the required standards of work and behaviour explained to you? AC 1.1

3. How do team members work together and support each other? AC 1.2

4. Do you have any current issues that are likely to give rise to conflict? AC 2.1

5. Have you identified any issues in your organisational structures that are likely to give rise to conflict? AC 2.1

6. Do you have any potential conflict situations between team members? AC 2.2

7. What action is required or used to avoid potential conflict situations? AC 2.3

8. Describe an agreed or proposed strategy to avoid conflict. AC 2.3

9. Why is it important to encourage team members to identify and resolve their own problems and conflicts? AC 3.1

10. What methods are used to maintain team members' respect for each other? AC 3.2

11. What might happen if you did not follow the legal and organisational requirements concerning conflict? AC 4.1

12. What are the legal and organisational requirements used in your work area? AC 4.1

13. What documentation or forms do you use to record confidential records of conflicts and outcomes? AC 4.2

14. Where are the documents and forms you use to record confidential records of conflicts and outcomes held? AC 4.2

15. Give three methods you use to document reviews with team members. AC 4.2

Pulling it all together and gathering evidence

You and your assessor will need to agree the most appropriate sources of evidence. Here are some suggestions:

- An electronic portfolio: you could upload your evidence to an e-portfolio package or simply store the evidence in electronic format.
- A paper-based portfolio: you could build a folder with hard copies of your evidence.

Types of evidence:

- Observation: a record by your assessor when observing you taking part in a meeting.
- Work product: copies of work produced by you that demonstrate your competence, for example agenda, your notes, minutes.
- Discussion: a record of you and your assessor discussing examples of things that happened in a meeting and how you dealt with them.
- Questioning: a record of your assessor asking questions to test your knowledge.
- Personal statement, reflective account or case study based on the activities in this unit: this should have sentences which start with 'I …' and should tell a story giving real-life examples.
- Witness testimony from your line manager confirming your competence, in writing or recorded as a discussion with your assessor.

It is a good idea to include a range of evidence from different sources. Your evidence should cover a period of time and not be a 'one-off'. However, try to keep the evidence to a minimum. Your assessor can make a note of product evidence they have seen so it can be left in the workplace.

Remember:

Less is more – quality not quantity!

Be holistic – can you use this evidence again for other units?

EVALUATION

What have you learned from completing this unit?

What new skills and techniques are you using?

How has this affected the people you work with?

How has your organisation benefited? How might it benefit in the future?

Introduction and learning outcomes

Learning outcomes for Unit D11:
1. Be able to prepare to lead a meeting.
2. Be able to manage meeting procedures.
3. Be able to chair a meeting.
4. Be able to undertake post-meeting tasks.

These learning outcomes say what you will have learned by the end of this unit. Each learning outcome is further broken down into assessment criteria which we will look at in detail in the following sections of this unit.

This Unit Guide is a resource to help you gather the evidence you require to achieve Unit D11. It can be used as a learning resource if you are new to the role, are studying team leading in preparation for work or as a refresher if you are already an experienced team leader.

You and your assessor will agree what you need to do to meet the assessment criteria and show you are competent. This Unit Guide provides some theory to develop your understanding of leading and managing meetings, gives some case studies for you to examine and then an opportunity for you to reflect, with a virtual adviser, on how you can develop your own skills and gather evidence of competence. Some ideas are provided in the 'Pulling it all together' section at the end of this unit.

So, the purpose of this unit is to develop the skills and knowledge you need to lead and manage meetings.

Why call a meeting?

It is unfortunate but true that many people dread meetings. How often have you thought, 'Oh no, not another meeting, what a waste of time' or 'I seem to spend my whole life in meetings!'?

Figure D11.1

These are some of the common complaints about meetings:

- too many items on the agenda
- the meeting goes on too long
- we go round and round in circles
- I couldn't get a word in edgeways
- it was so dull.

You can probably think of a few more from your own experience.

Of course, it does not have to be like this. We could look at meetings in a different way to avoid some of the common pitfalls. There are several steps to successful meetings which leave everyone feeling positive:

- Be clear about the reason for calling a meeting.
- Invite the right people.
- Be well prepared.
- Manage time during the meeting.
- Manage contributions during the meeting.
- Communicate the outcome of the meeting.
- Follow up any agreed actions.

The main reasons for calling a meeting are:

- to make a decision
- to gather ideas
- to share information.

If you are unclear about the purpose, you will not invite the right people for the job, the attendees won't be prepared and you won't have thought about the process involved.

When a decision needs to be made it is best to have only a few people who are directly affected by the issue. Most decisions involve change and the aim should be to get everyone on board. It is unlikely that everyone will have the same views, so you need to be prepared. If there is disagreement, can you delay making a decision or does it need to be made immediately? Would it work best to go with a majority vote? If so, everyone needs to agree to this at the beginning and you must be prepared to accept that not everyone is on board. If you need a consensus, there may be more negotiating to establish what people need in order to say 'yes'. If there has to be a total consensus on new working hours, you must be prepared to suggest other forms of compensation that would help everyone come to an agreement.

If the aim of the meeting is to gather ideas you may want to invite more people, but not too many so that individuals cannot have their say. You may want to prepare some brainstorming activities and you will need to have flip charts, pens or some way of capturing what has been suggested. This takes preparation. Individuals need to know the purpose of the meeting in advance so that they can do some research and come prepared.

Before you call a meeting for sharing information, consider whether there is a better option. Could it be circulated by email? If the information concerns the launch of a new product you may want the energy of a room full of people to generate a buzz. If the information concerns new procedures and you think this would be an opportunity to ask questions and ensure everyone has understood, then a meeting may be the best way.

Some meetings may have a mixture of purposes and desired outcomes on the same agenda. The key messages are:

- Be clear about the purpose.
- Communicate the purpose to others before the meeting.

Learning outcome 1 – Be able to prepare to lead a meeting

In this section we will explore each of the assessment criteria in more detail to develop your knowledge and understanding.

Assessment criterion 1.1 Perform activities in preparation for a meeting

As we discussed above, before calling a meeting at all it is essential to be clear about the purpose of the meeting. As part of your preparation, think about the type of meeting that will best achieve this purpose and whether, in fact, there is another way.

Meetings are time-consuming and can occasionally be inconvenient. The fact that all other work stops for a meeting means that they are expensive in terms of resources and loss of productivity. Individuals are taken away from their work; some may have to travel to get to the meeting. Meetings cannot always be arranged to suit the working schedules of all individuals. It is important to consider whether the meeting is essential or whether there is another way of achieving the same outcome.

Consider whether decisions can be made one to one, whether information could be shared in another way, for example documented, posted on the intranet, sent by email. Video- or tele-conferencing are especially useful if your participants work some distance from each other. Test the equipment before the meeting to ensure it will work smoothly on the day. If you have a visual connection, think about the seating – can everyone see and hear the remote participants? If you are using tele-conferencing, you may need different skills, for example greater use of names so everyone knows who is speaking, speaking in turn so everyone knows when to come in, and not everyone speaks at the same time.

Only call a meeting when you have a very good reason!

We briefly mentioned venue and how it may affect the outcome of a meeting. It is worth considering, especially if your meetings have become tedious and you want to make some changes. You may be limited for choice due to company protocol, but there may be certain venues that either help or hinder your agenda. If you have weekly meetings in the same room, a change of scenery can help to alter how participants contribute. If your meeting room is dark, or cramped, or very formal it may not be the best place to generate ideas. Meeting outdoors or in a café, however, can be distracting and does not offer much privacy.

A fixed venue for meetings can still offer opportunities to change the layout to suit the purpose of the meeting. Here are some possible arrangements:

- Everyone standing – good for very short meetings, no one falls asleep.
- Seated in rows – useful if they all need a forward-facing view of a speaker or presentation.
- Seated round a table – good for taking notes.
- Seated in a circle – encourages more open communication.
- Seated around small tables – good for small group work.

Figure D11.2: Change the layout of a room to suit the purpose of a meeting

Invite the right people

Not everyone needs to come to every meeting. Meetings should involve those who are directly affected by the agenda items. The number of participants should also depend on the type of meeting. If the meeting is being called in order to make a decision, then the number of people who can reach an agreement is fairly small, somewhere between three and eight individuals. Any more can lead to confusion and dissent.

Figure D11.3

A meeting called to generate ideas can benefit from larger numbers, different perspectives, varied points of view. When carrying out any form of brainstorming, it works best when you have a number of people to bounce ideas around and spark ideas in others; a small group of less than six can make for slow progress. Everyone will want to make a contribution and have their ideas heard, so more than 20 people would become difficult to manage and leave some participants dissatisfied.

There is no upper limit to numbers when it comes to sharing information, especially if you want to generate a buzz or some excitement about a new product or development. The more the merrier!

Assessment criterion 1.2 Produce documentation in support of activities

Meetings are regular events in the running of a business so it is worth having a procedure or a checklist to ensure you are well prepared. This checklist might include:

- decide on the purpose of the meeting
- decide who to invite
- speak to people before the meeting
- produce an agenda
- book a venue
- book any equipment
- send out invites with any pre-meeting documents
- buy biscuits.

Your organisation may have particular procedures or meeting protocols that you need to follow – we will look at this in section 2 below.

When preparing for a meeting, there are many ways in which technology can make life easier. As well as emails for sending out invitations, it may be worth considering systems for booking venues and there are virtual diary packages which allow individuals to select dates when they are available and for you to see the most popular date and time for a meeting.

When preparing an agenda there may be standard items such as health and safety that are covered at every meeting. A template agenda can then be customised for each meeting. The agenda lets everyone know what will be discussed at the meeting so they can come prepared. It is also a useful tool to communicate the amount of time you hope to spend discussing each item and who will lead the discussion.

Participants should come to a meeting prepared, having read the documents you sent them with the agenda and done some research of their own. So make sure you send out this information in plenty of time.

Figure D11.4

The case study below provides an opportunity for you to read about a team leader or team leading scenario. The case study highlights some of the issues discussed. You can use this to reflect on the situation and answer some questions. You do not have to write down your answers unless your tutor or assessor has asked you to do so.

CASE STUDY 1

Shelly is the regional team leader of 12 sales representatives who travel around South Wales and are based in offices in Swansea and Newport. She calls a monthly meeting which is held alternately at each site so that the burden of travelling is shared. This is especially useful as the meetings are always on a Friday afternoon and the weekend traffic can be quite heavy.

She feels the meetings are important to allow the individual sales reps, who often work in isolation, to get together and support each other. She also uses this occasion to share company updates and find out how individuals are progressing towards their targets.

During the annual appraisals, when asked for feedback, 8 out of 12 of her team said they found the meetings a waste of time and they would prefer to be out meeting their sales targets.

What do you think?

1. What were Shelly's reasons for calling the meetings?
2. Do you think any of these outcomes could be achieved in a more effective way?

3. If you were Shelly, how would you do things differently?

4. How often would you meet with the whole team?

5. Where and when would you hold the meetings?

6. What would you introduce to make the team appreciate the benefits of the meeting?

DEVELOPMENT ACTIVITY 1 with your virtual adviser

I am here to demystify the assessment criteria and help you relate what you have learned to your own job role. We will look at what you are currently doing and how you can develop your skills and have a real impact in your workplace.

Draw up a simple table with three columns. In the first column write **Where am I now?** and, as if you were explaining to me, make a few notes about your strengths and weaknesses when planning work for your team. Be specific and provide some examples. Be honest with yourself – this is not part of your assessment, and identifying weaknesses is the first step to making improvements.

The questions below may help you.

Where am I now?
Tell me about the meetings you run and how you prepare for them.

1. Can you identify a clear reason for holding each meeting?

2. Where and when are the meetings held?

3. Who is invited to the meeting?

4. What documentation is sent out? How and when is this sent?

Now, in your second column, write the heading **Improvements** and in the third column **Action**.

Improvements and action
Are there any areas where your planning could be improved?

What action do you think you could take to make those improvements happen?

Some of the changes you have identified might affect the way things are done in your organisation and you may need to discuss them with your line manager. Some changes can be made by you. Remember, small changes can make a big difference.

When you plan to make a change, remember to make your new objectives SMART!

You can discuss the notes you have made with your assessor. They may provide evidence of your competence.

An example

Sales Team Meeting re New Product Launch

Agenda

Wednesday 5 July
14:00 – 16:00

Carver House
Room 209

Attendees: Shelly, Bill, Kate, Amir, Rosie, Angelika

14:00	Welcome Update from last meeting	
14:15	Outline of new product range (see attached documentation)	Amir
14:20	Chance to ask questions	
14.30	How to promote new range Group ideas gathering	Rosie
15:00	Promotional budget Decision on promotional event	Shelly
15.30	Update on recruitment drive	Bill
15:40	Any other business	

Figure D11.5: Example of a typical agenda

Learning outcome 2 – Be able to manage meeting procedures

In this section we will explore each of the assessment criteria in more detail to develop your knowledge and understanding.

Assessment criterion 2.1 Identify any formal procedures that apply in your own organisation

Procedures are usually introduced to make sure that everyone in an organisation is following a minimum standard of good practice every time they do a particular job. You could think of them as a checklist to make sure the job gets done properly.

The procedure for managing a meeting may vary from organisation to organisation, and from industry to industry. There may be industry guidelines on how often meetings should take place:

- Local authorities, for example, are expected to have regular meetings with local residents to involve them in decision making and get feedback on the services provided.
- Care homes must have regular meetings with residents, advocates and other stakeholders to ensure the care meets the individual's requirements.
- In retail environments that are driven by sales targets, it is not unusual to have a team briefing every day to outline the targets and get the team psyched up for the day ahead.
- In construction, it is common to have a daily or weekly toolbox meeting to allocate jobs.

In each environment, procedures, whether written or understood, will exist governing the frequency of meetings, where they take place and who attends. There may be an unspoken agreement about who buys the biscuits, makes the coffee, takes notes and types the minutes.

Areas that may be covered by company procedures include:

- fixed agenda items
- informing line managers
- meeting room protocol.

Meetings are a convenient opportunity to cover essential items such as health and safety. Minutes of the meeting provide an auditable record of any discussions proving that they have taken place. So health and safety may be a fixed item on the agenda.

It is usually part of any protocol to inform the line manager that an individual is attending a meeting. It may be useful to think more broadly about who else may be affected if the individual is unavailable for an hour or more. Will urgent work need to be reallocated? Will there be enough people left on the shop floor? Will cover be needed? Are colleagues aware they are covering? Will the individual need to redirect calls?

There may be a standard protocol for the meeting room. A good booking system is essential when meeting rooms are in demand. Nobody wants to turn up and find the room has been double-booked. If you do not arrange the layout of the room yourself, you should be able to request the correct seating and table layout to suit your needs. You may also need to set up and test equipment: the projector and screen for a presentation, flip chart and pens for gathering ideas, video- or tele-conferencing technologies. You may also need a procedure for ordering refreshments – they do not appear by magic.

And finally the chair: does your organisation have the same manager chairing all the meetings or does everyone take it in turns (this is called a rotating chair)?

Formal meetings and the law

Meetings range from the informal get-together involving two or three people where nothing is recorded to very formal company meetings. Here are a few notes regarding those formal meetings.

Private companies can hold general meetings or annual general meetings (AGMs) with their shareholders, although there is no longer a statutory requirement to do so, or board meetings/directors' meetings. Decisions cannot be made at these meetings if there are not enough people in attendance. A sufficient number of people is known as a quorum.

Once the minutes are produced, they must be signed by the chair. The Companies Act 2006 states that proper minutes must be kept of all members' and directors' decisions and must be stored for ten years. These minutes can be important as evidence of what occurred and could be used if the parties disagree or there are disputes with third parties. Minutes of meetings are increasingly being used as evidence in court cases to prove or disprove that a director has fulfilled their duties. Without these minutes it may be harder to sell a company, as due diligence cannot be carried out by the purchaser without such records.

Now it is time to think about the procedures for running meetings in your organisation.

The case study below provides an opportunity for you to read about a team leader or team leading scenario. The case study highlights some of the issues discussed. You can use this to reflect on the situation and answer some questions. You do not have to write down your answers unless your tutor or assessor has asked you to do so.

CASE STUDY 2

Shelly decides to try a different strategy for her meetings, holding them on a Monday morning at a venue mid-way between the two offices, and to make it more interesting she plans to do a brainstorming exercise to find out the team's ideas of what would be relevant and useful for them to cover at the team meetings.

She sends an email round a week before the meeting with details of the new time and venue. Although most people were able to come at short notice, she was disappointed that they did not seem to respond to the exercise with as much enthusiasm as she had hoped.

What do you think?

1. Why do you think the team may have been less than keen on the new arrangement?

2. How could Shelly have organised the meeting to ensure a more enthusiastic response?

DEVELOPMENT ACTIVITY 2 with your virtual adviser

I am here to demystify the assessment criteria and help you relate what you have learned to your own job role. We will look at what you are currently doing and how you can develop your skills and have a real impact in your workplace.

Draw up a simple table with three columns. In the first column write **Where am I now?** and, as if you were explaining to me, make a few notes about your strengths and weaknesses when making contributions and acknowledging the contributions of others in a meeting. Be specific and provide some examples. Be honest with yourself – this is not part of your assessment, and identifying weaknesses is the first step to making improvements.

The questions below may help you.

Where am I now?

Think about the way meetings are run in your organisation.

1. Are there any written procedures telling you what to do?

2. Who needs to be informed that a meeting is taking place?

3. Who prepares documentation? How much notice do they need?

4. How do you send out invites and how much notice is given?

5. How do you book a room? How do you prepare the room? How do you check health and safety? How do you order refreshments?

6. Who takes the notes and types up minutes? Is there a standard format for minutes?

Now, in your second column, write the heading **Improvements** and in the third column **Action**.

Improvements and action

Are there any areas where your contribution to meetings could be improved?

What action do you need to take to make those improvements?

Some of the changes you have identified might affect the way things are done in your organisation and you may need to discuss them with your line manager. Some changes can be made by you. Remember, small changes can make a big difference.

When you plan to make a change, remember to make your new objectives SMART!

You can discuss the notes you have made with your assessor. They may provide evidence of your competence.

Learning outcome 3 – Be able to chair a meeting

In this section we will explore each of the assessment criteria in more detail to develop your knowledge and understanding.

Assessment criterion 3.1 Manage the agenda in cooperation with participants to ensure objectives are met

Managing the agenda means managing two factors, namely:

- people
- time.

Here we will look at some simple techniques you can try in your own meetings to get the very best out of your team and how to do it on time. First let's look at people and the way they behave in a meeting. When you call a meeting you hope that everyone will arrive full of enthusiasm and willing to cooperate – this is not usually the case. People may arrive tired. Their heads may be full of the previous job they were doing, or a piece of work with an urgent deadline. There may be someone who is worrying about a situation outside of work. You don't know, but you can be certain they will all have different thoughts buzzing round their heads.

At the start of a meeting it is good to:

- welcome everyone
- talk about housekeeping
- break the ice
- clarify the purpose of the meeting.

People feel more relaxed, open and positive if they are welcomed to the meeting. It is also nice to thank people for coming – it acknowledges that people have given up their time and put other work on hold.

Housekeeping may not seem very exciting, but people need to know where the toilets are and whether there will be a testing of the fire alarm and where the nearest emergency exit is. It shows you care about their comfort. This may also be a good time to say when the refreshments will be arriving.

If the group do not know each other you could make some introductions, maybe a round robin, where each person in the group takes a turn to say something about themselves, or a smaller exercise to break the ice in pairs or small groups. You can choose to keep this activity brief if the team know each other well, or be creative and get people to share their star sign, hobby, best achievement, pet, burning ambition, secret hideaway, favourite food.

If this team have been working together, it may be useful to think about what stage they are at. Bruce Tuckman, an educational psychologist, is probably best known for his theory that explains how groups go through these various stages in their development:

1. Forming
2. Storming
3. Norming
4. Performing.

When forming, members tend to be very polite, not knowing each other well, all trying to get along. That politeness wears off when the differences between them come to the surface and during the storming phase we see differences of opinion, individuality, clashes of ideas and maybe disagreements. With time and greater understanding and acceptance of each other there is a period of norming or settling into a way of working. And finally we get to performing, when everyone is working effectively towards a common goal.

If you know which stage your group is at, you can vary your approach:

- spending more time on ice breaking in the forming stage
- allowing everyone to be heard and building bridges during the storming phase
- checking the norming is working for the project and the whole group
- monitoring performance.

Even in a well-established team, there will be differences of opinion from time to time. It is an essential part of any creative process and in order to generate new ideas and make improvements it is necessary to challenge the old ways of doing things. It is reassuring to think of some level of disagreement as healthy and positive. However, if you are running a meeting, dealing with conflict can be quite a scary prospect. It is good to have some techniques ready to use in these situations:

- Acknowledge the differences.
- Make sure all parties are heard.
- Use other opinions in the group to defuse confrontation.
- Look for areas where there is agreement.
- Step back and look at the process.
- Outline different ways to resolve the situation.

The worst thing you can do when there is a disagreement is to ignore it, or ignore one side of it. It will only come back and bite you later. Of course, if it is a personal issue between two individuals, you may agree a time to discuss it outside of the meeting. But relevant differences of opinion need to be acknowledged and both parties need to be heard. You can say how important these contributions are to the process and write both ideas on a flip chart – when they are on paper, it can take the heat out of an argument.

You can involve the rest of the group, whose opinions can defuse a more intense one-on-one disagreement. Other ideas may lend weight to one argument, showing the other to be less feasible. More ideas can shed more light and make it easier to see the practicalities of the situation. This exploration of ideas can also help to establish common ground.

At any point during the meeting you can take a step back and look at the process. This can help move things on. If you say, 'OK, we've got two very different approaches, and a decision has to be made today. We can explore each of these ideas in a bit more detail and then we will have to take a vote on it', the team may not agree on the ideas but you *can* get everyone to agree on the next step in the process. Other members of the team may also be able to suggest ways of resolving the situation. Don't forget to ask them.

Once your group has resolved any disagreements and is working well together, you need to be aware of any patterns that might be emerging. Is there someone who is quiet and rarely participates? Is there someone who manages to brush certain topics to one side? Does one person tend to have the final say when influencing decisions? Does someone seem critical of all new ideas?

Belbin's Team Roles identify nine different ways in which individuals tend to behave when interrelating with others in a group. Most people do not fit neatly into one role and usually combine several roles. It can be interesting to notice any tendencies in others or in yourself. There are plenty of quizzes online to help you with this. This is a brief outline of the roles Dr Meredith Belbin, the renowned management consultant, identified in three categories:

Action-oriented roles:

- Shaper shakes things up, suggests improvements.
- Implementer turns ideas into practical plans.
- Completer/Finisher gets the job done, detailed and thorough.

People-oriented roles:

- Coordinator leads the team, is calm, good natured, delegates.
- Team worker is supportive, negotiates, is flexible and diplomatic.
- Resource investigator explores options, is enthusiastic.

Thought-oriented roles:

- Plant has new ideas, approaches, is creative.
- Monitor/Evaluator analyses others' ideas, is objective, strategic.
- Specialist has technical, specialist knowledge.

An awareness of the role you and others play in the group, or the group dynamics, can help you understand what is going on and can help you get the right balance in the team. For example, if the conversation often becomes bogged down in too much technical detail, you may have too many specialists in the team who are not seeing the bigger picture. Ideally, you want a balance of all the roles.

In the 1980s Dr Edward de Bono invented the Six Thinking Hats to try to separate the performance of individuals from their personalities or egos. Each colour hat indicated a way of thinking:

- white hat – data, facts, figures, information
- red hat – intuition, emotional responses
- black hat – logical, advising caution, finding barriers
- yellow hat – logical, finding positive benefits
- green hat – creativity, finding alternatives
- blue hat – commenting on the process.

All the group members would wear the same hat at any one time, encouraging everyone to use all types of thinking and broaden the contributions. This is just one tool that can be used when gathering ideas in a group.

There are various techniques for managing time during the meeting. The first step is to allocate and agree a time limit for each agenda item. Then comes the difficult bit: getting everyone to stick to that time limit. If you need to be involved in discussions, it can be useful to ask someone else to be a time-keeper. Time-keeping does not mean blowing a whistle when the allocated time is up. It may involve steering someone who has been talking for a long time or has wandered off the point: 'That's a good point, Bill, I'd like to hear what everyone else thinks.' 'So if I summarise what you've said, Kate …' 'Our ten minutes on this item is up, can I suggest we move on and discuss this further outside the meeting, by email, one-to-one, at the next meeting?'

On very rare occasions, an issue may need to be extended, in which case agree an additional time limit. It may mean something else has to be sacrificed.

Assessment criterion 3.2 Produce minutes of the meeting and allocate action points after discussion

During the meeting it is essential to have someone who takes notes. Sometimes there is a dedicated person who is not actively involved in the meeting but has specialist skills in shorthand or speedwriting who can record the discussions and decisions. If you do not have a note taker, this role needs to be given to a participant, maybe someone different each time. It is not easy to chair a meeting and take notes, or to be a key presenter and take notes.

A note taker does not have to record every word that is said. They need to develop the skill of capturing the key issues, the most important aspects of the discussion. A top tip is to ask for a summary of the key points that need to be minuted at the end of each agenda item. It is important to respect personal issues that may come up at a meeting that are 'off the record' and shouldn't be in the minutes.

The main items that should be minuted are:

- date and time of the meeting
- names of those attending
- names of those who sent apologies
- summary/main points of a discussion
- summary of any brainstorming activities
- reference to key individual contributions
- record of any decisions made
- detailed record of any actions to be taken, stating exactly what is to be done, by whom, by when.

The case study below provides an opportunity for you to read about a team leader or team leading scenario. The case study highlights some of the issues discussed. You can use this to reflect on the situation and answer some questions. You do not have to write down your answers unless your tutor or assessor has asked you to do so.

Shelly has prepared well for her team meeting. She has asked everyone for items they wish to discuss and agreed to set aside time for an update on the recruitment drive. She has issued an agenda and relevant documentation, giving everyone plenty of time to read them. She has indicated the desired outcome of each agenda item, involved other members of the team in delivery and clearly allocated time slots for each item to help individuals prepare.

The meeting itself starts late because Amir is held up in traffic and his item is first on the agenda. While they are waiting, Shelly welcomes Kate, the new member of the team, and everyone introduces themselves. They also go over the outline of the meeting and agree the overall purpose, which is to share ideas about promoting the new product range and make a decision about how best to spend the promotional budget.

Amir arrives and delivers his agenda item. He's a little flustered and manages to overrun by about five minutes. Kate is new and has quite a few questions to ask and the team then spend nearly an hour bringing her up to speed on a range of company issues.

Half an hour is spent gathering ideas on how to promote the product range. Suddenly time is running out. The decision on how to spend the promotional budget is not made as no one can agree on the best event. The recruitment update is covered in five minutes and a date hurriedly agreed for the next meeting.

Shelly goes home feeling disappointed that things had not gone according to plan.

What do you think?

1. Could Shelly have been better prepared for her meeting?

2. What went wrong in the meeting? What do you think could have caused these problems?

3. If you were Shelly, what techniques could you have used to ensure the meeting was a success?

DEVELOPMENT ACTIVITY 3 with your virtual adviser

I am here to demystify the assessment criteria and help you relate what you have learned to your own job role. We will look at what you are currently doing and how you can develop your skills and have a real impact in your workplace.

Draw up a simple table with three columns. In the first column write **Where am I now?** and, as if you were explaining to me, make a few notes about your strengths and weaknesses when chairing a meeting. Be specific and provide some examples. Be honest with yourself – this is not part of your assessment, and identifying weaknesses is the first step to making improvements.

The questions below may help you.

Where am I now?

Think about your skills in managing people in a meeting. Think of a specific example of when you used that skill.

1. What situations have arisen where, as chair, you have had to guide the discussion?

2. When and how have you dealt with conflict?

3. What techniques have you used to bring out the best in others in a meeting?

Now, in your second column, write the heading **Improvements** and in the third column **Action**.

Improvements and action

Are there any areas where your skills could be improved?

What action do you need to take to make those improvements?

Some of the changes you have identified might affect the way things are done in your organisation and you may need to discuss them with your line manager. Some changes can be made by you. Remember, small changes can make a big difference.

When you plan to make a change, remember to make your new objectives SMART!

You can discuss the notes you have made with your assessor. They may provide evidence of your competence.

An example

Sales Team Meeting re New Product Launch **MINUTES** **Wednesday 5 July** **14:00 – 16:00** **Carver House** **Room 209** **Attendees:** Shelly, Bill, Kate, Amir, Rosie **Apologies:** Angelika				
ITEM	**DISCUSSED**	**ACTION AGREED**	**BY WHOM**	**BY WHEN**
Update from last meeting	Minutes from last meeting were agreed as an accurate record of that meeting. All agreed actions had been addressed. Bill outlined quotes he had received for new office equipment.			
Outline of new product range	Amir outlined the new product range, handing out promotional material.	Copies to go to Angelika	Amir	12 July
Questions	Bill was interested to compare costs with current stock. Rosie asked if competitors were selling this range. Amir said it is not advertised on their website.	Costs to be emailed to Bill	Shelly	7 July
Promoting new range	Everyone brainstormed promotional ideas. The main ones were: • A theatrical event in shopping mall • Local TV/radio broadcast • Article in local free press • Stall at local trade fair	Costs to be emailed to Bill	Shelly	7 July
Decide on event	There was not enough time to make a decision so this has been put off until next meeting.	Add to next agenda	Shelly	7 July
Recruitment drive	Shelly gave an update on number of applicants for new sales posts. There has been a good response with some promising candidates. Interviews will be held next Monday.			
Any other business	Kate apologised in advance for not being able to make the next meeting as she has a booked holiday.			
Next meeting:	Wed 19 July			

Figure D11.6: Example of minutes of a meeting

Learning outcome 4 – Be able to undertake post-meeting tasks

In this section we will explore each of the assessment criteria in more detail to develop your knowledge and understanding.

Assessment criterion 4.1 Explain that the minutes of the meeting provide an accurate record of proceedings

There are a number of important jobs that need to be done after a meeting:

- Produce minutes of the meeting.
- Distribute the minutes.
- Communicate key issues.
- Follow up any action points.
- Evaluation.

The minutes of a meeting provide a written record of what was discussed and agreed, when and by whom. These can be kept for many years and if there is any disagreement about decisions at a later date, the minutes are a valuable piece of evidence. For this reason it is important to get them right. It is advisable to produce the minutes as soon as possible after the meeting when everything is fresh in your mind.

It is important that they give sufficient detail. It is not usually enough to say 'new staffing rota discussed'. Later on, an employee may want to prove that they had objected to the new rota because they would have difficulties changing their shift as they act as a carer for a member of their family. And before you send out the minutes to everyone, make sure they are approved by the relevant person, the chair or a manager.

The minutes need to be distributed to:

- those at the meeting
- those who sent apologies
- other interested parties.

Those at the meeting need a record of any action they have agreed to take. Those who missed the meeting and sent their apologies may need to catch up on any shared information or decisions made. It may not be too late to have their say. There may be others who are interested in the discussions but not directly involved, for example more senior management find minutes a quick way of knowing what happened in a meeting without having to attend, or other departments in the company may be interested in what colleagues are doing and be able to identify how a change in staff rota might affect payroll or security.

It is important not to rely on copies of the minutes as the sole method of communicating what happened in a meeting. These may not be distributed to all interested parties; they may be sent round but not read; or they may be read but if not clear, there is a danger they could be misinterpreted.

Figure D11.7

Assessment criterion 4.2 Communicate and follow up meeting outcomes to relevant individuals

Following a meeting it is important to have various one-to-one discussions:

- to check someone has all the resources they need to carry out their agreed action
- to clarify issues for any new members of the team
- to explain points in more detail to anyone who was not at the meeting
- to check on anyone who seemed quiet or was involved in any conflict.

Your team may not always carry out the agreed actions by the specified deadlines. Someone may be off sick or had to reprioritise their workload. They may lack the necessary resources or the cooperation of busy colleagues. They may have been tasked with getting a quote from another organisation which hasn't got back to them. And they may have seen how busy you are and decided not to bother you with their problems. Many of these hurdles can be overcome if you follow up the agreed action points, checking on progress at appropriate intervals.

Assessment criterion 4.3 Evaluate whether the meeting's objectives were met and identify potential improvements

The final step in the process is to evaluate whether the meeting was successful. Did it achieve what it set out to do? Did it meet its original aims? Did the benefits of the meeting outweigh the costs in terms of time and money? These are not always easy questions to answer. Some of the benefits are difficult to measure; some deliver only at a point in the future.

Sometimes you can ask yourself a few questions:

- Was the general purpose met?
  - For example, if the purpose was to make a decision, was that decision made?
  - Could it have been achieved in a different way?
- What went well?
  - Did the team emerge more positive, better informed than before?
- What didn't go so well?
  - Did you encounter any difficulties while running the meeting?
- What would you do differently next time?
  - What skills do you need to develop?

The case study below provides an opportunity for you to read about a team leader or team leading scenario. The case study highlights some of the issues discussed. You can use this to reflect on the situation and answer some questions. You do not have to write down your answers unless your tutor or assessor has asked you to do so.

CASE STUDY 4

Shelly always ensures that notes are taken at the meeting and she checks the minutes are accurate before they are distributed. The minutes record the discussions held and also the names of all those who attended.

At a recent meeting it was agreed that Thomas would present information to the team on new products at the next month's meeting, as he was attending the product launch in London the following day. Shelly asked him especially to make a note in his diary to pick up any promotional material that could go out with the next agenda.

At the next meeting, the product launch was not on the agenda and it was only when one team member asked Thomas how the event had gone that everyone remembered his input. It was rearranged for the next meeting.

What do you think?

1. What are the possible effects of forgetting Thomas's input to the meeting? On Thomas? On the rest of the team? On the organisation?

2. How could Shelly have ensured that Thomas's presentation to the team was not forgotten?

DEVELOPMENT ACTIVITY 4 with your virtual adviser

I am here to demystify the assessment criteria and help you relate what you have learned to your own job role. We will look at what you are currently doing and how you can develop your skills and have a real impact in your workplace.

Draw up a simple table with three columns. In the first column write **Where am I now?** and, as if you were explaining to me, make a few notes about your strengths and weaknesses when chairing a meeting. Be specific and provide some examples. Be honest with yourself – this is not part of your assessment, and identifying weaknesses is the first step to making improvements.

The questions below may help you.

Where am I now?
Think about all the things you do after a meeting.

1. Were there any written minutes of your last meeting?

2. Look at the minutes of your last meeting. Do they clearly record the time and date and all those in attendance?

3. Do they outline important discussions in sufficient detail?

4. Are any agreed action points clearly noted as specific, measurable, achievable, realistic, time-bound?

5. Are they attributable to a specific individual?

6. Were the minutes agreed? Distributed? When?

7. Where are the minutes kept? How long are they kept?

Now, in your second column, write the heading **Improvements** and in the third column **Action**.

Improvements and action
Are there any areas where your performance could be improved?

What action do you need to take to make those improvements?

Some of the changes you have identified might affect the way things are done in your organisation and you may need to discuss them with your line manager. Some changes can be made by you. Remember, small changes can make a big difference.

When you plan to make a change, remember to make your new objectives SMART!

You can discuss the notes you have made with your assessor. They may provide evidence of your competence.

Further information

More information about the Companies Act 2006 can be found at:

www.legislation.gov.uk

There are various websites where you can search for information about: Group Dynamics, Bruce Tuckman, Belbin's Team Roles, and other writers about groups such as Edward de Bono and R.F. Bale.

TEST YOUR KNOWLEDGE

Here are some questions to test your knowledge and understanding of the issues explored in this unit. You can write the answers down or discuss them with your assessor. They could provide good evidence for your NVQ.

1. What activities must be carried out in preparation for a meeting? AC 1.1

2. What documentation do you produce prior to a meeting? AC 1.2

3. What procedures relating to meetings must be followed in your organisation? AC 2.1

4. Name three things you can do during a meeting to ensure its objectives are met and explain why they would work. AC 3.1

5. Name the key pieces of information that make up the minutes of a meeting. AC 3.2

6. What is the purpose of minutes? AC 3.2

7. Who receives copies of minutes in your organisation and how are these distributed? AC 4.1

8. How do you assign actions to individuals and how are these followed up? AC 4.2

9. How do you know whether your meetings are effective? AC 4.3

10. What improvements could you make to the effectiveness of future meetings? AC 4.3

Pulling it all together and gathering evidence

You and your assessor will need to agree the most appropriate sources of evidence. Here are some suggestions:

- An electronic portfolio: you could upload your evidence to an e-portfolio package or simply store the evidence in electronic format.
- A paper-based portfolio: you could build a folder with hard copies of your evidence.

Types of evidence:

- Observation: a record by your assessor when observing you chairing a meeting.
- Work product: copies of work produced by you that demonstrate your competence, for example agenda, notes, room bookings, invites, minutes.

- Discussion: a record of you and your assessor discussing examples of how you have chaired a meeting, the techniques you have used to manage people and time, difficult situations that have arisen and how you dealt with them.

- Questioning: a record of your assessor asking questions to test your knowledge.

- Personal statement, reflective account or case study based on the activities in this unit: this should have sentences which start with 'I …' and should tell a story giving real-life examples.

- Witness testimony from your line manager confirming your competence, in writing or recorded as a discussion with your assessor.

It is a good idea to include a range of evidence from different sources. Your evidence should cover a period of time and not be a 'one-off'. However, try to keep the evidence to a minimum. Your assessor can make a note of product evidence they have seen so it can be left in the workplace.

Remember:

Less is more – quality not quantity!

Be holistic – can you use this evidence again for other units?

EVALUATION

What have you learned from completing this unit?

What new skills and techniques are you using?

How has this affected the people you work with?

How has your organisation benefited? How might it benefit in the future?

D12 PARTICIPATE IN MEETINGS

Introduction and learning outcomes

Learning outcomes for Unit D12:

1. Be able to prepare for a meeting.
2. Be able to participate in a meeting.
3. Be able to communicate information to relevant stakeholders.

These learning outcomes say what you will have learned by the end of this unit. Each learning outcome is further broken down into assessment criteria, which we will look at in detail in the following sections of this unit.

This Unit Guide is a resource to help you gather the evidence you require to achieve Unit D12. It can be used as a learning resource if you are new to the role, are studying team leading in preparation for work or as a refresher if you are already an experienced team leader.

You and your assessor will agree what you need to do to meet the assessment criteria and show you are competent. This Unit Guide provides some theory to develop your understanding of meetings, gives some case studies for you to examine and then an opportunity for you to reflect, with a virtual adviser, on how you can develop your skills and gather evidence of competence. Some ideas are provided in the 'Pulling it all together' section at the end of this unit.

So, the purpose of this unit is to develop the skills and knowledge you need to participate effectively in meetings.

Why do we have meetings?

Humans are sociable beings and have been gathering together to worship, celebrate, socialise and trade since the beginning of their existence. It is difficult to imagine a world that does not have meetings of some kind or another. Throughout history and across all cultures meetings have been held. Around 500 BCE, in the Greek state of Athens, one of the first-known democracies, the people did not elect representatives but turned up in person to vote on matters of state.

Before the widespread use of technology, and in the days when many people did not read, meetings were an important way of announcing information, telling people about new laws or going to war. But many things have changed in the way we live and do business. It is essential to ask ourselves why we have meetings today. What is their purpose? Are they effective? Is there a better way of achieving the same aim?

Meetings can seem like a waste of time. All other work comes to a halt. People spend time travelling to and from meetings. Sometimes the meeting does not seem relevant. Sometimes very little is achieved. All this can cost an organisation time and money.

Figure D12.1

No one wants to see their work pile up and have their time wasted, so it is important to make sure your meetings work for you. The purpose of a meeting is usually to:

- pass on information
- make a decision
- gather ideas.

Most meetings have a combination of these aims. If the aim is to pass on information, we need to ask whether there is a better way of doing this: via email, post, notice board, verbally. Or is it essential that the information, like the launch of a new product, be an event that will generate energy and enthusiasm from all the people gathered in the room? If the aim is to make a decision, we need to check the relevant people are involved and we need to agree how the decision will be made. Will the majority win in a vote? Or do we need the consensus of everyone to agree the way forward? If the aim of the meeting is to gather ideas, we need enough people but not too many. Everyone will want their ideas to be heard.

Whatever the purpose, meetings involve people and provide an ideal opportunity to develop your networking skills.

In the sections below we will explore how to make your meetings more effective by:

- being prepared
- participating
- communicating with relevant stakeholders.

Learning outcome 1 – Be able to prepare for a meeting

In this section we will explore each of the assessment criteria in more detail to develop your knowledge and understanding.

You may be running a meeting for your team or you may have been asked to lead on a particular agenda item. You need to be well prepared. We will also look at why you need to be prepared even if you are attending a meeting as a participant.

Assessment criterion 1.1 Explain meeting objectives prior to the meeting

As with most things in life, preparation begins well before the actual event. It is the same with a meeting. Before you even think about calling a meeting you must be clear about the objectives. What is it exactly you want to achieve? What is the desired outcome? The clearer you can be about your objectives, the more effective your meeting will be. You need objectives so you can measure whether the meeting was effective.

You may have heard about the need for objectives to be SMART, that is:

- specific
- measurable
- achievable
- realistic
- time-bound.

Let's see how these can be applied to your meeting.

A meeting needs to have specific items on the agenda so that people can come prepared. It is not helpful to call a meeting to discuss 'workloads' – everyone will wonder whether they are going to be shared or increased, or whether people will be made redundant. Do you want participants arriving anxious and defensive? So be specific. The item could be 'Make decision on shared workloads during busy holiday period'. Then everyone can look at their own workloads and come prepared with some ideas.

To know whether a meeting has been effective, we need to be able to measure its success. You need to ask the question: 'How will I know it was a good meeting?' The answers may be quite straightforward, for example a decision was made, we stuck to the agenda, we started and finished on time. If building a good rapport in the team is an objective, then a lively meeting with full participation may be a measure of success. If there are new members in the team, a measure of success may be their inclusion and opportunity to contribute. You need to know what you are aiming to achieve to know whether you have achieved it.

A meeting has limited resources of time and people's attention span. It is not achievable to cover too many items in one meeting. In fact, it could be counter-productive to rush through too many items or lose the attention of half the people in the room. One rule is never to have more than three items on the agenda, but this is a general guide and may vary a little.

Your expectations of a meeting need to be realistic. You may hope to gather ideas for a promotional event but if, in reality, the budget is limited then you may have to sacrifice the fireworks.

And lastly, time-bound. Everyone likes to finish a meeting on time. This usually means starting on time and keeping to time on each item discussed. You may have to build this into your plans, allowing time for people to arrive, greet each other and settle down, then allocating a realistic amount of time for each item, including questions that may arise. Check there is a good timepiece in the room. Ask an individual to be time-keeper. It is good to delegate and share the roles involved in running a meeting.

Once you are clear about the objectives of the meeting you need to ensure you have explained them clearly to others.

Assessment criterion 1.2 Identify own role and prepare as necessary

Now that you are clear about **why** you need to have a meeting and what the objectives are, you need to prepare:

- **who** will have an input, what your role will be
- **what** will be discussed at the meeting
- **what** will be sent out in preparation
- **when** the meeting will be held, and for how long
- **where** the meeting will be held.

And let everyone know!

Prior to the meeting, someone needs to:

- invite all the participants
- prepare an agenda
- prepare input for each item
- prepare any documents and send them out with an agenda
- book the meeting room and any equipment
- book refreshments.

During the meeting, someone needs to:

- manage the time
- manage the contributions
- take notes.

After the meeting, someone needs to:

- type up the minutes and have them approved
- distribute the minutes
- inform other stakeholders of the outcome of the meeting
- follow up any agreed action points.

One person does not have to do all these jobs, they can be shared among the team.

There are benefits to asking members of the team to take a lead on a particular agenda item:

- It is more interesting for people to hear input from a varied range of speakers.
- It is motivating to acknowledge the expertise of individuals in the team.
- It increases the level of participation from the team as a whole.

During the meeting, it is difficult for one person to introduce the topic, encourage contributions from individuals and keep an eye on the time. These aspects can be delegated to different individuals, with one person, the chair, taking an overall coordination role. Many meetings have a rotating chair, with individuals taking it in turns to run the meeting.

People are generally busy and need plenty of notice so they can clear a space in their diary for a meeting. The more notice you give, the better. Regular meetings are much easier as everyone knows there will always be a meeting, for example on the first Monday of each month. Often the date is agreed at the previous meeting. This is an effective way to ensure everyone is available for the next meeting as it saves lots of emails and phone calls later. There are also IT packages freely available on the internet which help to find the most suitable date for an event.

It may be that you do not have a role in running the meeting but are attending as a participant. It is also important for you to be prepared so that you can contribute fully. This will be discussed further under assessment criterion 2.1.

The case study below provides an opportunity for you to read about a team leader or team leading scenario. The case study highlights some of the issues discussed. You can use this to reflect on the situation and answer some questions. You do not have to write down your answers unless your tutor or assessor has asked you to do so.

CASE STUDY 1

Jim leads a small team of builders, plumbers and electricians who carry out repairs to houses for the rental market. Every Monday morning he attends a toolbox meeting where the owner of the company allocates a list of jobs for the week.

This Monday, the boss announces that they have had to lay off one team and will be reallocating their work equally across the other teams. This seems fair and everyone accepts their lists.

After the meeting, Jim realises that the additional work is on the other side of town and when he looks at the route finder he calculates that he and his crew will not have enough time to get all the work done. He knows these jobs should have been given to a more local crew but now it is too late to say so.

What do you think?

1. How do you think Jim is feeling?

2. Was the purpose of this meeting any different from the usual Monday morning meeting?

3. How well do think Jim was prepared for the meeting?

4. What difference would it have made if the team leaders had been told beforehand that there was going to be a change in the company structure and work would need to be reallocated?

DEVELOPMENT ACTIVITY 1 with your virtual adviser

I am here to demystify the assessment criteria and help you relate what you have learned to your own job role. We will look at what you are currently doing and how you can develop your skills and have a real impact in your workplace.

Draw up a simple table with three columns. In the first column write **Where am I now?** and, as if you were explaining to me, make a few notes about your strengths and weaknesses when preparing for a meeting. Be specific and provide some examples. Be honest with yourself – this is not part of your assessment, and identifying weaknesses is the first step to making improvements.

The questions below may help you.

Where am I now?
Tell me about the various meetings you attend.

1. How clear were you about the objectives of those meetings? Or the objectives of different agenda items? Do you have a copy of an agenda with clear objectives that you could show me?

2. Are all participants aware in advance of the purpose of the meeting? How do they know that there will be decision making, gathering of ideas or sharing of information? Could you show me any emails where you have made the purpose of meetings clear?

3. What was your role in these meetings? You can use the checklist below to establish who does what:

Prior to the meeting:

- invite all the participants
- prepare an agenda
- prepare input for each item
- prepare any documents and send them out with an agenda
- book the meeting room and any equipment
- book refreshments.

During the meeting:

- manage the time
- manage the contributions
- take notes.

After the meeting:

- type up the minutes and have them approved
- distribute the minutes
- inform other stakeholders of the outcome of the meeting
- follow up any agreed action points.

4. What do you do to prepare for a meeting and ensure that each of the roles above is carried out? Do you have any emails showing room bookings? Do you have any notes showing preparation?

Now, in your second column, write the heading **Improvements** and in the third column **Action**.

Improvements and action
Are there any areas where your preparation for meetings could be improved?

What action do you think you could take to make those improvements happen?

Some of the changes you have identified might affect the way things are done in your organisation and you may need to discuss them with your line manager. Some changes can be made by you. Remember, small changes can make a big difference.

When you plan to make a change, remember to make your new objectives SMART!

You can discuss the notes you have made with your assessor. They may provide evidence of your competence.

Learning outcome 2 – Be able to participate in a meeting

In this section we will explore each of the assessment criteria in more detail to develop your knowledge and understanding.

Assessment criterion 2.1 Contribute to the meeting discussions using evidence to support own opinions

Let's consider the communication skills we use when making a contribution at a meeting. Communication is a complex thing and it is difficult to generalise. Two people can use the same words but one will come across as aggressive, the other funny. There are layers of body language, tone of voice and use of humour that add interest and nuance to the way we communicate. So here are a few ideas for you to consider when looking at the way you communicate in meetings.

There is often a gap between what we say and what other people hear. When we want to make a point, it is essential that everyone hears and understands what we are saying. Table D12.1 shows some examples.

Table D12.1: Examples of what we say and what other people hear

What we say	What people hear	How people respond
It must be done by Friday	What I say goes, there is no room for discussion	Reluctant Disengaged
You should have this done by Friday	And there will be trouble if it's not done	Pressured
If we get this done by Friday, we'll meet the customer's deadline	We're in this together as a team	Don't let the team down Motivated
I'd like this done by Friday, can you manage that?	That's clear. Now I have to say 'yes' or 'no'.	Involved Committed

We can see in the first two examples that some words like 'must' and 'should' are stronger and apply more pressure. These are appropriate when the situation is critical and not up for discussion. They give an order but do not encourage discussion or participation. The second two examples are gentler and more inclusive, they invite more discussion and encourage involvement. These may work better in situations where you are trying to bring everyone on board. The final example has a question, which ensures the other person makes a commitment.

Some of the contributions made at meetings will be in the form of questions and it's good to think about how to ask those questions in order to get the response you are looking for. For example, see Table D12.2.

Table D12.2: Questions and responses

Type of question	Question	Response
Closed	Will that be ready by Friday?	Yes/No
Open	How will you make sure it's ready by Friday?	I'll need to prioritise and clear my other work

Sometimes all you need is a Yes/No answer as confirmation or clarification of a point. But if you need some detail then make sure you are asking an open question.

Let's look at a few typical contributions you might make at a meeting and explore why it is important to have evidence to support your opinions.

First, imagine you are meeting to gather ideas about a promotional event. You recently attended a flash mob in the local shopping mall and suggest something similar might generate interest. No one seems to take your idea seriously, some people don't know what a flash mob is, and when asked how they are organised, you can say only that you will find out.

With the wisdom of hindsight, you might say it would have been a good idea to have a video clip of a flash mob event to show everyone in the meeting. And to have thought of some of the questions you might get asked. It is usually a good idea to run through the who, what, why, when, where, how questions to cover all angles. The visual evidence may have sparked everyone's imagination. Having facts and figures ready to answer questions will ensure your point is taken more seriously.

At another type of meeting, you may be asked to decide on new opening hours for your restaurant. Everyone prefers to open a little later in the evening, but you feel there are many people who eat earlier, after work or before the cinema. You are unable to convince everyone that earlier is better and a majority vote could tip the decision in favour of opening later.

The outcome might be different if you have some facts and figures at your fingertips. If you have carried out a review of the competition, noting how busy they were at different times of the day, or completed a customer survey, you may have enough evidence to persuade people your idea is feasible.

However fantastic your idea, it may not be taken seriously unless you have some evidence to back it up.

Assessment criterion 2.2 Acknowledge other viewpoints presented at the meeting

The key objectives of a meeting are more likely to be met if people are actively listening. You can show you are actively listening by:

- nodding your head
- looking at the speaker.

If the listener does not make eye contact it does not mean they are being inattentive – some people concentrate better if they are looking elsewhere or making notes. Some cultures avoid eye contact more than others. Don't be too quick to make judgements.

It is best to avoid:

- looking around the room or out of the window
- looking at the clock or at your watch
- checking your mobile phone for messages (apparently Barack Obama collects all BlackBerries in a basket at the beginning of a meeting)

- crossing your arms and legs
- closing your eyes.

Acknowledging another person's point of view can be a good way to move things forward at a meeting. If someone has a point they feel strongly about they can go on making the same point in several different ways until they feel they have been heard.

One way of acknowledging what someone else has said might be to rephrase it: 'So, Jim, are you saying your team are having difficulties with the amount of travelling to site?'

Once people feel they have been understood, they are usually more open to adapting their view or understanding a different point of view. This technique works well when there is disagreement.

Assessment criterion 2.3 Seek clarification of own understanding of outcomes

Participating in a meeting is a two-way process. It is important to communicate clearly both when you want to make a point and when listening to the views of others. But, as we have seen, it is not always easy to communicate clearly. It therefore becomes important to clarify or double-check that we have understood what has been said and what has been agreed. Typical misunderstandings include being unsure about who has agreed to do something. Occasionally someone's attention may wander and they miss part of the discussion. Or sometimes people just hear one thing and have a completely different understanding.

It is always useful to paraphrase what has been said: 'So you are saying *all* work on this project needs to be completed by Friday.' Or a question to clarify: 'Is the Friday deadline for *all* work on the project?' This can also be a useful technique to summarise what has been going on and draw the discussion to a close. It helps move the discussion on to the next topic. It enables the chair person to manage time more effectively.

At the end of a meeting it is important to confirm the outcomes. Everyone needs to leave the meeting with a clear understanding of what has been discussed, what decisions have been made and what action needs to be taken next. A useful technique at the end of a meeting is to ask people to state what action they have agreed to take. Once this has been said in front of others, people are more committed to seeing it through.

The outcomes also need to be confirmed in writing, in the form of notes or minutes of the meeting (see Figure D11.6 for an example of minutes taken at a meeting). This ensures no one forgets what has been discussed and agreed. It provides a permanent record for reference at a later date.

The case study below provides an opportunity for you to read about a team leader or team leading scenario. The case study highlights some of the issues discussed. You can use this to reflect on the situation and answer some questions. You do not have to write down your answers unless your tutor or assessor has asked you to do so.

Figure D12.2: At the end of meetings it is important to run through what has been agreed

CASE STUDY 2

Jim and his crew managed to finish the work but it took a lot longer than expected and they were not happy. He has promised them he will sort it out at the meeting on Monday. He comes prepared, with a map of the town and some notes he made on the actual time his journeys have taken.

Jim's boss hears that the team leaders are not happy with the new arrangements but is quite defensive and says several times that there is not enough work or enough money to recruit another team. Jim realises they are reaching a stalemate because the boss and the team leaders have taken up opposing sides of the argument. He acknowledges the fact that another team cannot be taken on, and his boss visibly relaxes and asks the team: 'What choice have I got?'

Other team leaders then chip in, offering to swap some of their work so none of them has to travel too far. They get out Jim's map and make a new geographical division of the area. Everyone seems quite happy. Then on Friday, confusion breaks out when two teams turn up to the same job.

What do you think?

1. Was Jim better prepared for this meeting?

2. How do think the evidence he brought supported his own opinion?

3. How might others have reacted differently if he had not had any back-up evidence?

4. How did things change when he acknowledged his boss's point of view?

5. Why do you think this technique is effective?

6. The meeting seemed to be going so well, so why did everything go wrong on Friday?

7. How could this have been avoided?

DEVELOPMENT ACTIVITY 2 with your virtual adviser

I am here to demystify the assessment criteria and help you relate what you have learned to your own job role. We will look at what you are currently doing and how you can develop your skills and have a real impact in your workplace.

Draw up a simple table with three columns. In the first column write **Where am I now?** and, as if you were explaining to me, make a few notes about your strengths and weaknesses when making contributions and acknowledging the contributions of others in a meeting. Be specific and provide some examples. Be honest with yourself – this is not part of your assessment, and identifying weaknesses is the first step to making improvements.

The questions below may help you.

Where am I now?

Think about the various meetings you attend.

1. Can you think of a time when you really wanted to make your opinion heard? How well had you prepared for that meeting and what evidence did you bring that helped convince your colleagues?

2. Can you remember using any particular phrases or language that helped communicate your point? Did you say anything that had a negative response from others?

3. How did you acknowledge other people's points of view?

4. How did you double-check that you had correctly understood the points made and the agreed outcome of the meeting?

Now, in your second column, write the heading **Improvements** and in the third column **Action**.

Improvements and action

Are there any areas where your contribution to meetings could be improved?

What action do you need to take to make those improvements?

Some of the changes you have identified might affect the way things are done in your organisation and you may need to discuss them with your line manager. Some changes can be made by you. Remember, small changes can make a big difference.

When you plan to make a change, remember to make your new objectives SMART!

You can discuss the notes you have made with your assessor. They may provide evidence of your competence.

Learning outcome 3 – Be able to communicate information to relevant stakeholders

In this section we will explore each of the assessment criteria in more detail to develop your knowledge and understanding.

Assessment criterion 3.1 Communicate information from the meeting to those who have an interest, in line with any organisational protocol

Not everyone attends a meeting, not everyone is invited. A meeting should involve those directly affected by the issues being discussed. A meeting about new sales targets should be attended by the sales team, but others in admin, purchasing or HR may also need to be informed of the outcome.

Not everyone who has been invited can make it. For various reasons, some people will send their apologies but will need to be informed of the outcome. Many more are affected by the decisions made and need to be informed. So let's look at some of the ways this can happen.

Often, information from one meeting is cascaded down in another team meeting. A new product range may be discussed by regional managers, who then share the information with their local teams. This is an effective way of sharing important information. Information is often passed on verbally, one-to-one. This is a quick method of ensuring a particular individual is brought up to speed, but would be time-consuming for a large number of people. As the verbal passing on of information changes slightly with each telling, as in the traditional game of 'Chinese Whispers', it is always essential to have a written copy of minutes to refer to. These minutes can be posted, emailed or uploaded to the company intranet to allow access by various groups or individuals. By themselves, they do not provide any guarantee that they will be read or understood.

A combination of communication channels could be used, depending on the desired outcome. Many companies have their own procedures or protocols which dictate how and when information from meetings will be communicated to all relevant stakeholders.

The case study below provides an opportunity for you to read about a team leader or team leading scenario. The case study highlights some of the issues discussed. You can use this to reflect on the situation and answer some questions. You do not have to write down your answers unless your tutor or assessor has asked you to do so.

CASE STUDY 3

Jim has come away from the meeting feeling quite pleased with himself. He has achieved his objective, which was to renegotiate the allocation of work so that the jobs he and his team take on are more local.

He sees one of his team, Mike, coming out of the petrol station and shares the information from the meeting with him. Mike is a very sociable team member, who gets on well with the others, so he tells Mike to pass on the good news.

Mike tells the next team member he sees and then assumes Jim will tell everyone else.

What do you think?

1. Can Jim be sure that everyone in the team has heard the news?

2. What are the implications of one person missing out on this information?

3. Is it important that everyone hears at the same time, in the same way?

4. If you were Jim, how would you have handled this situation?

DEVELOPMENT ACTIVITY 3 with your virtual adviser

I am here to demystify the assessment criteria and help you relate what you have learned to your own job role. We will look at what you are currently doing and how you can develop your skills and have a real impact in your workplace.

Draw up a simple table with three columns. In the first column write **Where am I now?** and, as if you were explaining to me, make a few notes about your strengths and weaknesses when communicating after a meeting. Be specific and provide some examples. Be honest with yourself – this is not part of your assessment, and identifying weaknesses is the first step to making improvements.

The questions below may help you.

Where am I now?
Think about the various meetings you attend.

1. Who usually prepares the minutes of the meeting? How are they distributed? Who gets a copy? How long after the meeting does this happen?

2. How do you identify interested parties other than those at the meeting?

3. How and when do you update others about the meeting?

Now, in your second column, write the heading **Improvements** and in the third column **Action**.

Improvements and action
Are there any areas where your follow-up and communication after meetings could be improved?

What action do you need to take to make those improvements?

Some of the changes you have identified might affect the way things are done in your organisation and you may need to discuss them with your line manager. Some changes can be made by you. Remember, small changes can make a big difference.

When you plan to make a change, remember to make your new objectives SMART!

You can discuss the notes you have made with your assessor. They may provide evidence of your competence.

TEST YOUR KNOWLEDGE

Here are some questions to test your knowledge and understanding of the issues explored in this unit. You can write the answers down or discuss them with your assessor. They could provide good evidence for your NVQ.

1. What was the purpose of a recent meeting you attended? AC 1.1

2. How was this purpose explained to you? AC 1.1

3. What was your role in the meeting? AC 1.2

4. How did you prepare for the meeting? AC 1.2

5. What might happen if you did not know the purpose of a meeting, your role or you arrived unprepared? AC 1.2

6. What points did you contribute during the meeting? AC 2.1

7. What evidence did you have to back up your points? AC 2.1

8. What skills did you use to acknowledge the viewpoints of others? AC 2.2

9. Why is it important to acknowledge the views of others? AC 2.2

10. What skills did you use to clarify points or confirm your understanding? AC 2.3

11. What might happen if you did not clarify or confirm understanding? AC 2.3

12. Who else needed to know what was discussed and decided at the meeting? AC 3.1

13. How did you inform these interested parties or stakeholders? AC 3.1

14. Give three reasons why it is important to communicate information from the meeting to those who have an interest. AC 3.1

Pulling it all together and gathering evidence

You and your assessor will need to agree the most appropriate sources of evidence. Here are some suggestions:

- An electronic portfolio: you could upload your evidence to an e-portfolio package or simply store the evidence in electronic format.

- A paper-based portfolio: you could build a folder with hard copies of your evidence.

Types of evidence:

- Observation: a record by your assessor when observing you taking part in a meeting.
- Work product: copies of work produced by you that demonstrate your competence, for example agenda, your notes, minutes.
- Discussion: a record of you and your assessor discussing examples of things that happened in a meeting and how you dealt with them.
- Questioning: a record of your assessor asking questions to test your knowledge.
- Personal statement, reflective account or case study based on the activities in this unit: this should have sentences which start with 'I …' and should tell a story giving real-life examples.
- Witness testimony from your line manager confirming your competence, in writing or recorded as a discussion with your assessor.

It is a good idea to include a range of evidence from different sources. Your evidence should cover a period of time and not be a 'one-off'. However, try to keep the evidence to a minimum. Your assessor can make a note of product evidence they have seen so it can be left in the workplace.

Remember:

Less is more – quality not quantity!

Be holistic – can you use this evidence again for other units?

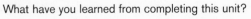

EVALUATION

What have you learned from completing this unit?

What new skills and techniques are you using?

How has this affected the people you work with?

How has your organisation benefited? How might it benefit in the future?

Introduction and learning outcomes

Learning outcomes for Unit E10:

1. Be able to identify circumstances that require a decision to be made.
2. Be able to collect information to inform decision making.
3. Be able to analyse information to inform decision making.
4. Be able to make a decision.

These learning outcomes say what you will have learned by the end of this unit. Each learning outcome is further broken down into assessment criteria, which we will look at in detail in the following sections of this unit.

This Unit Guide is a resource to help you gather the evidence you require to achieve Unit E10. It can be used, as a learning resource if you are new to the role, are studying team leading in preparation for work or as a refresher if you are already an experienced team leader.

You and your assessor will agree what you need to do to meet the assessment criteria and show you are competent. This Unit Guide provides some theory to help you make effective decisions, gives some case studies for you to examine and then an opportunity for you to reflect, with a virtual adviser, on how you can develop your own skills and gather evidence of competence. Some ideas are provided in the 'Pulling it all together' section at the end of this unit.

So, the purpose of this unit is to develop the skills and knowledge you need to make effective decisions.

Why do we need to make effective decisions?

I used to be indecisive, I am not so sure now. We encounter decisions daily: 'Should I get out of bed and go to work today?' In your mind you have already set an objective: I need to go to work as I am responsible and if I don't, perhaps

I won't get paid. That decision is fairly straightforward, a simple choice tempered with your own beliefs.

In business, decisions are required that are based upon a number of factors, for example the buying and selling of shares is based upon market conditions generally but outside influences may also affect those decisions. These influences could be the weather, war or a change in government. Depending on the shares, grain, oil or gas perhaps?

When you arrive at work, the need to make decisions may commence as soon as you get to your desk or in some cases as soon as you open the door.

It would be good to have some sort of 'magic' dice that makes an effective decision for you based on a throw. But sadly this is not available – if you have one please send it to us!

Some decisions are easy, straightforward – yes or no. Others may take time to consider (time you may not have, however). The more difficult the decision, the more time you need to mull over your options. As a team leader the team need you to make decisions for them at times, as the decision may be out of their range of responsibilities or scope of work. In team work, when a decision is required the need to respond effectively and in line with the agreed protocol is both desirable and expected.

Learning outcome 1 – Be able to identify circumstances that require a decision to be made

Assessment criterion 1.1 Explain the circumstances requiring a decision to be made

Circumstances change and situations develop that require decisions. Let's look at a few and consider the potential need to intervene and apply decisions.

Work-based issues requiring decisions could be:

- changes in the normal work routines
- planned changes
- operational changes
- review of work practices.

A change in a normal routine at work may alter a number of factors. The team may be unsure as to how to continue or reluctant to offer an idea to progress. In these situations your role is to provide the alternative solution to move on.

The team may offer proposals on how to progress and may present a number of options, but the option selection will be down to you.

Conditions that affect any disruption are generally too hot to handle for team members – they are scared that if it is their decision they will be blamed and perhaps disciplined if all goes wrong. Planned changes are set into the work routines, so as team leader you may have to set the plan and provide guidance through your decision to move on to another facet of the team's work. Targets and timings may need to be reset and the team leader will generally consider the plan and make the decision to do so.

During operational changes a number of decisions may be required and the team leader could be involved in making those decisions. For instance, in such an operational change involving a head count reduction, the team leader's manager may be removed from their post and in the interim decisions may be left to the team leader. Or there could be a new strategy to review business practices. Decisions may focus around the need to remove staff, cut hours, and freeze salaries and benefits. Such circumstances lead to hard final or participative decisions, possibly made by the team leader. Reviews of work practices also require a decision. Consideration of skill levels and application within the team could lead to a change in a work practice, procedure, policy or process.

Assessment criterion 1.2 State the desired objective(s) for making the decision

With each decision you make during your time at work, an objective or reason needs to be applied – why we do something or decide to do something needs to be understood. In some cases you may need to refer to your reasons or objective later as a review is conducted on a particular event.

Let's consider some of the objectives for decisions.

- prioritising
- best use of work-related resources
- increased workload.

When a situation arises at work so that a number of events occur at the same time, it is useful to understand your priorities. So you must be clear in defining your objectives. The first question must be, 'Which will I attend to first?' while giving consideration to the current position of your team's overall task. Once established, priorities can allow you to 'label' the order in which you deal with events that have occurred together. Say, for example, you are a team leader in a manufacturing environment and the team has one maintenance team member. If there are breakdowns on various points on the same production line, chances are you would request that the team member works in reverse order on the line so gradually the line moves forward. By doing this and clearing the output section first, the line will slowly move towards targets and your team will still produce.

During any task at work the team leader needs to ensure that they use the supply of resources in the best manner to serve the objectives of the team. Resources are defined as a supply from which a benefit is produced. Therefore all areas of your work that meet the objectives of the team are resources. If your resources are depleted, you need to use them to the best effect. Our friendly maintenance team member is a human resource and they were used to good effect by keeping the line moving forward.

Ideally, resources need to be made available at all times. However, we all know that is not always possible and when you are presented with a decision to optimise resources, clear facts need to be available on what the team 'has to hand'. Work into a team area does not always flow at a static and measured pace. When extra work is presented the decision on how to meet the work needs to be made by you, the team leader. Decisions on who does what, how it affects other duties and overall targets must be made. Contingency plans need to be considered and developed through the decision-making process.

Assessment criterion 1.3 Establish criteria on which to base the decision, in line with own organisation

Certain issues may creep into your decision-making choices or options and obviously there is some uncertainty as some of the facts may not be known. The background information might be highly complex and you may have to consider other factors. So the consequences may carry some high-risk element and the impact of the decision may be quite significant.

We have looked at options in decision making based on the factors that could be around to assist the selection. In a number of organisations set criteria are in place to follow to assist the process. Take, for example, a decision-making procedure such as a fire evacuation plan. Decisions are set in that procedure based upon the actions needed to remove employees from danger. The procedure may be as follows:

- Upon hearing the fire alarm all personnel must evacuate the building.
- Note: do not return to your place of work for belongings.
- In an orderly manner proceed to your allocated assembly area.
- The use of lifts during an evacuation is not allowed.
- Fire marshals will take a roll-call to ascertain all personnel are accounted for.
- Wait in the assembly area until advised otherwise by the fire marshal.

In this case, decisions regarding evacuation are set out in the plan. The evacuation plan will be reviewed often and the alarm will be tested at agreed times so the employees identify the alarm. Reaction time to evacuate will also be assessed through evacuation drills.

So any decision-making criteria need to be based upon a number of factors, but information regarding the decision process needs to be:

- sufficient
- accurate
- reliable
- relevant.

Organisational needs may require the development of a decision tree to look at perhaps a process, reporting route or procedure. By placing the requirements in a graph similar to a family tree, the user can determine their decision based on the interlinked information within the tree. Environmental conditions or issues in a manufacturing workplace are normally set out in a decision tree. The process following a chemical spill, perhaps, needs to determine a quick decision and the responsive points in the tree help to determine the actions needed.

Accident reporting follows a similar process in a number of organisations and the reports are used to decide upon safety conditions or initiatives.

So by taking the four factors listed above, let's look at the accident-reporting decision tree. Sufficiency reports and near misses need to be recorded and supply enough detail to react to a safety concern. Accurate information – photographs, witness statements and direct consultation with the person involved in the accident – is needed to explain the conditions at the time of the accident. The reports need to reliable and give accounts that can be verified if necessary. If the accident is serious the report will go on to the Reporting of Injuries, Diseases and Dangerous Occurrences Regulations 1995 (RIDDOR).

Relevance to the accident is obvious and the need to investigate and apply a process that is set in law is part of the overall decision process.

As a team leader you may be requested to consider a decision-making process to a work-based condition. It may be linked to quality of your team's outputs, what are the set criteria for your key performance indicators and how you pass or fail an output. A decision method for the absence of staff perhaps may be pertinent, who fills in for whom for example during a reported absence or if the team member needs to be relocated for other duties.

The case study section provides an opportunity for you to read about a team leader or team leading scenario. The case study highlights some of the issues discussed. You can use this to reflect on the situation and answer some questions. You do not have to write down your answers unless your tutor or assessor has asked you to do so.

CASE STUDY 1

Naomi works as a team leader. Her team prepare and coordinate events for a large function suite, which has a wide range of facilities offering training rooms and a large interactive area for sales conferences and private functions.

Today Naomi has arrived following her holidays and one of the team has noted that the flower show that started at 08:00 does not finish until 17:00. A private party is due to arrive at 18:00 to use the same room. The team member indicates that they do not have enough time to clear the room ready for the other booking.

The main flower show has finished and the judging is complete. A number of the stalls have already moved out of the suite. It is 14:00. A smaller room is available but will not seat the party booking due at 18:00. It will take one and a half hours to clear the main room.

What do you think?

1. What in your opinion is the best decision for the team leader based on the information you have?

2. Who should Naomi advise of her decision and what should she say?

3. Does Naomi have all the facts upon which to base her decision?

DEVELOPMENT ACTIVITY 1 with your virtual adviser

I am here to demystify the assessment criteria and help you relate what you have learned to your own job role. We will look at what you are currently doing and how you can develop your skills and have a real impact in your workplace.

Prepare a personal statement regarding any circumstances during which you have had to make a decision based upon established criteria. The heading should be: **Where am I now?** As if you were explaining to me, make a few notes about your strengths and weaknesses in identifying when decisions should be made. Remember to include your decision tree or chart. Be specific and provide some examples. Be honest with yourself – this is not part of your assessment, and identifying weaknesses is the first step to making improvements.

The questions below may help you.

Where am I now?
Tell me about the types of decisions required during your work.

1. Do you use decision charts or trees?

2. How do you assess the objective of a decision?

3. Describe circumstances leading to your required decision.

Now, in your personal statement, extend your points to consider **improvements** and then **action**.

Improvements and action
Are there any areas where you identify circumstances that require a decision to be made that could be improved?

What action do you think you could take to make those improvements happen?

Some of the changes you have identified might affect the way things are done in your organisation and you may need to discuss them with your line manager. Some changes can be made by you. Remember, small changes can make a big difference.

When you plan to make a change, remember to make your new objectives SMART!

You can discuss the notes you have made with your assessor. They may provide evidence of your competence.

An example

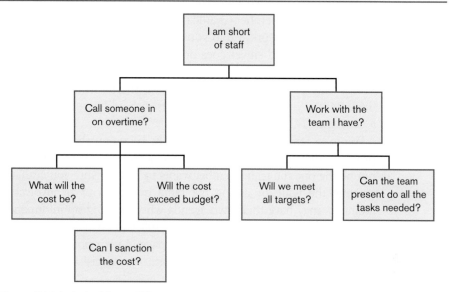

Figure E10.1: A decision-making process

Learning outcome 2 – Be able to collect information to inform decision making

In this section we will explore each of the assessment criteria in more detail to develop your knowledge and understanding.

Assessment criterion 2.1 Identify information needed to inform the decision-making process

Let's start by listing the types of information needed during the decision-making process and what it needs to be:

- accurate
- current
- factual
- reliable
- adequate.

Remember your full notebook from previous units – perhaps this is time to ensure you have space or a new book.

Decisions are based on the level of information you have. Some information will be linked to criteria used in the workplace. Those criteria of course do not totally support your final decision but offer a 'map' to follow while you pick up the detail along the way. Identifying information during decision making is almost like being involved in a crime scene – required information needs to be noted and those involved in the issue interviewed.

To ascertain accurate, current, factual, reliable and adequate information is a daunting task. But by viewing all aspects requiring a decision certainly helps. So when your team member Charlie comes up to you and says, 'I need a decision on this point in our work, I told you about it two weeks ago and nothing has been done yet', if a cold shiver goes down your spine this probably means you have forgotten about the issue. However, if you have your trusted notebook with you, things may be different as you will have the information or full circumstances documented and will certainly be closer to addressing the problem by offering a decision.

Points to remember are obvious really. Focus on the information regarding the problem, then enlightenment will come, although in some cases your decision may not be the one the team member wants to hear. Ensure you evaluate the problems creating the issue by asking the same questions of all involved as some team members may have their own agenda when offering up information – don't base your decision on one point of view; a full consensus is required. Remember the list above and put it at the top of the page in your notebook and refer to it when identifying relevant information to inform your decision-making process.

Assessment criterion 2.2 Communicate with stakeholders affected by the decision-making process

Let's look at a 'crime scene' at work and get the notebook out. This decision is based on a potential environmental spill. Potential stakeholders may be:

● team members

● linked managers

● suppliers

● planning or sales

● customers.

This particular incident will review whom you decide to inform during an incident of this nature.

You are a team leader in a company that uses some chemicals on site. As you come round a corner at the product intake bay you see an upturned drum gently discharging its contents into a drain. What would you do first?

1. Do you quickly ring the environmental agency at that point?

Or

2. Would you assess all the conditions first?

You may want to locate any team members around the area and determine whether they were aware of the issue and seek their assistance. If none of the team knew about the drum, it may be appropriate to have the unit uprighted and checked for detail of the contents, using the information on the side of the drum. You could determine its material data and see whether it has any control measures. The Control of Substances Hazardous to Health (COSHH) details will give you this information on the specification data sheet.

Using that information, what would you decide to do?

1. Ask a team member to contact the supplier to seek advice on the contents' properties?

Or

2. Prior to deciding on your next step have the contents sent away to be analysed?

The drain type could be storm or waste, so that needs to checked, along with the direction of flow. So who would you contact?

1. Advise the environmental control at the relevant controlling body for the drains?

Or

2. Ask your colleague in Engineering the route of the drains?

What other points can you pick up from this exercise? What may happen later if this decision is incomplete?

Thus we have a list of potential information to communicate. We now need to ensure those who need to know are informed of all the facts.

First, you have assessed the work area and your decision was to advise the Environmental Agency. However, this condition presents a number of issues and concerns because your decision may have other high-profile repercussions, so you must consider others who need to be aware of your decision. They could be other team members not involved directly, linked managers, and suppliers who have the information and could replace the drum if required. Thus in ongoing decisions the communication links need to be set and along the way those who need to know must be advised.

Some decisions are such that those who ask for a decision invariably are aware of the answer, for example unexpected requests for time off from team members who know you have just enough staff to run the department. However, other conditions may prevail so that as a team you do not have enough resources to operate or fulfil your obligations to others. You may, for example, have determined that you need to stop your team activities and advise your stakeholders that they will not see any outputs from the team. This 'last resort' situation will need to be documented and communicated clearly to the affected groups.

Assessment criterion 2.3 Explain how to inform stakeholders about the decision-making process

Once a decision goes through the full information-gathering stages, responding to the parties involved must be carried out effectively, a process which is normally down to the protocol in your workplace.

Delayed decisions can have a demotivational effect which clearly needs to be considered, particularly in a team environment as the team working with you wait for you to decide the credibility of the situation and how the issue is affected. You may hear 'management take their time over decisions as they cannot make them'. Conversely, if a decision is offered quickly you may hear 'that decision was already made'. The team member involved obviously did not get their requested holidays! So the turnaround of a decision, albeit slow or quick, will in most cases be 'challenged' or questioned.

We are considering informed decision making that needs time generally to determine the next action. The decisions that are made following a report or an investigation of some kind at work tend to follow a prescribed course. The process may be the decision to recruit following interview or perhaps the decision to offer a contract to a supplier following a presentation. These types of decisions need the formality of a procedure or guidelines to follow.

Using direct and timely contact in these decisions is appropriate and desirable, with the affected stakeholder contacted first.

The case study section provides an opportunity for you to read about a team leader or team leading scenario. The case study highlights some of the issues discussed. You can use this to reflect on the situation and answer some questions. You do not have to write down your answers unless your tutor or assessor has asked you to do so.

CASE STUDY 2

Naomi has considered the oversight regarding the booking in the function suite. She has approached the flower show president to ask whether they can accommodate her and the team by exiting the large room early. The lady advises Naomi that would not normally be a problem but some of the stallholders need to use the room for a post-event meeting. They have a buffet arranged and the function suite kitchen team are providing it.

The customer who pre-booked the large room is due to arrive in three and a half hours. Naomi rings him and explains the problem. The man is extremely annoyed and declares the room is his as he has paid his booking fee upfront.

What do you think?

1. Was the contact with the second customer timely?

2. Was all the decision information identified?

3. What other options does Naomi have?

4. Who else should Naomi involve?

DEVELOPMENT ACTIVITY 2 with your virtual adviser

I am here to demystify the assessment criteria and help you relate what you have learned to your own job role. We will look at what you are currently doing and how you can develop your skills and have a real impact in your workplace.

List the types of information you have identified to form a decision. Include in your list the stakeholders involved and detail how they were affected by the process. Mark each method to indicate whether you felt the process was successful. Also indicate whether your organisation uses any other methods that you have not yet experienced or used in your role.

Your list should be titled: **Where am I now?** Write as if you were explaining to me. Make a few notes about your strengths and weaknesses when collecting information for decision making. Be specific and provide some examples. Be honest with yourself – this is not part of your assessment and identifying weaknesses is the first step to making improvements.

The questions below may help you.

Where am I now?
Think about the information you or your organisation use during decision making.

1. When have you used a certain information-gathering method?

2. What was the decision you were considering?

3. Who were the stakeholders at this time?

Now, alongside your list, write the heading **Improvements** and in another column **Action**.

Improvements and action
Are there any areas where your information to inform decision making could be improved?

What action do you need to take to make those improvements?

Some of the changes you have identified might affect the way things are done in your organisation and you may need to discuss them with your line manager. You can make some changes. Remember, small changes can make a big difference.

When you plan to make a change, remember to make your new objectives SMART!

You can discuss the notes you have made with your assessor. They may provide evidence of your competence.

Learning outcome 3 – Be able to analyse information to inform decision making

In this section we will explore each of the assessment criteria in more detail to develop your knowledge and understanding.

Assessment criterion 3.1 Identify information for validity and relevance to the decision-making process

During the decision-making process a number of pieces of evidence may be presented, but as with the earlier 'crime scene' reference, some of the information may have little or no relevance. Once again the need to look at the factors involved becomes clear, this time to ensure all aspects are reviewed and there are no inconsistencies during the decision-making process.

Using the same list as previously, the process needs to be:

● factual

● accurate

- reliable
- current
- adequate.

The need now is to break down the information presented and dig deeper to try to remove some preconceived assumptions. This method, sometimes called 'critical thinking', examines all the assumptions, evaluates the evidence and moves on to clarify goals or objectives of the decision. It is almost like filtering out the rubbish and applying some clarity.

The main skills for the process are observation, interpretation and analysis.

It is a bit like a jigsaw – some of the pieces look the same but they fit in a different part of the puzzle, or in our case they are not relevant for the decision in the area of work we are looking at.

The decision that needed to made earlier during the drum spill incident was whether or not to call the external agencies. Now we need to decide on the actions following such a high-profile incident. As the incident needs to be reported, the cause needs to be included. All assumptions need to be checked and fully evaluated.

News reporters would perhaps follow a process like this example:

- Who
- What
- Where
- When
- Why
- How.

Two of the process points are apparent:

- What happened – the drum overturned.
- Where it happened – the location was identified as the intake bay.

So the progress would be to determine who was involved in order to understand when, why and how. In that case all parties around the area need to be identified and interviewed to see whether they saw the active participants in relation to the drum overturning. Once the parties are identified, the questions how and why could be asked.

One of the security team has indicated that a delivery had been made on and around the time of the drum spill. The point of delivery was the intake bay. The delivery driver had left ten minutes later, according to security records. The delivery was a drum of the chemical as identified during the spill.

The team leader contacts the delivery company and advises them of the situation. Company management advise that they will interview the driver and report back with a written statement from him. The team leader requests that the driver rings into the site to speak directly to him. The company advise that the request is not possible as they have a procedure to follow and they will forward the statement once they have carried out their own interview.

Assessment criterion 3.2 Analyse information against established criteria

Decision-making processes need to be followed with care at all times, so building up background information to support your decision is very important. That information needs to be retained either by the team leader in their notebook or in records that are available for the event or issue. Keeping clear records has been covered through a number of the units.

The decision-making processes in all areas of a team leader's work need to be concise, clear and in some cases controlled. The decision to change a procedure, for example, will involve a number of records, including the prime reasons for the change. The history of a change and the reasons behind it may then be referred to or considered for future similar changes. This will offer a template for change or indeed information on certain pitfalls or conditions that may affect the reviewer's final decision.

Information of this kind offers references to established criteria so any analytical requirements have some detail already supplied to start the decision-making process once more. If you as a team leader have some trends or known patterns to follow, then making the decision is perhaps easier and probably timely.

The team leader in the drum spill situation has looked at the previous deliveries of the chemicals. The delivery timings viewed on the delivery notes show times and dates not agreed with the supplier. The times were set in a contract and are due to the workload of the team on site; production days do not offer the access to the site as the team are otherwise engaged. The last four deliveries have been out with these agreed timings.

Questions to the team on the previous deliveries offer responses that advise that they had noticed that the material was just left on the loading dock at the intake bay. The team had assumed that this delivery was agreed and just brought the chemical into the factory at a later time. Team members also indicated that due to the door on the loading dock being closed, the drum was very close to the edge of the access platform.

The team leader then questions the planning department, who coordinate orders, and asks whether a change in delivery had been agreed from their perspective. The response is that no change was requested. Armed with this information, the team leader waits for the supplier's report from the driver.

This type of information gathering is critical when as a team leader you require good points of reference to enable your decision-making process.

The critical thinking is applied by expanding into other areas for more information.

The case study section provides an opportunity for you to read about a team leader or team leading scenario. The case study highlights some of the issues discussed. You can use this to reflect on the situation and answer some questions. You do not have to write down your answers unless your tutor or assessor has asked you to do so.

Naomi is looking at her options. She has considered the booking arrangements and the party due in at 18:00 has paid for the room in advance, so she cannot use the other room for them.

The committee from the flower show are about to start their meeting. Naomi decides to start moving the flower show tables out of the main room to give the team a chance to prepare for the later booking.

The team move into the room and start folding the tables so they can move them. The flower show president asks them to leave as they are disturbing the meeting. The team members advise Naomi of this and she then starts to consider her next move.

What do you think?

1. Has Naomi identified all of her decision-making information?

2. Was it important to find out whether the later booking had paid?

DEVELOPMENT ACTIVITY 3 with your virtual adviser

I am here to demystify the assessment criteria and help you relate what you have learned to your own job role. We will look at what you are currently doing and how you can develop your skills and have a real impact in your workplace.

Think of a time when you had to analyse information when making a decision in your workplace. Draw a simple table with four columns. Above the first and second columns write the heading: **Where am I now?** In the first column, list the information you considered using to make a decision. In the second column place a tick against some of the information that you actually used to make your decision.

Under the table, as if you were explaining to me, make a few notes about your strengths and weaknesses when identifying information for this particular decision. Be specific and provide some examples. Be honest with yourself – this is not part of your assessment, and identifying weaknesses is the first step to making improvements.

The questions below may help you.

Where am I now?
Think about this situation when you identified information to inform your decision-making process.

1. How did you ensure the information was relevant?

2. How did you reference the information against an established analytical criterion?

3. Have you used any analyses in your decision making before?

Now, in your second column, write the heading **Improvements** and in the third column **Action**.

> **Improvements and action**
>
> Are there any areas where your analytical methods of information in decision making could be improved?
>
> What action do you need to take to make those improvements?
>
> Some of the changes you have identified might affect the way things are done in your organisation and you may need to discuss them with your line manager. You can make some changes. Remember, small changes can make a big difference.
>
> When you plan to make a change, remember to make your new objectives SMART!
>
> You can discuss the notes you have made with your assessor. They may provide evidence of your competence.

Learning outcome 4 – Be able to make a decision

In this section we will explore each of the assessment criteria in more detail to develop your knowledge and understanding.

Assessment criterion 4.1 Apply decision-making techniques to determine a decision

A number of decision-making techniques are available and these are generally known and proven. Some may be in use in your organisation and you may have come across them before. Some team decisions are made through consensus of opinion, often at a team meeting or team talk. Others used are condition based and look at the factors that present themselves for the problem requiring a decision. A number of the identified points in your place of work will help you in selecting an appropriate decision-making technique.

Let's look at a small selection:

- brainstorming
- pros and cons
- SWOT.

Brainstorming can be used in most team environments as it involves a group who view a problem and consider the possible solutions through mass opinion. The obvious attraction for team working is that everyone is involved – ensuring that all those on the team are invited is crucial as in theory no one can offer a counter opinion on the final decision as everyone has participated. The team leader as facilitator is central to the success as they need to act as referee.

The process considers the problem, then discussion ensues. Later, points on how to attend to the problem are listed and a decision is made on the final outcome. Similar to this process, with some modifications depending on the group:

1. Define and agree the objective.
2. Brainstorm ideas and suggestions, having agreed a time limit.

3. Categorise/condense/combine/refine.

4. Assess/analyse effects or results.

5. Prioritise options/rank list as appropriate.

6. Agree action and timescale.

7. Control and monitor follow-up.

A weighted decision-making template shows the pros (for – advantages) set against the cons (against – disadvantages). The weighted score is down to the group and could be up to 10 or 20 or 100. This type of decision-making tool removes emotional ties to one of the factors as the decision is based upon an overall score assessed against other measures. (See Table E10.1.)

Table E10.1: Pros v. Cons

Question/Decision/Option:			
Pros (for – advantages)	Score	Cons (against – disadvantages)	Score
Total		Total	

SWOT analysis looks at the strengths, weaknesses, opportunities and threats of a particular response to a problem or potential problem, so this type of analysis is of more use when linked to other types of decision-making techniques.

Table E10.2: SWOT analysis

Strengths	**Weaknesses**
Examples:	**Examples:**
Advantages of proposition? Capabilities? Competitive advantages?	Disadvantages of proposition? Gaps in capabilities? Lack of competitive strength?

Opportunities	Threats
Examples:	**Examples:**
Market developments? Competitors' vulnerabilities? Industry or lifestyle trends? Technology development and innovation?	Political effects? Legislative effects? Environmental effects? IT developments? Competitor intentions – various? Market demand?

The examples applied as the criteria in each section can be altered, increased or reduced depending on the workplace or review.

Assessment criterion 4.2 Explain the decision made in line with desired objectives

When the process of decision making is drawing to a close, references should be made to the overall objectives to detail that the decision is in line with them. Your summary should also include how the decision is based upon current information. This re-emphasis of the objective needs to be mentioned and detailed in the final report.

If we go back to our problem with the chemical spill, the objective of the team leader was to determine how the spill was caused so he could provide that information in an environmental report. The report from the supplier's driver has arrived, indicating that indeed the driver did leave the drum on the loading dock as that was the point of delivery detailed in his paperwork. He also stated that the drum was near the end of the loading dock access platform and was stable when he left.

While waiting for the supplier's report, the team leader had carried out some experiments using a drum filled with water. The team leader had measured the drum diameter and determined that more than 40 per cent of the drum would overhang the loading dock. When the drum with water was positioned on that area, the drum tipped back on three of the five times due to uneven surface. Photographs were taken of the experiment and the health and safety representative from the team was present to monitor the exercise and assist.

Reviewing all the conditions in any circumstance that needs a decision gives you as a team leader the opportunity to offer detailed explanations of your findings. In most cases you do not need to relive an event or condition, but the use of all information around you that is current and in keeping with your desired objectives allows you to give your final decision credibility and support when an explanation is due.

In the case of the chemical spill scenario, in the exercise to review how the incident happened the involvement of the team's health and safety representative offers added value to the internal explanation. So the practice of keeping others actively involved in certain decisions is productive as the witness or participant supplies more information to add to the explanations.

Assessment criterion 4.3 Communicate the decision taken to relevant stakeholders

It is really important that all concerned in any decision-making process are advised of the final outcome. Others interested in the situation may also require an update, particularly if they have similar roles or situations that may develop within the organisation.

Affected stakeholders first! If the decision affects someone in a personal manner, they need to be advised first. Direct communication is best in these situations and depending upon the decision, that may be one-to-one, a telephone call or a formal letter. The manner in how to communicate may be detailed in a protocol. If the decision offers sensitive information and you have no protocol, seek advice from others on how to approach the contact.

During all communication your explanation on how you arrived at your decision may (and probably will) be required. So your records need to be available to detail this information if the situation is suitable. Once again, seek guidance if necessary and refer to your organisational guidelines. If you were involved in a recruitment and selection process, the response in a decision on a job role might not perhaps include the detail on how someone was selected. Such information may have been supplied prior to the selection process. Feedback on a selection process is generally offered, however, and that will include the criteria for selection and how the candidate was appraised against those criteria.

Those decisions that occur daily or frequently still need some explanation and detail. Your communication on operational plan changes may have a knock-on effect for others involved in the outputs of your team. Clear background information on the plan change and why it was decided upon supports and sustains relationships, as it is then included in the reasons.

Let us return to the drum spill scenario for the final communication. In the team leader's report he commented that based on current information and experiments with the drum, the spill was accidental due to the inappropriate storage of the drum. Upon reading the communication and speaking directly to the team leader, the supplier conceded that the problem was with the activity of the driver. Soon after this the deliveries were brought in at the correct time and the driver had extra training on customer contact and storage methods. So in this decision-making process all went well and the situation was resolved, although not without some work and effort applied to ensure proper assessment, management and presentation.

Some decisions you make will not meet your objectives. These learning situations still need the same process of ensuring you follow a pre-determined path and gather enough information to present why things were done. Remember this quote, which is attributed to President Roosevelt:

'In any moment of decision the best thing you can do is the right thing, the next best thing is the wrong thing, and the worst thing you can do is nothing.'

The case study section provides an opportunity for you to read about a team leader or team leading scenario. The case study highlights some of the issues discussed. You can use this to reflect on the situation and answer some questions. You do not have to write down your answers unless your tutor or assessor has asked you to do so.

CASE STUDY 4

Naomi has looked at all of the issues affecting the booking arrangements today. She asks her team to gather and have a quick brainstorming session on the available options.

A team member advises that the small room is available adjacent to the large room. It would be easy for the team to set up the buffet in that room. It offers a private place for a meeting and the tables are set in a meeting arrangement. The kitchen team member indicates that actually would be more suitable for them as they have better access for the food. Another team member indicates that by doing this the time to set up the large room ready for the large party would be manageable.

Naomi quickly gathers this information and provides the information to the flower show president and asks whether this would be suitable. The president is happy with the arrangements and asks the meeting attendees to move to the meeting room.

Naomi rings the lead person for the evening event and assures him that all will be ready for him. She apologises for her previous contact.

What do you think?

1. Was the situation finally addressed correctly?
2. Did the final decision meet all of the objectives?
3. Should any other information be recorded or documented?

DEVELOPMENT ACTIVITY 4 with your virtual adviser

I am here to demystify the assessment criteria and help you relate what you have learned to your own job role. We will look at what you are currently doing and how you can develop your skills and have a real impact in your workplace.

Draw up a simple table with three columns. In the first column write **Where am I now?** and, as if you were explaining to me, make a few notes about the decision-making techniques in use in your place of work. Think about the strengths and weaknesses when using these techniques and methods. Be specific and provide some examples. Be honest with yourself – this is not part of your assessment, and identifying weaknesses is the first step to making improvements.

The questions below may help you.

Where am I now?
Think about a time when you have used decision-making techniques and methods. Do you review or reflect on the technique in use and are others involved?

1. Consider your preferred decision-making technique. Is it a method that has had positive results?
2. When considering a problem and making a decision, do you document the process?
3. Do you communicate your decision to all stakeholders involved?

Now, in your second column, write the heading **Improvements** and in the third column **Action**.

Improvements and action
Are there any areas where your decision-making techniques could be improved or modified?

What action do you need to take to make those improvements?

Some of the changes you have identified might affect the way things are done in your organisation and you may need to discuss them with your line manager. You can make some changes. Remember, small changes can make a big difference.
   When you plan to make a change, remember to make your new objectives SMART!
   You can discuss the notes you have made with your assessor. They may provide evidence of your competence.

TEST YOUR KNOWLEDGE

Here are some questions to test your knowledge and understanding of the issues explored in this unit. You can write the answers down or discuss them with your assessor. They could provide good evidence for your NVQ.

1. What types of decisions do you make during your daily tasks? AC 1.1

2. What types of decisions have you made that have a real impact on your role? AC 1.1

3. What types of objectives do you consider when making a decision? AC 1.2

4. Describe the criteria you use in the various decisions you make. AC 1.3

5. How do you identify the information required to inform the decision-making process? AC 2.1

6. Give some examples of situations when you have communicated to stakeholders affected by the decision. AC 2.2

7. Describe how you explain and inform stakeholders about the decision-making process. AC 2.3

8. Describe how you identify information for validity and relevance in the decision-making process. AC 3.1

9. How do you analyse information against your decision-making criteria? AC 3.1

10. Do you apply any decision-making techniques? If relevant, describe them. AC 4.1

11. How do you explain the decision made in line with final objectives? AC 4.2

12. How do you communicate your final decisions? AC 4.3

13. Who do you communicate your final decision to? AC 4.3

Pulling it all together and gathering evidence

You and your assessor will need to agree the most appropriate sources of evidence. Here are some suggestions:

- An electronic portfolio: you could upload your evidence to an e-portfolio package or simply store the evidence in electronic format.
- A paper-based portfolio: you could build a folder with hard copies of your evidence.

Types of evidence:

- Observation: a record by your assessor when observing you during a chosen decision-making technique.
- Work product: copies of work produced by you that demonstrate your competence, for example emails, presentations, briefing notices and team talk minutes.
- Discussion: a record of you and your assessor discussing examples of things that happened during decisions and how you dealt with them.
- Questioning: a record of your assessor asking questions to test your knowledge.
- Personal statement, reflective account or case study based on the activities in this unit: this should have sentences which start with 'I …' and should tell a story giving real-life examples.
- Witness testimony from your line manager confirming your competence, in writing or recorded as a discussion with your assessor.

It is a good idea to include a range of evidence from different sources. Your evidence should cover a period of time and not be a 'one-off'. However, try to keep the evidence to a minimum. Your assessor can make a note of product evidence they have seen so it can be left in the workplace.

Remember:

Less is more – quality not quantity!

Be holistic – can you use this evidence again for other units?

EVALUATION

What have you learned from completing this unit?

What new skills and techniques are you using?

How has this affected the people you work with?

How has your organisation benefited? How might it benefit in the future?

E11

COMMUNICATE INFORMATION AND KNOWLEDGE

Introduction and learning outcomes

Learning outcomes for Unit E11:

1. Be able to identify the information required, and its reliability for communication.

2. Be able to understand communication techniques and methods.

3. Be able to communicate information and knowledge using appropriate techniques and methods.

4. Be able to adapt communication techniques and methods according to target audience response.

These learning outcomes say what you will have learned by the end of this unit. Each learning outcome is further broken down into assessment criteria, which we will look at in detail in the following sections of this unit.

This Unit Guide is a resource to help you gather the evidence you require to achieve Unit E11. It can be used as a learning resource if you are new to the role, are studying team leading in preparation for work or as a refresher if you are already an experienced team leader.

You and your assessor will agree what you need to do to meet the assessment criteria and show you are competent. This Unit Guide provides some theory to develop your understanding of communicating information and knowledge, gives some case studies for you to examine and then an opportunity for you to reflect, with a virtual adviser, on how you can develop your own skills and gather evidence of competence. Some ideas are provided in the 'Pulling it all together' section at the end of this unit.

So, the purpose of this unit is to develop the skills and knowledge you need to communicate information and knowledge.

Why do we need to communicate information and knowledge?

In all stages of development humans need to communicate and pass on information and knowledge. This process is vital for our survival, our well-being and progression.

Communication methods have altered radically and are now moving on with a pace, for example who would have thought that social media sites would have such an influence on how we interact since their development over the last few years.

The way we do business is also changing – the requirement to communicate effectively and with speed is essential.

We need to decide and determine the most suitable communication methods for the operational section of any business; the type of information and knowledge should also be considered.

Information may be sensitive, operational or feedback to questions posed by your team. To pass on general information it may be appropriate to do this: via email, post, notice board, verbally or a daily planned team meeting.

Direct information for selected individuals needs to be personal and responsive, for example during a training session the expectancy would be feedback to ensure understanding.

Sensitive information regarding changes in work practices or terms and conditions needs to be planned. These situations tend to use a wide range of communication methods to ensure all involved are aware of the proposed changes.

Learning outcome 1 – Be able to identify the information required, and its reliability for communication

In this section we will explore each of the assessment criteria in more detail to develop your knowledge and understanding.

Assessment criterion 1.1 Explain the information and knowledge that needs communicating

Before embarking upon communicating information you need to check your own understanding of the content required. This is vital preparation for anyone delivering information as the 'source' of information and knowledge. As the 'receiver' we all tend to measure communication skills with reference to content, clarity, knowledge and attitude.

The content of the information needs to be considered as you may be communicating information and knowledge to a wide range of people.

For effective communication you need a good understanding of the people you are communicating with, their needs, motivations and ways in which they prefer to communicate. It also requires careful planning, the use of a variety of techniques to retain people's interest and attention, flexibility to adapt the communication in response to feedback and ensuring people have received and understood the information and knowledge.

Assessment criterion 1.2 Identify the target audience requiring the information and knowledge

Managing people and processes requires communication methods that are relevant and appropriate for all involved, bearing in mind changing business needs. It is therefore important to identify your target audience. Agreeing your target audience may seem obvious, but understanding who represents your wider group of colleagues can be more difficult to grasp at times.

Your own working structure should give you the general reporting levels. However, some operational or process changes in condition may need your skills. This understanding of how your role may link into the system for exchanging information is an important part of your work. So, it is important to identify:

- what are the benefits of communication of information and knowledge
- who your target audience are, both internal and external
- why the most commonly used methods and techniques are in use in your organisation or section to communicate information and knowledge.

The consequences of not knowing this information may mean you will not perform to the standards required by your line manager or your organisation as a whole.

The case study below provides an opportunity for you to read about a team leader or team leading scenario. The case study highlights some of the issues discussed. You can use this to reflect on the situation and answer some questions. You do not have to write down your answers unless your tutor or assessor has asked you to do so.

CASE STUDY 1

Alan has just been promoted to logistics team leader for a supplier of janitorial and cleaning materials whose prime customers are public houses and hotels. The company prides itself on the success rate of delivery, with the average delivery rate nationally being 85 per cent. Alan was one of the delivery drivers but he also has extensive experience of the warehouse operations, hence his promotion.

Alan's team currently has an 87 per cent success rate. However, the company has had some external pressure to improve these targets from the lead pub companies, which want to standardise deliveries into their premises.

Sharon, Alan's line manager, has tasked Alan to introduce a highly innovative logistics planning system, which has been used in a pilot warehouse site where the delivery success rate has increased to 95 per cent, with focused times of deliveries available. Alan has viewed the system and is trained on the simple but effective computer input. He can therefore see the benefits as an experienced driver and warehouse operator.

So a number of operational conditions need to be communicated, for example delivery times will have to change to accommodate the system and stock into the site will need to be adjusted to ensure progression. The system will be installed in two weeks' time.

What do you think?

1. Who is the internal target audience for the communication of the change in planning system?
2. Who should Alan consider as the potential external target audience?
3. Does Alan have enough information?

DEVELOPMENT ACTIVITY 1 with your virtual adviser

I am here to demystify the assessment criteria and help you relate what you have learned to your own job role. We will look at what you are currently doing and how you can develop your skills and have a real impact in your workplace.

Draw up a simple chart with an outline of your current flow of communication practices. The heading should be **Where am I now?** As if you were explaining to me, make a few notes about your strengths and weaknesses when communicating information and knowledge to your team. Remember to include in your flow chart the manner in which you receive information to communicate to your team. Be specific and provide some examples. Be honest with yourself – this is not part of your assessment and identifying weaknesses is the first step to making improvements.

The questions below may help you.

Where am I now?
Think about the types of information you communicate to your team.

1. Do you hold regular updates with the management group with specific information to pass on to your team?
2. How do you receive information and knowledge to pass on to your team?
3. Do you have regular team talks or briefings to discuss operational targets, conditions or performance?
4. Do these meetings have an agenda and is the content noted?
5. Do you have a structured, planned one-to-one discussion with team members?

Now, in your information flow chart, against each communication point write the heading **Improvements** and then **Action**.

Improvements and action
Are there any areas where you gather or process information for team communication that could be improved?

What action do you think you could take to make those improvements happen?

Some of the changes you have identified might affect the way things are done in your organisation and you may need to discuss them with your line manager. Some changes can be made by you. Remember, small changes can make a big difference.

When you plan to make a change, remember to make your new objectives SMART!

You can discuss the notes you have made with your assessor. They may provide evidence of your competence.

Learning outcome 2 – Be able to understand communication techniques and methods

In this section we will explore each of the assessment criteria in more detail to develop your knowledge and understanding.

Assessment criterion 2.1 Identify what techniques and methods can be used to communicate information and knowledge

During communication, one aspect is vital: the source of the information must be trusted and therefore the techniques and methods we use to communicate must also be trusted.

Maybe you have heard of or played the game 'broken telephone', during which a phrase or statement is passed along a line of people – at the end, the initial statement bears no relationship to the starting phrase! This communication method obviously cannot be trusted, so how do we ensure our techniques are trustworthy and are in line with our team's and organisation's requirements? There is often a gap between what we say and what other people hear. So during the communication of information and knowledge it is essential that all team members understand what has been passed on.

We are presented with various communication methods, which may be dynamic and speedy. However, while they may be technically brilliant, they may not be appropriate for your target audience.

Let's list some of them and consider how they could be used:

- briefings
- presentations
- one-to-one discussions
- team talks
- workshops
- email
- memos
- notices.

The list is extensive but not exhaustive and not listed in any preference. Also, the description of the method may vary from organisation to organisation.

Briefings are normally held to pass on information to a group of people. The information tends to be one way, more like a 'state of the nation' address. The formality of briefings tends to make them structured and they are often used when changes are imminent.

Presentations tend to be a little more interactive, they offer more information and generally are supported by some form of pictorial or visual display.

One-to-one discussions can either be formal or informal. They offer more of an opportunity to raise questions or issues that directly affect the individual. They are often used during a performance review or direct training.

Team talks can be formal or informal and when structured offer full contribution of the team. They assist team development, offering two-way feedback that can be documented and referred to, thus establishing a progressive and interactive forum.

Workshops tend to be used when a message needs to be reinforced or at a point when something new is introduced to the team. They are interactive and allow the participants to ask questions and develop material using the group's ideas and knowledge.

Emails are direct and offer instant contact with the recipient. They are ideal when information needs to be circulated quickly. They are, of course, remote and do not offer the direct human contact required when a topic is perhaps sensitive.

Memos are similar to emails with regard to the interaction with the recipient. However, they offer a record of communication to others. They are normally read and passed on, with the recipient signing to indicate they have been read but sadly (as with emails) not necessarily understood.

Notices supply a direct point for a group to read information. They supply a medium to reach a wider audience as long as the group is aware of the notice location and frequency of notices being posted.

So when identifying the technique and method to use to communicate information and knowledge we have a number of options. The decision to use one particular communication format may not always be yours; however, as a team leader you should be able to identify the method that suits your team and lends itself to better understanding of the information as it is communicated.

Assessment criterion 2.2 Explain how to select the most appropriate techniques and methods

So, with our list of potential communication techniques and methods, the next phase of the process is to select a method (or methods) that works for you and the team.

Of course, organisational procedures may already be in place, tried-and-tested practices or guidelines to deliver information. If this is the case then the communication process is defined and you should follow the set guidelines.

Nevertheless, at times you may need to offer opinions on the process and therefore as a team leader your understanding of the potential to select communication methods is invaluable.

During team development communication is vital. The team dynamics are generally based on team members' individual contributions through both sound communication and input to form the group. The team leader role tends to be the conduit that links the team to the rest of the organisation. So the level of information and knowledge to communicate can be highly varied and complex.

As team communication methods develop, the group will grow to expect a structured approach in the delivery methods used. At times, however, the formality of the information will alter the normal communication process, and others may be involved on the edge of the team structure. As the target audience changes, so will the method of communicating information and knowledge.

The case study below provides an opportunity for you to read about a team leader or team leading scenario. The case study highlights some of the issues discussed. You can use this to reflect on the situation and answer some questions. You do not have to write down your answers unless your tutor or assessor has asked you to do so.

CASE STUDY 2

Alan, the newly promoted team leader, now needs to consider how he will identify an appropriate method to communicate the information and knowledge regarding the new logistics planning system. The system is new but it has most of the conditions that are already in place on the existing planner.

Alan's main problem is the demographics of his target audience, as the delivery team are based in the office and warehouse area only early in the morning, prior to going off to customer delivery points.

He considers his methods and comes up with the following options:

- Email all concerned with a link to the planning system's website and advise they must reply to indicate they understand the changes.

- Have a short briefing at 08:00 prior to the delivery team leaving.

- Put up a notice explaining the process and advise everyone of the times the system will be active.

- Call a team meeting for all involved, with a workshop to show the changes. This will involve some disruption to delivery schedules but could be managed by contact with suppliers and customers.

What do you think?

1. Which option, if any, would you suggest Alan uses?

2. Why would you use this option? Explain why, in your opinion, the others are not appropriate.

3. Who else would you suggest Alan involves in identifying his method?

4. What is Alan's timeframe for communicating this information and knowledge?

5. Should the selection of the method be based on formal or informal communication methods?

DEVELOPMENT ACTIVITY 2 with your virtual adviser

I am here to demystify the assessment criteria and help you relate what you have learned to your own job role. We will look at what you are currently doing and how you can develop your skills and have a real impact in your workplace.

Using the list of communication techniques and methods mentioned in this section, prepare a list that you have either used or participated in as a source of information and knowledge or a recipient of information and knowledge.

Mark each method to indicate whether you felt the technique was successful. Also indicate whether your organisation uses any other methods that you have not yet experienced or used in your role.

As if you were explaining to me, make a few notes about your strengths and weaknesses when communicating information and knowledge. Be specific and provide some examples. Be honest with yourself – this is not part of your assessment, and identifying weaknesses is the first step to making improvements.

The questions below may help you.

Where am I now?

Think about the various communication methods and techniques you use or are in use in your organisation.

1. When have you used a certain communication method?

2. What was the information and knowledge you delivered?

3. Who were the recipients at this time?

Now, alongside your list, write the heading **Improvements** and then a column headed **Action**.

Improvements and action

Are there any areas where your communication techniques and methods could be improved?

What action do you need to take to make those improvements?

Some of the changes you have identified might affect the way things are done in your organisation and you may need to discuss them with your line manager. Some changes can be made by you. Remember, small changes can make a big difference.

When you plan to make a change, remember to make your new objectives SMART!

You can discuss the notes you have made with your assessor. They may provide evidence of your competence.

Learning outcome 3 – Be able to communicate information and knowledge using appropriate techniques and methods

In this section we will explore each of the assessment criteria in more detail to develop your knowledge and understanding.

Assessment criterion 3.1 Communicate to target audience using the appropriate techniques and methods

The decision to use a communication technique or method depends on the information and knowledge to be passed on to your team. Effective communication needs to be clear and concise, especially when communicating to the team as a whole. An ambiguously worded message can be interpreted in different ways, so the message needs to be clear.

The examples mentioned in this section offer discussion points as a combination of communication methods could be used. Many companies and organisations have their own protocols and procedures which dictate how and when information should be cascaded.

Sales may be reduced in an organisation. Therefore the information and knowledge for the team will be the reasons why sales are declining. In this instance a formal presentation may be appropriate to highlight the circumstances, with graphs or charts to show the areas of concern.

A change in partnership agreements in a foreign country could be formally briefed using a format that gives information but does not provide much of an opportunity for debate. Opportunities for debate in such circumstances would perhaps be raised during team talks and one-to-one consultations.

Team talks are generally meetings to review operational and procedural issues. They can be highly interactive as debate is encouraged to ensure the team contribution levels are considered and examined.

Emails are normally used to give instant responses and as such are a fairly reactionary form of communication. Details of a production plan change or a delivery change into a warehouse may be communicated effectively by email as they need to be acted upon urgently.

Notices tend to communicate information that has a generous timeframe, such as forthcoming events or historical information (e.g. records and minutes of previous meetings).

Assessment criterion 3.2 Explain how the target audience has received and understood the information communicated

When communicating information and knowledge it is vital to check understanding. We have discussed the 'broken record' problems that can occur when communication methods are not used to good effect. For example, if a change in procedure affects only certain people or departments, be sure that your message clearly indicates this to prevent your team from thinking that it affects the whole organisation.

Communication is generally a two-way process – checking someone's understanding is fundamental for team working. Teams do not generally work with only one individual having all the information and knowledge. A check on your target audience can be undertaken by reviewing the responses from your team members to your chosen communication method and technique. During the delivery of a communication these responses are critical as they reflect understanding. Questions raised by the team will also show this, and as a team leader you should be aware of your target audience. For example, you may have some strong personalities in your team with set views and entrenched beliefs and their interpretation of the information communicated may differ from that of others.

The case study below provides an opportunity for you to read about a team leader or team leading scenario. The case study highlights some of the issues discussed. You can use this to reflect on the situation and answer some questions. You do not have to write down your answers unless your tutor or assessor has asked you to do so.

CASE STUDY 3

Alan has conducted a training session on a planning system for his delivery drivers and warehouse team. He developed a presentation method to show the various screens the team would use to access the overall plan for delivery and how this would fit into an overall schedule. This is the second time he has used this type of communication method – the first time he was a little concerned as the event covered all areas, but he had no way to show the team understood the system.

What do you think?

1. How would you ensure the information from the training session was understood?

2. What other methods would you use linked to Alan's presentation?

DEVELOPMENT ACTIVITY 3 with your virtual adviser

I am here to demystify the assessment criteria and help you relate what you have learned to your own job role. We will look at what you are currently doing and how you can develop your skills and have a real impact in your workplace.

Draw up a simple table with three columns. In the first column write **Where am I now?** and, as if you were explaining to me, make a few notes about your strengths and weaknesses when communicating to your team. Be specific and provide some examples. Be honest with yourself – this is not part of your assessment, and identifying weaknesses is the first step to making improvements.

The questions below may help you.

Where am I now?

Think about a situation when you have communicated information and knowledge to your team.

1. How did you ensure the information and knowledge was understood?

2. How did the team indicate they had received the information and knowledge?

3. Have you ever had to review the information and knowledge with the team since the initial delivery?

Now, in your second column, write the heading **Improvements** and in the third column **Action**.

Improvements and action

Are there any areas where your communication techniques and methods could be improved?

What action do you need to take to make those improvements?

Some of the changes you have identified might affect the way things are done in your organisation and you may need to discuss them with your line manager. Some changes can be made by you. Remember, small changes can make a big difference.

When you plan to make a change, remember to make your new objectives SMART!

You can discuss the notes you have made with your assessor. They may provide evidence of your competence.

Learning outcome 4 – Be able to adapt communication techniques and methods according to target audience response

In this section we will explore each of the assessment criteria in more detail to develop your knowledge and understanding.

Assessment criterion 4.1 Explain how to modify communication techniques and methods in response to verbal or non-verbal feedback

Not all communication methods and techniques will be successful – the simple fact is that some team groups will respond to different approaches. With various team compositions from a wide range of disciplines, a definitive method cannot be applied in a generic manner. The forms of interaction must consider the differing target audience groups, all using and requiring different skills. To establish how information is received during communication, direct feedback is essential. Questions and discussions on how information was received and understood should take place soon after delivery.

Let us review some practices that we use as a normal day-to-day activity. Emails are commonplace and quick, and once sent the sender believes they have communicated effectively. However, a direct two-way discussion may be much more effective to ensure understanding of the topic.

Presentations may be a highly visual communication method, and in some instances the same presentation is used to communicate information for all groups. However, while the sales team will understand the requirements of the customer and how certain sales have increased due to promotional activities, using that same presentation for the manufacturing team will confuse them and add extra questions over your communication method. In a similar manner, key performance indicators from the factory will not assist the flow of information for the sales team.

So the reduction of jargon and non-essential technical data will assist understanding and ensure the target audience have the information they require and are comfortable with their operational section of the organisation.

Effective communication needs to be clear and concise, especially when communicating to the group as a whole. Effective business communication requires us to keep asking questions – 'What do you mean by that?' – because most of what goes awry with communications is that generally people and team members make assumptions.

The case study below provides an opportunity for you to read about a team leader or team leading scenario. The case study highlights some of the issues discussed. You can use this to reflect on the situation and answer some questions. You do not have to write down your answers unless your tutor or assessor has asked you to do so.

CASE STUDY 4

Alan has reviewed his communication methods with the team in the warehouse. They indicate a good understanding of the planning system. The drivers, however, have some concerns. They have been presented with unfamiliar terminology regarding collection points in the warehouse.

Also, changes to plans are emailed to the warehouse team, for reasons which are not explained, and the drivers have indicated they are not included as they find out about such changes only prior to a delivery run.

What do you think?

1. How should any new terminology be used?

2. Is an email an appropriate communication method in this instance?

3. Should any other communication methods be included?

DEVELOPMENT ACTIVITY 4 with your virtual adviser

I am here to demystify the assessment criteria and help you relate what you have learned to your own job role. We will look at what you are currently doing and how you can develop your skills and have a real impact in your workplace.

Draw up a simple table with three columns. In the first column write **Where am I now?** and, as if you were explaining to me, make a few notes about your strengths and weaknesses when modifying or considering communication techniques and methods. Be specific and provide some examples. Be honest with yourself – this is not part of your assessment, and identifying weaknesses is the first step to making improvements.

The questions below may help you.

Where am I now?
Think about a time when you have used communication methods. Do you review or reflect on the manner in which a communication technique has been used and received?

1. Consider your preferred communication method. Is it a method that your 'receivers' of information prefer?

2. When delivering/communicating knowledge or information, do you review with your team the techniques used?

3. Do you use jargon or non-essential information during communication methods?

Now, in your second column, write the heading **Improvements** and in the third column **Action**.

Improvements and action
Are there any areas where your communication methods and techniques could be improved or modified?

What action do you need to take to make those improvements?

Some of the changes you have identified might affect the way things are done in your organisation and you may need to discuss them with your line manager. Some changes can be made by you. Remember, small changes can make a big difference.

When you plan to make a change, remember to make your new objectives SMART!

You can discuss the notes you have made with your assessor. They may provide evidence of your competence.

TEST YOUR KNOWLEDGE

Here are some questions to test your knowledge and understanding of the issues explored in this unit. You can write the answers down or discuss them with your assessor. They could provide good evidence for your NVQ.

1. What types of information and knowledge do you communicate? AC 1.1

2. Who are your target audience, internal and external? AC 1.2

3. What are the types of techniques and methods used to communicate information and knowledge? AC 2.1

4. Describe the selection of appropriate methods and techniques in use in your organisation. AC 2.2

5. How do you select the most appropriate for the topic being communicated? AC 2.2

6. Give some examples of situations when you have communicated to a specific target audience. AC 3.1

7. Describe how you ensure your target audience has received and understood the information communicated. AC 3.2

8. Describe how you modify and review your chosen communication techniques and methods. AC 4.2

Pulling it all together and gathering evidence

You and your assessor will need to agree the most appropriate sources of evidence. Here are some suggestions:

- An electronic portfolio: you could upload your evidence to an e-portfolio package or simply store the evidence in electronic format.

- A paper-based portfolio: you could build a folder with hard copies of your evidence.

Types of evidence:

- Observation: a record by your assessor when observing you during a chosen communication method or technique.

- Work product: copies of work produced by you that demonstrate your competence, for example emails, presentations, briefing notices and team talk minutes.

- Discussion: a record of you and your assessor discussing examples of things that happened during communication and how you dealt with them.

- Questioning: a record of your assessor asking questions to test your knowledge.
- Personal statement, reflective account or case study based on the activities in this unit: this should have sentences which start with 'I ...' and should tell a story giving real-life examples.
- Witness testimony from your line manager confirming your competence, in writing or recorded as a discussion with your assessor.

It is a good idea to include a range of evidence from different sources. Your evidence should cover a period of time and not be a 'one-off'. However, try to keep the evidence to a minimum. Your assessor can make a note of product evidence they have seen so it can be left in the workplace.

Remember:

Less is more – quality not quantity!

Be holistic – can you use this evidence again for other units?

EVALUATION

What have you learned from completing this unit?

What new skills and techniques are you using?

How has this affected the people you work with?

How has your organisation benefited? How might it benefit in the future?

E12 MANAGE KNOWLEDGE IN OWN AREA OF RESPONSIBILITY

Introduction and learning outcomes

Learning outcomes for Unit E12:

1. Be able to understand existing knowledge management in own area of responsibility.
2. Be able to develop knowledge.
3. Be able to share knowledge.
4. Be able to monitor and evaluate knowledge management in own area of responsibility.

These learning outcomes say what you will have learned by the end of this unit. Each learning outcome is further broken down into assessment criteria, which we will look at in detail in the following sections of this unit.

This Unit Guide is a resource to help you gather the evidence you require to achieve Unit E12. It can be used as a learning resource if you are new to the role, are studying team leading in preparation for work or as a refresher if you are already an experienced team leader.

You and your assessor will agree what you need to do to meet the assessment criteria and show you are competent. This Unit Guide provides some theory to help you manage knowledge in your own area of responsibility, gives some case studies for you to examine and then an opportunity for you to reflect, with a virtual adviser, on how you can develop your skills and gather evidence of competence. Some ideas are provided in the 'Pulling it all together' section at the end of this unit.

So, the purpose of this unit is to develop the skills and knowledge you need to manage the team's knowledge and skills.

Why do we need to manage knowledge in own area of responsibility?

You may have heard it said that the most valuable asset in an organisation is its staff. If knowledge is left untapped then as soon as a team member or colleague is not around, the question comes up: 'How do we carry out their function again?'

To counter this problem you need to tap into the staff's knowledge and ensure others are able to pick up the reins, with sound access to the knowledge required to keep the organisation operating successfully in their business area.

Individuals within a team have varied levels of knowledge required for their roles. The focus in most organisations is to develop a team that can change roles to supply support for the whole team. In some teams this will not work at all times as the roles are too defined. However, the necessary knowledge needs to be documented or stored in some form so that viable stand-ins can act in the role until a suitable alternative can be either trained or developed for the role.

Good team leaders are enablers – they help people and organisations to perform and develop. So they may not be the font of all knowledge, but they are able to access the knowledge and provide a platform for the team to progress through the development process.

Figure E12.1

Learning outcome 1 – Be able to understand existing knowledge management in own area of responsibility

In this section we will explore each of the assessment criteria in more detail to develop your knowledge and understanding.

Assessment criterion 1.1 Describe how knowledge is gained and applied in own area of responsibility

Most teams in organisations have distinct overall responsibilities, with requirements and set objectives for the team. To meet those objectives the team need to have sufficient knowledge to carry out their roles. The operational procedures or guidelines in place at work generally set the requirements for the team members' set of skills and required capabilities.

Imagine walking into a place of work without any form of guidance being offered. Left to your own devices you may start by asking questions and hope the responses are forthcoming. Not the best start to your work in an organisation!

The application of knowledge in the workplace normally offers some guidance that may be in your area of responsibility:

- sharing knowledge
- group activities
- individual activity
- networks
- communities.

In factories years ago knowledge was passed on through 'sitting with Nellie'. Through observation and then participation the learner would pick up the skills from 'Nellie'. This learning from experienced workers is also called the buddy system. The system is still used in some areas, as the skill level required for some tasks needs repetition and a person to observe that the skills have been developed.

On-the-job one-to-one training is a cost-effective way to transfer skills as the job progresses as the new team member develops their skill. Sharing knowledge is also developed through training approaches such as the apprentice programme, in which, with a mix of classroom-based training and participation in the workplace, the apprentice develops their skills. Some organisations offer new employees an extensive induction during which they are shown the work of the organisation and through a group, they work on some of the tasks they have viewed in the workplace. The group activity can range from new methods applied in the workplace to presentations on new and diverse applications of a new system. Such activities could be a new intranet system or database for your place of work, or application of a new device to transport material in a factory, such as a forklift truck.

Individual activities can be varied and diverse, depending on your working environment. Familiarisation with new practices and developments in technology often requires the actual use of a system, process or technical instrument. Take, for example, the development of new software for a system in the workplace. Training and instruction will be required, but the actual operations may need to be navigated by the ultimate user in isolation so that they can access inputs and see how they react and operate in actual conditions that the user or learner can identify with.

Community knowledge is the crossover of information over a wide group. The internet offers this, with social networking sites and databases evolving to share knowledge and skills. This type of collaboration of work does have its pitfalls, as like-minded individuals can work together to 'promote' an idea or perspective through the community.

The above information will assist you in ascertaining how knowledge is gained. Some of these aspects you will be aware of, but others may be specific to your organisation or team.

Assessment criterion 1.2 Explain how knowledge is shared in own area of responsibility

Once a process or condition is decided upon, a device or system needs to be in place to share the knowledge required for the workplace. A number of options are available to catalogue and then ultimately share the practices as we acquire them for our business. Management standards are used to provide a group of operational systems that, when linked together, form the basis of a potential knowledge list or template for an organisation to follow and develop. Quality management standards offer a framework for a business to manage its processes and activities. They can help improve the business and offer a standard to achieve at a particular recognised level.

The management systems in a workplace can be varied depending on your organisation's culture. These are systems within frameworks that look at your organisation's policies, procedures and processes. Generally these systems offer direct links to the requirements of team working by sharing information, benchmarking and working to the highest principles in terms of quality and environmental values. You may be aware of some of them – a number look at direct business challenges such as profitability, competition, change, adaptability, growth and the use of technology. All needs are checked using management systems, a number of which started in Japan while others have origins in America and were developed to assist in the required technology advancement of high-quality manufacturing techniques.

Within these management systems we have some tools to help us develop and access knowledge that is shared. These tools may not be physical; they may be procedures or protocols to allow things to take place. For example, we may use collaborative software, which allows people involved in a common task to achieve goals and objectives by coordinating their work. It may aid communication by having built-in calendars so the team are aware of others' movements and planning can then be supported.

Process management is the application of knowledge, skills, tools, techniques and systems to define the processes required to meet your customers' needs, a mix maybe of your team's objectives and those of another team to offer the final package. The team that delivers sales needs to be aware of production requirements from that particular team; that interplay is vital to establish the management needs of your organisation.

Assessment criterion 1.3 Outline how intellectual property is protected in own area of responsibility

In our place of work we have to ensure that our organisation is protected and our systems and work-based materials and support are kept confidential. For example, we don't want our information to fall into our competitors' hands. During the sharing and delivering of work-based knowledge it is therefore critical that when we give new team members information they understand that the information must be not be shared with anyone, and not detailed in the linked procedures or guidelines.

A lot is at stake. Some of the following can be protected by these conditions:

- patents
- design patents
- trademarks
- trade secrets
- copyrights.

Some companies and organisations have exclusive rights to such intellectual property. Well-known cola manufacturers have fought for years to ensure that their brand of cola is not copied, for example.

A US computer manufacturer with a fruity name does not release its new equipment until a specified date, much to the annoyance of its competitors. Such companies have built up a reputation for their goods and therefore they are highly protective of any information leaking from their sites. This gives them the maximum impact on the marketplace and in some cases means that competitors cannot keep up with their developments in their specified field.

Generally, other aspects need to be kept safe also, such as our supplier list and what we pay. The grade of metal used in a manufacturing site and perhaps even the type of person we employ may be useful to others. In manufacturing, other countries have copied our designs and in some cases copies have arrived on our shores that look and feel the same.

In order to safeguard these conditions, processes and procedures we normally have built-in security such as:

- passwords
- safe systems
- locked resources.

Passwords are used from the log-in to the personnel files to the start button on a production line. Safe systems can be defined as procedures establishing who is involved in a particular function and their accessibility to the stages before and after. Locked resources are those that are physically locked and padlocked, such as a store facility, or those that need two people to activate a condition or system.

The case study section provides an opportunity for you to read about a team leader or team leading scenario. The case study highlights some of the issues discussed. You can use this to reflect on the situation and answer some questions. You do not have to write down your answers unless your tutor or assessor has asked you to do so.

CASE STUDY 1

Annette is a team leader for a printing organisation specialising in printing advertisements for hoardings or billboards. The team she manages not only prints general advertisements but also provides special prints for organisations that want to have an immediate impact with a perhaps secret launch for a particular product.

Within the team Annette has specialists who have been with the company a number of years. One particular team member, Trevor, is due to retire in two years. His skills are such that he has printed using all mediums and printed using old screen methods. One such method was patented by the organisation and the only individual who understands that particular process in full is Trevor.

Max, a young printer, has a very high skill level using computer printing, which is instant and offers the client responsive solutions to their needs. Currently the company has no standards for the printing process – they rely on the team members' collective knowledge to get the tasks done and the team like this process as it offers them a creative challenge. Annette, however, is concerned about the reliance on this approach.

What do you think?

1. Should Annette be concerned over the approach to knowledge?
2. What would the consequences be if the team members moved on to other organisations?
3. Who else should be aware of the team's collective knowledge?
4. How should Annette protect her organisation and team?

DEVELOPMENT ACTIVITY 1 with your virtual adviser

I am here to demystify the assessment criteria and help you relate what you have learned to your own job role. We will look at what you are currently doing and how you can develop your skills and have a real impact in your workplace.

Write a personal statement describing your knowledge of your organisation's knowledge management process. Consider your organisation's expected guidelines for knowledge management and your part in that.

The questions below may help you.

Where am I now?
Tell me how your organisation provides a guide to its employees to manage knowledge in your area of responsibility.

1. How does the system work?
2. Are all of your team aware of the requirements of the knowledge management system?
3. Who are your knowledge (trainers) specialists?
4. Do you have a list of the intellectual property that needs protecting?

Now, write the heading **Improvements and action**.

Improvements and action
Are there any areas in your personal statement where your role in understanding knowledge management in your area of responsibility was unclear?

What action do you think you could take to ensure that all information is shared using your organisation's guidelines?

Write these improvements and actions in your personal statement to reflect on your findings. This reflection will assist you in considering your options, which could include a change in the way you communicate, the style, method or timing.

Some of the changes you have identified might affect the way things are done in your organisation and you may need to discuss them with your line manager. Some changes can be made by you. Remember, small changes can make a big difference.

When you plan to make a change, remember to make your new objectives SMART!

You can discuss the notes you have made with your assessor. They may provide evidence of your competence.

Learning outcome 2 – Be able to develop knowledge

In this section we will explore each of the assessment criteria in more detail to develop your knowledge and understanding.

Assessment criterion 2.1 Identify established processes and procedures which can develop knowledge

Business needs mean that organisations must keep pace with new initiatives and developments. The knowledge that the team you manage has to support the organisation is vital for survival of the organisation. It also means that the team is organised, professional and well informed of the requirements needed to support the organisation.

Let's look at some of the established methods – as an organisation you may use one of the methods and in some cases more:

- supervisions
- performance management
- professional development
- one-to-one discussions.

Supervisions are planned meetings to discuss with the team member the overall task in general. They follow a distinct agenda and training or knowledge needs are part of that agenda.

Performance management systems offer a more structured route, with applied measures. In each case part of the measure is a list of objectives, some of which will be linked to the knowledge requirements of the organisation.

Professional development refers to skills and knowledge in both the workplace and on a personal level, for example it may be that the team member has an interest in other facets of the organisation's work and this could be accommodated through this system to provide the organisation with a team member with another skill set. All types of facilitated learning may be used and the approach may have some form of evaluation to view progression.

One-to-one discussions offer either formal or informal contact with the team member to consider options and progress with learning initiatives.

Assessment criterion 2.2 Explain how to support individuals to ensure knowledge development processes are followed

The outcomes of the established procedures and processes such as those above need to be followed up and reviewed. As the enabler, the team leader must try to progress these to ensure that the team are best suited to the internal market. This will ensure that the team offer the correct skill set for the organisation's requirements. In all of these cases clear commitment to the team members' knowledge base must be made apparent.

As the circumstances for each method vary slightly, we will take an example from each one. Supervisions prepared after the meeting supply a section generally that gives clear goals in terms of the team members' knowledge. They:

1. provide clear direction for both team member and leader

2. clearly indicate success and objectives

3. help clarify the roles of the team member and leader.

Performance management systems offer a grading system that has known factors built in. The team leader will offer a grading based on the input into the performance management agreed targets. This grading is generally negotiable at the start of the process; however, the criteria adopted have definitive points of reference so both parties need to be aware of these and apply their own commitment to the process.

Professional development offers a variety of learning opportunities and these can range from college degrees to formal coursework. This approach can be highly participative for both team leader and team member. The provision of professional development can include evaluation, mentoring, coaching and technical support. Other methods may also be included depending on the job roles. Organisations developing this practice generally look towards succession planning and offer this as a method to retain employees.

One-to-one discussions lead generally into the more formal knowledge development processes. They offer the initial support and opportunities to progress are documented and taken up whenever possible.

The case study section provides an opportunity for you to read about a team leader or team leading scenario. The case study highlights some of the issues discussed. You can use this to reflect on the situation and answer some questions. You do not have to write down your answers unless your tutor or assessor has asked you to do so.

CASE STUDY 2

Annette has had to deal with a little professional jealousy from her team of printers. Darren and Jonny have complained that they have had to deal with the more mundane printing jobs while Trevor has had a number of 'one-offs' to do for a selective client using his patented method. Also Max has had some excellent feedback on his new 3D-style poster.

Darren and Jonny have both indicated they would like the opportunity to carry out these types of jobs in the future.

What do you think?

1. What course of action should Annette consider?

2. How do you think Annette should support the team as a whole?

3. What else should be in place in the printing team?

DEVELOPMENT ACTIVITY 2 with your virtual adviser

I am here to demystify the assessment criteria and help you relate what you have learned to your own job role. We will look at what you are currently doing and how you can develop your skills and have a real impact in your workplace.

Write a short personal statement regarding the development of knowledge in your workplace: **Where am I now?** As if you were explaining to me, make a few notes about your strengths and weaknesses when carrying out the processes and procedures you use to develop knowledge. Be specific and provide some examples. Be honest with yourself – this is not part of your assessment, and identifying weaknesses is the first step to making improvements.

The questions below may help you.

Where am I now?
Think about how your organisation supports individuals to develop knowledge.

1. Can you describe a time when you last supported a team member in developing their knowledge for your organisational needs?

2. Do you understand your responsibilities in the processes and procedures to develop knowledge?

3. Do you have any knowledge reviews planned for your team?

4. How have you at any time offered other knowledge advice to your team?

Now, in a second section, write the heading **Improvements** and in the third section **Action**.

Improvements and action
Are there any areas where your understanding of your organisation's knowledge development procedures or processes could be improved?

What action do you need to take to make those improvements?

Some of the changes you have identified might affect the way things are done in your organisation and you may need to discuss them with your line manager. Some changes can be made by you. Remember, small changes can make a big difference.

When you plan to make a change, remember to make your new objectives SMART!

You can discuss the notes you have made with your assessor. They may provide evidence of your competence.

Learning outcome 3 – Be able to share knowledge

In this section we will explore each of the assessment criteria in more detail to develop your knowledge and understanding.

Assessment criterion 3.1 Communicate established processes, which share knowledge across own area of responsibility

Many organisations offer some form of training and development opportunities for their staff. This requirement offers both parties the chance to progress as the training allows the teams to develop and offer more to their employer. Having said that, it is down to you as team leader to ensure they are aware of what is available. Team meetings and talks offer the opportunity to advise the team about what is on offer.

It may be desirable to get to know as much as you can regarding the programme, its content, the requirements of both parties and the time frame. Some direct training or insight into the initiative may be required in the first instance. The types of programme for imparting knowledge may be:

- work-based training
- job shadowing
- databases
- workshops
- one-to-one reviews.

Let's look at work-based training first. This type of training is generally directly linked to the job in hand. It may be a simple instruction process on a new piece of equipment or an extension of a role which needs to be offered to the team.

Job shadowing is similar to the buddy system. By following a trained team member around the work, gradually the hands-on approach will be adopted. The work will get done but during this time you will potentially lose two team members to the training environment.

Databases offer a credible alternative to job shadowing as the database generally has a wide range of examples to offer which may not be encountered on a stint with a colleague.

Workshops offer a number of opportunities to develop expertise, making others available to offer advice and experience in an environment away from the hustle and bustle of the workplace. Also it gives the participant the opportunity to ask direct questions that may be answered by a number of potential experts.

One-to-one reviews offer an opportunity for the team member to ask questions that they may not wish to raise in contact with their peers. One-to-ones offer a contact that is direct and totally involves the individual.

Other established methods may be as follows:

- case study
- consultation
- coaching
- lesson study
- mentoring
- reflective supervision
- technical assistance.

Many of these methods can be intertwined into the previous lists as generally the sharing of knowledge across own area of responsibility is a broad term and will encompass a range of people in your team, each with differing interests and approaches to their learning or ability to take in the requirements of each learning specific.

Assessment criterion 3.2 Explain how to support individuals to ensure knowledge sharing processes are followed

Have you ever heard of the phrase 'You can lead a horse to water but you can't make it drink'? Well, a lot of support is required when trying to develop the knowledge sharing process. Remember your role within the team is generally the 'enabler' and as such you need to have two primary skills: involvement and delegation. By using this enabling trait you will be able to support the team in making effective decisions regarding their knowledge sharing opportunities.

As team leader it is also desirable to create an environment of trust, open communication, creative thinking and constant improvement. Of course, these are the most suitable traits for your support of knowledge sharing processes.

However, here is another group of traits that also applies – in no particular order either:

- Ensure knowledge sharing is part of the team's quality policy.
- Allocate responsibilities for knowledge sharing.
- Define knowledge objectives.
- Implement and monitor knowledge sharing.

Others may be included to ensure support is given depending on your team make-up and the overall requirements and objectives of the organisation.

So how will you bring your team together to achieve this support? Try linking team members together to work on a review of work-based practices. It may be, for example, that you use team members who are inexperienced to cast a new viewpoint on a potential change. Workshops are an excellent forum for sharing knowledge, with all parties able to question and get answers. Databases offer the opportunity to review operational procedures and then consider them against the actual events in the workplace.

The case study section provides an opportunity for you to read about a team leader or team leading scenario. The case study highlights some of the issues discussed. You can use this to reflect on the situation and answer some questions. You do not have to write down your answers unless your tutor or assessor has asked you to do so.

CASE STUDY 3

Annette has requested that Trevor takes some time away from the team and develops some work-based information; the team have no specialist print jobs due in for a month. She has requested that he prepares a full breakdown of the patented print job and writes it up using a procedure template and then prepares a database for such information.

When he has completed that task she would like him to take Darren through the full procedure and physically show him how to follow the procedure when the work comes in the next month.

What do you think?

1. Who will benefit from this approach?
2. What other methods could Trevor adopt?
3. What other provisions would you consider if you were Annette?
4. What would the next stage be?

DEVELOPMENT ACTIVITY 3 with your virtual adviser

I am here to demystify the assessment criteria and help you relate what you have learned to your own job role. We will look at what you are currently doing and how you can develop your skills and have a real impact in your workplace.

Draw a simple table list. List the methods you use to communicate and explain the sharing of knowledge with your team. Give it the title **Where am I now?** Against each item on your list, as if you were explaining to me, detail the event explained and describe in a few words how successful you were in ensuring the sharing of information process was followed. Be specific with regard to methods you have used and provide some examples. Be honest with yourself – this is not part of your assessment and considering options in this manner will prepare you for any developments that may occur in the future.

The questions below may help you.

Where am I now?
Think about the sharing of knowledge process.

1. Describe the event and the knowledge shared.

2. How did you supply information on the knowledge sharing event with the team?

3. How was the event attended? Supply numbers and team orientation.

Now, add two sections to your list: **Improvements** and **Action**.

Improvements and action
Are there any areas where you could improve how you are able to share knowledge?

What action do you need to take to make those improvements?

Some of the changes you have identified might affect the way things are done in your organisation and you may need to discuss them with your line manager. Some changes can be made by you. Remember, small changes can make a big difference.
   When you plan to make a change, remember to make your new objectives SMART!
   You can discuss the notes you have made with your assessor. They may provide evidence of your competence.

Learning outcome 4 – Be able to monitor and evaluate knowledge management in own area of responsibility

In this section we will explore each of the assessment criteria in more detail to develop your knowledge and understanding.

Assessment criterion 4.1 Assess the knowledge development process in own area of responsibility

During the knowledge development process it makes sense to assess how well knowledge transfer is proceeding. It may be appropriate to assess your team's knowledge development by a desktop method. Look at the standards used to measure the organisation's knowledge levels overall and then review your team against those standards.

   Let's take an example in the food and drink industry. The industry operates using a number of practices that are monitored with rigour. Guidelines and high-level standards are in place to assess an organisation's ability to operate in the industry. Obviously that leads to the objectives of these standards and the associated knowledge being transferred to the operational points on where they apply. Any inspection or audit of these standards would not occur in the director's office alone, although the director is responsible for the overall management of the systems. So if you are a team leader in a food environment you need to be aware of all the prevailing conditions, assessments and audits that apply. The knowledge that is required by yourself and the team to carry out your duties is part of that assessment, audit or review.

So moving back to your own workplace, all of your conditions and external forces have an impact on your working environment in terms of knowledge required for the role and the records associated with the types of work you and your team need to do to get the job done. Overall knowledge for the team is not just about training, it is also about experience and the ability to recall a condition that prevailed and either document it or pass it on. The database we have referred to is an ideal area to hold the knowledge for the organisation. Auditors, when assessing against a standard, value the fact that they can see a knowledge base that reflects the needs of the organisation in relation to the operational sector.

Let's go back to that desk. You have your knowledge database and perhaps an assessment of how that is reflected in your team's knowledge. That may be expressed as a grid or a chart to show how knowledgeable your team are against the standards you use. That assessment will or should reveal the development process that is in place in your area of responsibility. Points you may consider in this assessment are as follows:

- Knowledge assessed against the standards.
- Reviews of practices and feedback from others.
- Take-up of development opportunities presented.

If any of these conditions reveals a stagnation of your team's knowledge development then you need to act upon that information and consider other options.

Assessment criterion 4.2 Implement any changes to improve knowledge management

So, how do you act and respond to improve the knowledge base and how it is managed? The knowledge database should give you a good starting point. If review schedules have not caused a reaction, you need to consider inserting conditions and management guidelines on how to respond. Audits offer an excellent opportunity to improve not during or after but before.

Let's consider our friends in the food industry once more. Organisations that produce food and drink are conditioned to provide information, statistics and records for auditors. Those who carry out the audit may be working for existing or potential customers to produce products that carry the customer's name. As these own-name products affect the customer's reputation, you can imagine how deep the auditor probes and 'questions' all facets of the organisation. When the auditor says jump, the response is normally, how high? So when records are required to advise on the knowledge management, they need to reflect the whole range of the company's knowledge cycle.

In this particular sector, to be forearmed is a vital condition for the full management team. Progressive changes are then considered far in advance of any external auditor visiting. In teams away from the food and drink sector, similar conditions obviously prevail. However, what we are looking for is what we need to do to implement changes to improve knowledge management.

A push in the right direction is one thing but the practice is another. Gaps in your knowledge database generally give the team leader an idea about what to focus on. Within the team the use of mentors and assessors will assist – individuals who can offer a wealth of expertise themselves, those who are aware of some of the pinch points in a process, procedure or general duties within the team. From this will develop the need to offer more on how to feed into the ever-growing knowledge pool.

A lot of organisations develop individual roles within the teams, expert or knowledgeable in health and safety perhaps or environmental issues. By accessing their views on the topic in which they have an interest they find a good resource that is keen, able and known to the group. Progressive workshops could be used to spread the activity of knowledge management and how it may fit into your organisation using these in-house resources.

The process of change on the improvement of knowledge management has offered up other arrangements within some organisations, such as drop-in learning zones for those primarily honing their computer skills, or a central point to gain knowledge on the needs of the organisation.

Assessment criterion 4.3 Monitor change and development in the knowledge development process

In some cases the monitoring of the knowledge development process is very difficult. For example, the developments in technology can leave us all behind if we turn our backs for long enough! We have discussed standards, which are very useful and obviously can illustrate the progression of something or someone. The standards we are using now for this qualification will be monitored, reviewed and checked on an ongoing basis to see whether they still fit business purposes. So, too, should the knowledge development process used in your workplace, and the skill set as it applies to the ever-changing market in which we all perform. We have training analysis tools which are all conditioned to the knowledge required for the role, and we can use our networks to see what other 'folks' are up to.

A number of like-minded organisations offer the use of benchmarking when it comes to knowledge development processes. Human resource departments offer examples in some instances on how they manage certain aspects of their knowledge base. Being a team leader, maybe in an environment in which you can share practices, offers another dimension. You can look to see how your opposite number on another site perhaps practises and manages their knowledge development processes for the team.

The case study section provides an opportunity for you to read about a team leader or team leading scenario. The case study highlights some of the issues discussed. You can use this to reflect on the situation and answer some questions. You do not have to write down your answers unless your tutor or assessor has asked you to do so.

CASE STUDY 4

Trevor has completed his input into the database and Darren has successfully carried out the printing method using the procedure.

Max has also started to write up some procedures. Jonny has looked at them and has indicated that he cannot make any sense of them due to the technical information regarding the new print processes.

Jonny has asked for more clarity regarding the jargon. Max has asked if he can do anything to help.

What do you think?

1. How should Annette progress with the sharing of information?

2. What would you do?

3. Should Annette take up Max's offer to help even though his procedures appear to be unsuitable?

DEVELOPMENT ACTIVITY 4 with your virtual adviser

I am here to demystify the assessment criteria and help you relate what you have learned to your own job role. We will look at what you are currently doing and how you can develop your skills and have a real impact in your workplace.

Prepare a personal statement on your current practices in monitoring and evaluation of knowledge in your organisation.

The questions below may help you.

Where am I now?
Think about any changes to improve knowledge management that you have been involved in.

1. Have you assessed the knowledge development in your area of responsibility?

2. Do you keep a database of knowledge development?

3. How are records kept and maintained?

Now, if you do not keep records or logs, write a short statement on how you would make **improvements** and then how you would implement any **action**.

Improvements and action
Are there any areas where you could improve your ability to monitor and evaluate knowledge management in your own area of responsibility?

What action do you need to take to make those improvements?

Some of the changes you have identified might affect the way things are done in your organisation and you may need to discuss them with your line manager. Some changes can be made by you. Remember, small changes can make a big difference.

When you plan to make a change, remember to make your new objectives SMART!

You can discuss the notes you have made with your assessor. They may provide evidence of your competence.

TEST YOUR KNOWLEDGE

Here are some questions to test your knowledge and understanding of the issues explored in this unit. You can write the answers down or discuss them with your assessor. They could provide good evidence for your NVQ.

1. How is knowledge gained and applied in your team? AC 1.1

2. How is knowledge shared in your area of responsibility? AC 1.2

3. Detail any intellectual property in your organisation. How is it protected? AC 1.3

4. Do you have any examples of established processes and procedures to develop knowledge? AC 2.1

5. How do you support individuals to ensure knowledge is developed through processes? AC 2.2

6. Have you communicated processes in use to share knowledge? AC 3.1

7. What action is used to share knowledge? AC 3.2

8. Describe how knowledge development processes are assessed. AC 4.1

9. How do you implement changes to improve knowledge management? AC 4.2

10. What are the main points in the monitoring processes when looking at development in knowledge? AC 4.3

Pulling it all together and gathering evidence

You and your assessor will need to agree the most appropriate sources of evidence. Here are some suggestions:

- An electronic portfolio: you could upload your evidence to an e-portfolio package or simply store the evidence in electronic format.
- A paper-based portfolio: you could build a folder with hard copies of your evidence.

Types of evidence:

- Observation: a record by your assessor when observing your interaction with your team.
- Work product: copies of work produced by you that demonstrate your competence, for example standards, your notes, minutes.

- Discussion: a record of you and your assessor discussing examples of things that happened in a knowledge review and how you dealt with them.

- Questioning: a record of your assessor asking questions to test your knowledge.

- Personal statement, reflective account or case study based on the activities in this unit: this should have sentences which start with 'I …' and should tell a story giving real-life examples.

- Witness testimony from your line manager confirming your competence, in writing or recorded as a discussion with your assessor.

It is a good idea to include a range of evidence from different sources. Your evidence should cover a period of time and not be a 'one-off'. However, try to keep the evidence to a minimum. Your assessor can make a note of product evidence they have seen so it can be left in the workplace.

Remember:

Less is more – quality not quantity!

Be holistic – can you use this evidence again for other units?

EVALUATION

What have you learned from completing this unit?

What new skills and techniques are you using?

How has this affected the people you work with?

How has your organisation benefited? How might it benefit in the future?

PROCURE SUPPLIES

Introduction and learning outcomes

Learning outcomes for Unit E15:

1. Be able to identify requirements for supplies.
2. Be able to evaluate suppliers that meet identified requirements.
3. Be able to select suppliers and obtain supplies.
4. Be able to monitor supplier performance.

These learning outcomes say what you will have learned by the end of this unit. Each learning outcome is further broken down into assessment criteria, which we will look at in detail in the following sections of this unit.

This Unit Guide is a resource to help you gather the evidence you require to achieve Unit E15. It can be used as a learning resource if you are new to the role, are studying team leading in preparation for work or as a refresher if you are already an experienced team leader.

You and your assessor will agree what you need to do to meet the assessment criteria and show you are competent. This Unit Guide provides some theory to develop your ability to procure supplies, gives some case studies for you to examine and then an opportunity for you to reflect, with a virtual adviser, on how you can develop your own skills and gather evidence of competence. Some ideas are provided in the 'Pulling it all together' section at the end of this unit.

So, the purpose of this unit is to develop the skills and knowledge you need to procure supplies.

Why do we need to procure supplies?

Through the ages, as far back as the development of civilisation, it became apparent that humans needed others to supply and source materials as well as to provide a service or assistance to others. Trading links were quickly set up, for instance transporting spices and fine silks from the Orient. These trading companies would bring the highly desired materials into other countries. When the materials arrived, specialists developed their trade to use the materials and provide a service. Going to market to buy supplies was perhaps the normal routine then. However, the time taken to go to market restricted the time that could be spent in producing goods to sell. So soon a delivery service offering the required materials developed.

Obviously this concept remains today; business infrastructure needs others to supply materials and expertise. Take the car industry, for example. Without others to supply the essential components on time and to a desired specification, the time to build a car would result in a fairly lengthy waiting list.

The business of supply and demand also offers the specialist a role in the marketplace. The needs of the customer and how to meet their demands are the underlining process. Procurement is the acquisition of goods and services; it is desirable to obtain these goods and services at the best possible advantage, in terms of cost or delivery time. In some organisations procurement of supplies is a highly specialised function and a team of people will be employed to monitor the process. Tendering for the business may be the preferred system involved, offering a comprehensive package to meet the overarching requirements of the customer.

Some industries have built trade links that are reliant on each other and the negotiated purchase of consumables may be planned for years. For example, a well-known soft drinks company requires cans for its products, so the can producer has built its factory next door to the soft drinks premises. This provides a highly reciprocal business model.

As a team leader we generally have a need to review supply requirements locally. This may be materials needed to produce something or support materials that are used in our work. Either way, a procurement process will be involved.

Figure E15.1

Learning outcome 1 – Be able to identify requirements for supplies

In this section we will explore each of the assessment criteria in more detail to develop your knowledge and understanding. You need to be able to identify supply requirements.

Assessment criterion 1.1 Select colleagues to agree requirements for supplies

It is imperative to involve others in agreeing supplies when working in an organisation. However, the ability to identify the individuals to involve is generally specific to the product required or the organisation constraints in the procurement strategy. Let's look at the possible individuals or groups that may be involved in a supply requirement.

Team members

Requests for materials to carry out their functional tasks will come direct from your team – you are their conduit generally for information and communication, so they will ask you to resource or how to resource a material need. However, in this instance the requirement is to select colleagues to agree supply needs. So the development of team members' involvement in the process is desired.

Once again we look at the interaction in a team. Certain functions will be carried out perhaps by distinct team members. These individuals should be involved in the procurement of materials that directly affect their duties or tasks. A performing team as defined by Bruce Tuckman's 1965 forming, storming, norming and performing model, due to their high degree of autonomy, will be able to ascertain the process needs of a function and the general usage of materials and therefore will be able to offer advice on requirements for the supply. If the requirement for supply is new, a team decision on the project needs may be required. The involvement of the team will contribute to the successful use and provide potential data that can be used in costing and evaluation of the overall needs.

Procurement specialists

In larger organisations a team of procurement specialists may be involved in agreeing your requirements for supplies. A systematic approach is normally adopted; the team may have a list of potential or existing suppliers. With agreed contacts, contracts and tendering processes, the procurement specialists will have carried out the organisation's checks on delivery and costing methods. So in these instances your colleagues may have already carried out a number of extensive checks and have preferred suppliers in place.

Many manufacturing firms enrol their procurement specialists direct from their workers or team leaders in company training programmes. These employees spend a substantial amount of time working with experienced procurement specialists to learn the details of their firm's practices (for example, about commodities, prices, suppliers and markets). They may also spend time working in the production planning department to gain insight into the inventory and material requirement systems the company uses to efficiently operate its production and replenishment functions.

Legal and financial specialists

It is best to ensure that your supplies meet with the financial profile for your organisation, so developing contact with legal and financial experts is desirable. If your supply requirements necessitate significant expenditure, then budget concerns may be affected. You also may consider using a different supplier from the norm, but this may be contrary to agreements with existing suppliers and could be to the detriment of future supply provision. To this end the legal specialist will be a useful participant to agree your future requirements.

Assessment criterion 1.2 Produce a specification for supply requirements

A specification is a defined standard for the products and services that you provide. Your organisation's customers will expect a product, service or provision to be supplied to the exacting detail they have requested. So the same applies for your organisational demands – your specification when presented to your suppliers needs to contain comprehensive detail that covers all aspects, including quality, delivery times, costs and implications if supply is not met.

When a team is brought together, generally they are required to work to expected organisational targets. They will have obvious tasks to perform, and they may have standard operating procedures to follow in order to carry out their role. Generally, the specification requirements are considered in both organisational targets and operating procedures. Included in these operational documents will be times and conditions that stipulate supply needs. Team work involves the contribution of everyone – defining a specification will in some form affect others within your team or structure. So the process of producing a specification for supply requirements is an inclusive task.

Part of your role as a team leader is to ensure tasks in the workplace are coordinated and effective to meet the desired outcomes of the team. Questions you may ask when developing a specification are similar to those you would ask when you consider the sales of your end product:

- quality expectations
- lead time of deliveries
- usage requirements
- terms of delivery
- cost
- consequences if either party fails to meet their contract conditions.

The list order may not be correct, but the detail will have some of the listed points, if not all; others may be added depending on your specific requirements. Once your specification is identified and presented to the potential supplier, more detail will be added as the supplier asks questions and starts a negotiation process.

The case study section provides an opportunity for you to read about a team leader or team leading scenario. The case study highlights some of the issues discussed. You can use this to reflect on the situation and answer some questions. You do not have to write down your answers unless your tutor or assessor has asked you to do so.

CASE STUDY 1

Stephanie works for a security company that supplies and installs alarms and other electronic security devices. The clients are from all sectors, including private and industry based.

Stephanie is a team leader in the sales and administration section of the company; the team is made up of five administration staff and four in direct sales. They receive and place orders for materials and also have direct contact with the firm's clients. Stephanie and her team often contact suppliers for materials and they have good relations with the partner organisations.

A supplier has rung in to say they can offer some cabling for installations. The cable is 20 per cent cheaper than the material currently used. The firm produce only the one type of material; the existing supplier provides all the installation cabling and components. Delivery times seem to be the same or similar to those of the current supplier.

The company has a team of 20 electricians/engineers who fit and service the security systems. Other parties in the firm are two accountants and the three directors.

Stephanie has checked the written specification for the cable and one of the engineers has confirmed 'it would do'. The new supplier indicates they have the offer on only until the end of the week.

What do you think?

1. Should Stephanie take up this offer to save the potential costs?
2. What would the consequences be if Stephanie decided to switch to the new material as soon as it was offered?
3. Who else should Stephanie involve in the process from the overall team?
4. How quickly should the firm respond to the supplier?

DEVELOPMENT ACTIVITY 1 with your virtual adviser

I am here to demystify the assessment criteria and help you relate what you have learned to your own job role. We will look at what you are currently doing and how you can develop your skills and have a real impact in your workplace.

Write a personal statement describing your knowledge of your organisation's requirements to identify supplies. Consider your organisation's expected guidelines for procurement of supplies and your part in the identification.

The following questions may help you.

Where am I now?

Tell me how your organisation identifies the requirements for supplies.

1. How does the procurement of new supplies work?

2. Are all your team aware of the specifications of the supply requirements?

3. Who are your procurement specialists?

4. Do you have a list of the supplies that you are accountable for?

Now write the heading **Improvements and action**.

Improvements and action

Are there any areas in your personal statement where you did not understand your role in identifying requirements for supplies?

What action do you think you could take to ensure the team understands the requirements for supplies?

Write these improvements and actions in your personal statement to reflect on your findings. This reflection will assist you in considering your options, which could include a change in the way you communicate, the style, method or timing.

Some of the changes you have identified might affect the way things are done in your organisation and you may need to discuss them with your line manager. Some changes can be made by you. Remember, small changes can make a big difference.

When you plan to make a change, remember to make your new objectives SMART!

You can discuss the notes you have made with your assessor. They may provide evidence of your competence.

Learning outcome 2 – Be able to evaluate suppliers that meet the identified requirements

In this section we will explore each of the assessment criteria in more detail to develop your knowledge and understanding.

Assessment criterion 2.1 Identify suppliers that meet resource, organisational and legal requirements

Business problems through the use of poor or inappropriate suppliers can in fact have a direct impact on your work and consequently most organisations implement an approved supplier list. The aim of any procurement process is to carry out activities in such a manner that all aspects that can be reviewed are, and with care. The overriding focus is to procure resources of the required quality, from the best source, and that they are priced correctly and can be delivered on time to the correct place.

Approved supplier lists are considered in different ways, as are the methods and techniques to 'measure' a supplier's ability. The list below considers a number of aspects that most procurement team members use. Suppliers should be or have most of these traits:

- competitive
- reliable
- provide quality goods
- managerially competent
- have suitable resources
- financially stable
- have technical support
- environmentally and ethically sound.

These factors can then be measured or weighted in accordance with your organisation's requirements for the particular resource or supply need.

So a potential supplier needs to be screened correctly to ascertain their ability to provide you with a service, a process which can slow your decision methods. However, to get a supplier that meets your needs is an important process and can determine how your team operates and performs against your business targets (depending on how critical the supply is in relation to your end product or service).

Imagine you are in a position in which ineffective delivery schedules and poor service levels affect your targets. Consider your customers' responses to these conditions. They will not say, 'It's OK, I will wait for your products'; they will move to another source quickly and your competitors will applaud your decision to use the rogue supplier.

Assessment criterion 2.2 Evaluate suppliers against requirements

Evaluation methods are varied. Once you have chosen a potential supplier, the need then shifts to comprehensive benchmarking. So let's look at a supplier audit. Once again there are no standard evaluation methods as each organisation may be looking for slightly different criteria. We would still use the basic premise to follow of:

- quality of product
- cost
- timeliness
- reliability.

However, the shift now is on full continuing appraisals; once an organisation is added to the approved supplier list, evaluation methods will still be used, such as questionnaires and supplier visits. Most suppliers are used to these conditions and the continuing process becomes part of the integrated supplier management process. So intermittent audits are commonplace, often on an annual basis to ensure performance or agreed conditions have not altered.

We need to remember also that not all supplies are as critical to the work we do; some are required but will not directly affect our targets. These supplies are still subject to certain evaluation methods and we still seek quality, cost, timeliness and reliability. Ancillary materials such as administration supplies or janitorial services will be monitored but we would perhaps not carry out a supplier audit on an annual basis. So the manner in which we evaluate these supply provisions may not be weighted as highly as direct components for, say, a production situation.

To run through the overall potential process, poor suppliers are weeded out prior to the evaluation stages. During ongoing evaluation, identified weaknesses of approved suppliers can be worked on. As an auditor the individual becomes an influencer and as such the customer service arrangements can be maintained between supplier and procurer.

The case study section provides an opportunity for you to read about a team leader or team leading scenario. The case study highlights some of the issues discussed. You can use this to reflect on the situation and answer some questions. You do not have to write down your answers unless your tutor or assessor has asked you to do so.

CASE STUDY 2

> The company that provided a specification for cable has contacted Stephanie again to see whether the product was suitable. Stephanie has advised them that the cable has potential but at this stage she is unable to commit to an order.
>
> The company representative reminded Stephanie that the offer on the price would remain for only a few more days. Stephanie indicated that she was aware of that point but at this stage needed more time to review. She invited the representative for a meeting to discuss the product and to bring along more samples.

What do you think?

1. Was Stephanie correct to decline the supply at a significant discount?
2. How do you think others in the company would react to her action?
3. What else should she have said (or missed) when responding to the potential supplier?
4. Do you think the meeting with the representative is a good idea?
5. If the meeting goes ahead, should prices be discussed with the representative?

DEVELOPMENT ACTIVITY 2 with your virtual adviser

I am here to demystify the assessment criteria and help you relate what you have learned to your own job role. We will look at what you are currently doing and how you can develop your skills and have a real impact in your workplace.

Draw a simple table with three columns. In the first column write **Where am I now?** and, as if you were explaining to me, make a few notes about your strengths and weaknesses when procuring supplies for your team and organisation. Be specific and provide some examples. Be honest with yourself, this is not part of your assessment, and identifying weaknesses is the first step to making improvements.

The questions below may help you.

Where am I now?

Think about the procurement process for supplies in your area of responsibility.

1. Can you think of a time when you required supplies quickly?

2. Do you understand your limitations when ordering supplies?

3. Do you have any evaluation procedures for the procurement of supplies?

4. How have you at any time put together a new specification for a supply need? If not, do you have a process to create a specification?

Now, in your second column, write the heading **Improvements** and in the third column **Action**.

Improvements and action

Are there any areas where your knowledge of your organisation's procurement evaluation methods could be improved?

What action do you need to take to make those improvements?

Some of the changes you have identified might affect the way things are done in your organisation and you may need to discuss them with your line manager. Some changes can be made by you. Remember, small changes can make a big difference.

When you plan to make a change, remember to make your new objectives SMART!

You can discuss the notes you have made with your assessor. They may provide evidence of your competence.

Learning outcome 3 – Be able to select suppliers and obtain supplies

In this section we will explore each of the assessment criteria in more detail to develop your knowledge and understanding.

Assessment criterion 3.1 Select supplier(s) that best meet requirements

Most suppliers are honest folk, reasonably reliable and down to earth. However, in order to win contracts to supply, some salespeople will be prone to 'bending the truth' in order to establish initial contact and to progress a potential order. Therefore care must be taken in ensuring all aspects of your supply and delivery needs are covered. That is why it is valuable to have an approved supplier list, although beware: even when the supplier obtains a place on your list, it may be a while before you need to use them and situations may change.

With comprehensive information on a potential supplier, it is easier to place your order for supplies knowing you have challenged their statements on supply through the systems and procedures used in your workplace. So prior to selection, confirmation and some verification on the capability of your supplier will need to be carried out. Table E15.1 details some example questions and expected responses from your chosen supplier.

Table E15.1: Example questions for a supplier

Procurer	Supplier
Confirm the type of supplies that are required	Provide specifications and quality identification
Confirm information on the supplies that need to be ordered	Quantity and rate of supplies required are clearly identified
Confirm information on the supplies' arrival	Quantity and delivery schedules of supplies are clearly identified
Confirm cost of supplies and agreed delivery charges	Agreed costing arrangements are clearly identified

If a supplier cannot meet your agreed needs, do you have another supplier to consider? An approved supplier list is vital so that alternative supplies can be obtained if a supplier has a problem with your expectations. Supply processes should be monitored regularly and operational relationships between organisations should be well maintained so they are mutually beneficial. Also consider the supplies you require, for example if one item on your list has a higher price from your supplier, consider the package that the organisation offers.

- Cost: it may be that overall the costs are lower when you consider all supplies on a potential inventory, so you will save overall if the other supply needs are resourced frequently.

- Quality: by using inferior products, are the costs a benefit or are you jeopardising your overall quality by using a sub-standard component?

- Time-bound delivery: the ability to supply on dates that suit your organisation may offer you an incentive to use the supplier. Arrival times of a component may mean you meet your performance or production targets and customer needs.

- Reliability: how quickly will your supplier respond to your needs? Do they assist when you need help with any of your requirements? This factor is difficult to quantify, so make sure you have records of such events for your evaluation team to consider.

- Added value: does your supplier offer any other requirements that assist the process in your organisation, such as training or call-out responses to repair items?

These additional benefits offer a sound resource for your organisation and can be added to your contractual agreements.

Thus the selection of a potential supplier must be an optimal mix of all factors on offer. How you choose may be down to your requirements at a particular time but also down to any procurement policies in place:

- quality of product
- cost
- time-bound delivery
- reliability
- added value.

Assessment criterion 3.2 Explain how to agree contractual terms with selected suppliers

Contractual arrangements work both ways. I start with this statement because you may feel you have the upper hand being the procurer – this is not the case.

Table E15.2: Agreeing contractual terms

What the buyer (procurer) thinks	What the seller (supplier) thinks
The supplier will provide everything we need.	The supplier will not commit to anything, apart from demanding prompt payment.
If we change our minds the supplier will still supply us with what we want.	Items supplied will be in any condition we see fit and the buyer must accept this.
All employees of the supplier will know everything about our requirements.	No compensation will be given to the buyer for anything we miss.
All employees of the supplier are available at all times and will respond to our requests straightaway.	Delivery times will be when we can be bothered and the buyer will be charged for any time over ten minutes that our delivery team are on their premises.
Training will be provided whenever we require it on any item sold to us.	
Any agreed usage can be exceeded or reduced at any time.	Prices will be flexible in our favour.
The supplier will agree any form of payment, can pay when they want and what they want.	Any supplies we cannot supply will be bought in from our competitor(s) and supplied to the buyer at a premium charge.
The supplier will not be paid at all if any of the above events are not forthcoming or followed.	

The thoughts in Table E15.2 may be near to the truth of what organisations would or may like in some cases. But generally contractual terms are discussed to the best advantage for both parties, with sensible agreements and workable arrangements that are considered with a long working future in mind, and remembering that both parties have reputations they value, for their customers and for other suppliers.

Contracts have a number of points but imbedded into the structure, costs, timescales and terms and conditions are the main areas. A supply contract or service agreement generally has the following structure:

1. Heading and title.

2. Description – the purpose of the supply or service.

3. Parties – those involved: procurer and supplier.

4. Date.

5. Territory – area covered.

6. Definitions – essential explanations of terms used.

7. Term – or the period of the agreement.

8. Pricing.

9. Pricing adjustment – may be linked to inflation.

10. Responsibilities of the provider.

11. Responsibilities of the client.

12. Payment terms.

13. Confidential information (may be specification of supply).

14. Dispute and arbitration process.

15. Termination clauses.

16. Renegotiation/renewal.

17. Laws.

18. Signatures and witnesses.

As the group seeking new business, the supplier will instigate the contract process. This is normal and is vital for both parties as it supplies the required reasonable business boundaries (unlike the procurer and supplier detailed in Table 1.2). Most organisations are familiar with business contracts and a solicitor will normally view the contract on behalf of the parties.

The discussion in the main will focus on the considerations of those directly involved; the actual mechanics of the operational requirements may involve the team leader or manager who made the supply request. So it is important to consider potential changes in your operational work that may effect a direct change in perhaps delivery times or specification alterations or reviews. Also, as supply components can directly affect key performance indicators, it is necessary to involve finance on costs, not only on the costs as detailed in the contract but how they will affect final product or services.

Some contracts will lead to other business relationships – supply of material may include handling equipment or some form of service charge if equipment is hired or loaned to the procurer's team. The contract for these functions may be added to the existing supply arrangement or another contract will be drawn up. So negotiations may be protracted or extended if agreements cannot be decided upon, and often the first draft of a contract will look nothing like the finished article. But they are essential as they build in confidence for supplier and procurer alike.

The case study section provides an opportunity for you to read about a team leader or team leading scenario. The case study highlights some of the issues discussed. You can use this to reflect on the situation and answer some questions. You do not have to write down your answers unless your tutor or assessor has asked you to do so.

Figure E15.2: Meeting a supplier

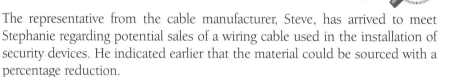

CASE STUDY 3

The representative from the cable manufacturer, Steve, has arrived to meet Stephanie regarding potential sales of a wiring cable used in the installation of security devices. He indicated earlier that the material could be sourced with a percentage reduction.

Stephanie meets Steve and asks whether he minds if a few of her colleagues are present at the meeting. Steve agrees and the meeting progresses.

Steve delivers a short presentation to describe his company and the products they supply. He is a little vague on the lead-time through manufacturing, although he does explain the manner in which the supplies are delivered into agreed delivery points. A bonus for Stephanie's company is that Steve's company can offer same-day delivery direct to installation points if the material requirement is large enough.

What do you think?

1. Who from the team (described in case study 1) would you invite to the meeting?

2. What questions would you ask Steve (consider the meeting is still in progress)?

3. What provisions would you like to apply to a potential contract if you were involved in this meeting?

4. What would the next stage be for Stephanie and the team?

DEVELOPMENT ACTIVITY 3 with your virtual adviser

I am here to demystify the assessment criteria and help you relate what you have learned to your own job role. We will look at what you are currently doing and how you can develop your skills and have a real impact in your workplace.

Once again, draw a simple table as a 'to do' list. In the list, view a supply contract and discuss its preparation with colleagues from your workplace. If you have not had an opportunity to deal with a supplier selection process, prepare a written statement, as if you were explaining to me, detailing how you would progress to the point when you would enter into contract to supply discussions.

Be specific with regard to methods you have used and provide some examples. Be honest with yourself – this is not part of your assessment, and by considering options in this manner will prepare you for any developments that may occur in the future.

The questions below may help you.

Where am I now?
Think about the selection of suppliers that you have been involved in.

1. Describe the supplier selection process in your area of responsibility.

2. Do you have any involvement in determining a potential supplier?

3. How are contractual terms agreed with suppliers in your place of work?

Now, in your second section, write up a reflective account on how you would make **improvements** and then how you would implement any **action**.

Improvements and action
Are there any areas where you could improve your approach to the selection of potential suppliers?

What action do you need to take to make those improvements?

Some of the changes you have identified might affect the way things are done in your organisation and you may need to discuss them with your line manager. Some changes can be made by you. Remember, small changes can make a big difference.

When you plan to make a change, remember to make your new objectives SMART!

You can discuss the notes you have made with your assessor. They may provide evidence of your competence.

Learning outcome 4 – Be able to monitor supplier performance

In this section we will explore each of the assessment criteria in more detail to develop your knowledge and understanding.

Assessment criterion 4.1 Identify how to monitor supplier performance and delivery against agreed contractual terms

It is quite normal for suppliers and procurers to agree the criteria on the monitoring of the supplier performance. The supply contract normally sets the agreed performance level: this is usually detailed in the following headed sections:

● Description – general supply arrangements

● Responsibilities of provider (supplier)

● Responsibilities of client (procurer)

● Dispute – the agreed procedure to follow.

Once established, these conditions need to be monitored by both parties, so once again good communication needs to be in place.

The responsibilities of both parties is perhaps the most important area for monitoring requirements as it determines the agreed measures and proposed actions for all involved.

Joint measures offer good practice, providing combined performance towards joint goals. For example, if a transport company rings in to one of the team to say they have a breakdown, it is probably worthwhile contacting the supplier to ensure they are aware of this condition.

In business, the need to continue your operational tasks needs to be fully monitored. Generally, a performance measure is applied to all facets of your team's work, so the issues that affect your output need to be removed, overcome or set in your plan.

Let's look at responsibilities and how they may be monitored. The assessment of supplier performance will be detailed in the contract and may have some of the following review points:

● product quality

● rejects

● service

● call-out times

● customer service response time

● performance against agreed delivery lead times

● relationship (account management)

● costs maintained or reduced.

Depending upon your sector, the points will be pretty similar and they are in no particular order of merit or level of importance; that will be set in the contract to supply.

Supplier performance monitoring needs to have a procedure to follow or guidelines from the offset. Good performance monitoring follows a path:

Risk – Records – Reviews – Result

Risk

When entering a new supply arrangement both parties have an element of risk involved. Agreements are made but a number of circumstances could lead to the best intentions of a contract failing early in the term. As the contract develops and the arrangements between supplier and procurer progress, the risk element begins to diminish as the initial assumptions of the working arrangements are challenged.

Records

Set against your measures, the need to keep records seems obvious. So what are we recording? Information recording is to ensure quality standards are being met and maintained; it must be factual and objective. Type of records will vary – some examples may be delivery times against schedules.

Flow charts in a manufacturing unit may perhaps review quality checks: was the supply of unit the correct quality and if not, did it affect the quality of your finished product? Store records: were all parts available for a garage to carry out a repair to keep a fleet on the road? Stock lists: is all print paper available to carry out administration tasks? All vital business needs and any lack of material or quality issues need to be recorded.

Reviews

So through good reports the information can be presented for a review and then with a supportive working relationship with the suppliers we begin to identify how together we can resolve the performance requirements of a supply need. For these reasons the development of good communication and reviews is essential – the elements of the review will probably be laid out in the responsibilities section in the written contract document.

Ensure you advise your supplier on any defect or non-compliance as soon as it occurs; the supplier will then have information to react quickly to your concerns. Do not wait until a planned review meeting to list all the problems – this may result in an escalation that will affect both parties.

Result

With joint measures in place that are workable and effective the supplier relationship can move on. Business plans and promises need results; compliance and performance must therefore be measured but only by adopting a circle of events that is agreed and practicable for all parties.

Some supplier relationships last for years, but they endure only if they are worked upon and maintained, resulting in contracts being reviewed successfully.

Assessment criterion 4.2 Explain the procedure for dealing with breaches of contract

In some cases an escalation of a supply situation may result in applying a procedure for dealing with breaches of contract. The detail of such circumstances will be in the overall content of the agreed contract; however, the specific information is generally located in the terms and conditions, and in the dispute and arbitration section, and in some cases sadly that can lead to the termination clause.

It should be remembered that a supply contract is a two-way document and the supplier may follow the procedure in some cases, as the contract is in place to protect their interests also. A breach of contract is basically when one or more of the terms and conditions laid out has been broken. Breaching a contract may lead to the contract breaking down completely and thus to legal action and claims for damages in a law court.

The types of breach of contract are as follows:

- Minor breach – could be defined as the substitution of materials for specified materials. The substituted materials may work just as well but this is still a breach of contract.

- Material breach – when there are serious consequences on the outcome of the contract.

- Fundamental breach – would be a breach so serious that the contract is terminated.

- Anticipatory breach – where one of the parties makes it known they will not be carrying out agreed work. This could lead to damages being sought.

The proof of the breach needs to be clear and well documented, hence the need for the reports and records when any issue is raised. As legal cases may ensue, preparation is vital and the use of the terms and conditions section in the contract will be used to earmark potential penalty clauses.

With regard to a supply contract, a breach may start with the following statement: 'Failure to meet agreed performance in relation to contractual terms and conditions.' Legal advice is required and should be taken early, prior to escalation – it is no good calling the supplier and shouting 'breach of contract' until you are fully aware of the pre-set conditions in the contract detail.

So each supply contract has its own intricate conditions and as the operational team leader you need to be aware of the clauses that directly affect your process or work flow. Once again you need to rely on communication channels and documented records of any communication with your supplier that lead or may lead to a contract breach.

Take, for example, the substitution of a replacement material. If the material works in your process or work flow, the breach needs to be identified and raised but escalation may not occur if the material offers no side effect to the process output. However, if this material was substituted and its addition created a recall of product, the escalation is clear. In both instances logs and records of the events are required with enough detail to show the breach of contract. If, for example, the first substitution was ignored, why bother with the contract anyway? Your specification for supply would become meaningless and worthless.

The case study section provides an opportunity for you to read about a team leader or team leading scenario. The case study highlights some of the issues discussed. You can use this to reflect on the situation and answer some questions. You do not have to write down your answers unless your tutor or assessor has asked you to do so.

CASE STUDY 4

One of the alarm installation engineers has telephoned the office to speak to Stephanie; the cabling for a job has not arrived. Jeff, the engineer, had rung the supplier to ask whether the material was on its way. They advised that it had not come in yet and was not due into their warehouse for two days.

The installation contract is for a school, which is due to reopen in five days, following the summer holidays.

This is the fifth time the supplier has not met a delivery. Stephanie has documented accounts of the previous delivery issues.

The cabling is pre-ordered and the supplier had agreed in the contract to hold stock for Stephanie's firm and call off the material as required.

Stephanie is about to call Steve, the representative for the supply company.

What do you think?

1. How should Stephanie handle this problem?
2. What would you do?
3. Should Stephanie consult anybody else about this issue?
4. Is this situation a breach of contract? If so, what type?

DEVELOPMENT ACTIVITY 4 with your virtual adviser

I am here to demystify the assessment criteria and help you relate what you have learned to your own job role. We will look at what you are currently doing and how you can develop your skills and have a real impact in your workplace.

Draw up a list. In the list, detail your involvement in monitoring supplier performance. How do you record events relating to supplier performance? List the methods in place.

The questions below may help you.

Where am I now?

Think about any issues regarding a supplier's performance that you have been involved in.

1. Have you documented all issues relating to the supplier performance in formal records?

2. Do you or the team keep a diary or a log on supplier defects that you could use to refer to a situation or event?

3. How are records kept and maintained?

Now, if you do not keep records or logs, write a short statement on how you would make **improvements** and then how you would implement any **action**.

Improvements and action

Are there any areas where you could improve your understanding of the way you monitor supplier performance?

What action do you need to take to make those improvements?

Some of the changes you have identified might affect the way things are done in your organisation and you may need to discuss them with your line manager. Some changes can be made by you. Remember, small changes can make a big difference.

When you plan to make a change, remember to make your new objectives SMART!

You can discuss the notes you have made with your assessor. They may provide evidence of your competence.

TEST YOUR KNOWLEDGE

Here are some questions to test your knowledge and understanding of the issues explored in this unit. You can write the answers down or discuss them with your assessor. They could provide good evidence for your NVQ.

1. Which of your colleagues would you involve in agreeing a supply specification? AC 1.1

2. How was the required process to agree supplier requirements explained to you? AC 1.1

3. How do you produce a specification for supply requirements? AC 1.2

4. Do you have any examples or guidelines in use to identify potential suppliers? AC 2.1

5. Do you have an evaluation process in place for potential suppliers? AC 2.2

6. Do you have a quality manual detailing supply requirements? AC 2.2

7. What action is required or used to avoid potential conflict situations? AC 2.3

8. Describe how suppliers are selected for your organisation. AC 3.1

9. Why is it important to agree contractual terms with your selected suppliers? AC 3.2

10. What are the main points in your contracts for suppliers? AC 3.2

11. How do you monitor your supplier performance? AC 4.1

12. What are the legal possibilities if either party does not perform in a manner agreed in a contract? AC 4.2

13. Name three terms documented in an example of a supply contract. AC 4.2

Pulling it all together and gathering evidence

You and your assessor will need to agree the most appropriate sources of evidence. Here are some suggestions:

- An electronic portfolio: you could upload your evidence to an e-portfolio package or simply store the evidence in electronic format.
- A paper-based portfolio: you could build a folder with hard copies of your evidence.

Types of evidence:

- Observation: a record by your assessor when observing you taking part in a meeting.
- Work product: copies of work produced by you that demonstrate your competence, for example agenda, your notes, minutes.
- Discussion: a record of you and your assessor discussing examples of things that happened in a meeting and how you dealt with them.
- Questioning: a record of your assessor asking questions to test your knowledge.
- Personal statement, reflective account or case study based on the activities in this unit: this should have sentences which start with 'I …' and should tell a story giving real-life examples.
- Witness testimony from your line manager confirming your competence, in writing or recorded as a discussion with your assessor.

It is a good idea to include a range of evidence from different sources. Your evidence should cover a period of time and not be a 'one-off'. However, try to keep the evidence to a minimum. Your assessor can make a note of product evidence they have seen so it can be left in the workplace.

Remember:

Less is more – quality not quantity!

Be holistic – can you use this evidence again for other units?

EVALUATION

What have you learned from completing this unit?

What new skills and techniques are you using?

How has this affected the people you work with?

How has your organisation benefited? How might it benefit in the future?

MANAGE CUSTOMER SERVICE IN YOUR OWN AREA OF RESPONSIBILITY

Introduction and learning outcomes

Learning outcomes for Unit F17:

1. Be able to establish and communicate measurable customer service standards for your own area of responsibility.

2. Be able to support staff in meeting customer service standards.

3. Be able to monitor and evaluate customer service performance, systems and processes.

These learning outcomes say what you will have learned by the end of this unit. Each learning outcome is further broken down into assessment criteria, which we will look at in detail in the following sections of this unit.

This Unit Guide is a resource to help you gather the evidence you require to achieve Unit F17. It can be used as a learning resource if you are new to the role, are studying team leading in preparation for work or as a refresher if you are already an experienced team leader.

You and your assessor will agree what you need to do to meet the assessment criteria and show you are competent. This Unit Guide provides some theory to help you manage customer service in your own area of responsibility, gives some case studies for you to examine and then an opportunity for you to reflect, with a virtual adviser, on how you can develop your own skills and gather evidence of competence. Some ideas are provided in the 'Pulling it all together' section at the end of this unit.

So, the purpose of this unit is to develop the skills and knowledge you need to manage customer service in your area of responsibility.

Who is a customer and what do we mean by customer service?

In today's workplace, we have a growing understanding of who is a customer. We can define this person as:

Someone who benefits from the service we provide.

The word 'customer' no longer conjures up an image of a person buying products from a shop. Money doesn't even have to change hands. Today's customer can be an external customer who buys the products or uses the services provided by your organisation, or an internal customer who works within the organisation and benefits from the work you and your team do.

The idea of 'customer service' is continually developing in response to changing markets. It has moved a long way from the need to 'process' a customer. Today, customer service has a language of its own. It is about 'going the extra mile', 'delighting' customers, 'exceeding their expectations'. And customers themselves are changing, and are more likely to complain as their expectations of good customer service become higher.

Organisations now have Customer Charters, Customer Promises, Customer Service Standards to explain how they will behave in relation to customers. These documents put the customer at the centre of all organisation procedures. Yet none of the grand promises will be fulfilled, none of the high standards met without one very simple and basic skill, a skill that has always been used by anyone who is good at working with people: listening.

You cannot exceed the expectations of your customer unless you know what those expectations are. You have to ask them and listen to what they say. You cannot 'go the extra mile' unless you know in which direction to go. You have to ask the customer and listen to what they tell you. You cannot manage customer service within your area of responsibility and you cannot achieve the learning objectives above unless you have a good understanding of what customer service is. Then you can start to develop some key customer service skills in your team:

- empathy
- confidence, assertiveness, handling of complaints
- problem-solving skills, pro-activity, creativity
- team working
- product knowledge
- commitment to the values of the organisation
- communication skills:
  - questioning
  - listening
- and just being human!

Learning outcome 1 – Be able to establish and communicate measurable customer service standards for your own area of responsibility

In this section we will explore each of the assessment criteria in more detail to develop your knowledge and understanding.

Assessment criterion 1.1 State organisational, legal and regulatory requirements for customer service

Legislation and regulations are designed to protect employees and customers. Some are common to all workplaces, for example:

- Health and Safety at Work Act
- Equality Act
- Data Protection Act.

Health and safety legislation requires the employer to make the premises and equipment safe, provide personal protective equipment (PPE) where necessary and train staff to use equipment. Employees are expected to behave in a way that does not endanger themselves or others. To keep customers safe there may be restrictions on areas they can visit unaccompanied and notices explaining that only trained staff can operate certain machinery. For more information about this and other health and safety legislation that may affect your particular sector, go to www.hse.org.uk.

The Equality Act can benefit customers in several ways. An organisation can use positive action to recruit from under-represented groups. They, in turn, can relate more closely to the needs of customers from diverse groups within the wider community. Customers are also protected from harassment by businesses providing goods, facilities or services. The language and behaviour of you and your team must not cause customers to feel humiliated or degraded in relation to one of the protected characteristics. (See Unit B11 for more information.)

The Data Protection Act protects customers by ensuring any information about them is held:

- with their knowledge and consent
- for a specific purpose
- only for as long as it is needed.

Customers also need to be informed if their phone calls are being recorded. This can protect customers as well as employees.

Other legislation may apply specifically to your sector. There are too many regulations to be covered here. To find out whether there are legal requirements governing aspects of your work, go to www.legislation.gov.uk. We will look at a few examples of areas covered by legislation just to get you thinking:

- CCTV code of practice
- consumer protection laws
- no smoking in a public place or workplace
- laws covering licensed premises
- selling of age-restricted goods
- use of chip 'n' pin machines
- playing of background music
- offering consumer credit.

The important thing is that you are aware of the legislation and that you know what is expected of your team in order to meet the requirements and how these protect your customers.

In addition to UK-wide legislation, there may be regulatory guidelines for your particular sector or industry. There may be a level of qualification needed to work in certain sectors, for example a CRB check for volunteers working with children and vulnerable adults, a registered nursing qualification for a registered manager in a nursing home, membership of a professional body for those offering alternative therapies, and an assessor qualification for those assessing NVQs. There will be an organisation that represents your industry, maybe a sector skills council or professional body. They will have a website with details of the guidelines for your sector. Make sure you access this information regularly and that you ensure your team is aware of the guidelines, how they improve the service to your customers and affect your team's expected standards of performance.

And last, but certainly not least, your organisation's customer service requirements. These can be expressed in many ways and will depend on the size and nature of your business. They may be:

- included in the mission statement
- targeted in key performance objectives
- written in a Customer Service Promise
- stated as a Customer Service Charter
- outlined as Customer Service Standards
- specified in a Service Agreement
- embedded in operating procedures.

For further information on customer service standards you can go to the Institute of Customer Service (ICS), which has provided guidance for setting up customer service standards. The British Standards Institution or BSI Group has also produced a BS 8477 Customer Service Code of Practice. Links to these organisations can be found at the end of this unit.

Many of the mission statements, charters and promises made to customers are general statements, often summarising the organisation's values, and are aspirational in nature. The important thing about customer service standards is that they are specific and can be measured. They should cover every aspect of your organisation's work that has an impact, directly or indirectly, on your customers. For example:

- information to customers: how and what information will be given to customers
- customer interaction: how you will engage and relate to customers
- responsiveness: stating how and when you will reply to enquiries, orders, deliveries, complaints
- documentation: how information will be captured and recorded
- corrective action: how problems and complaints will be identified and resolved.

You need to know exactly what standard of customer service is expected by your organisation and your customers and how these standards will be measured. And then you need to explain this to your team!

At the end of this section is a glossary of terms produced by the Institute of Customer Service. This gives definitions for the different names for customer service requirements. Whatever they are called, they all fulfil one purpose: to explain how your organisation will behave in relation to your customers.

Assessment criterion 1.2 Explain expected standards for customer service performance to employees in own area of responsibility

The first opportunity to explain expected standards for customer service is before a new employee starts work. They will be given essential information, for example what to wear and what time to arrive. During their induction and probationary period, there are many opportunities for you to explain the standards. You can also get the new employee to shadow a more experienced team member or have a 'buddy' who can show them how to behave in relation to customers.

Your job as a team leader is not over when an employee becomes an established member of the team. Your responsibility to deliver customer service standards is ongoing. You must ensure that all employees, even experienced team members, maintain and improve their levels of customer service.

Before you have any discussions about customer service with your team it is useful to look at the customer service language used in your organisation. Some of the key concepts of customer service are covered in the introduction to this unit. Make sure your team all share a similar understanding of these words and ideas so that when you talk about customers and customer service you are all speaking the same language.

Don't wait for a specific customer service target to arrive, or a change in company procedures. Build customers into every area of your work. So if you are discussing the hotel cleaning rota with your team, talk about ways of interacting with guests, building a rapport, respecting their privacy, inconveniencing them as little as possible. Discuss the internal customers – other hotel staff – and how the team provides a service to them and needs to communicate with them.

Whatever roles your team members perform, they need to be aware of promises that the organisation has made to the customer, what agreements have been made and what the customer has a right to expect. A shipping company may have an advertisement showing a smiling, friendly courier and a statement promising 'quick and friendly service'. You lead the team of couriers and need to tell them that customers will expect them to be on time and smiling. This is the promise that has been made and both the words and the picture will have created an expectation in the customer's mind. Your team's performance will be measured against this standard. They need to know what that standard of customer service is.

The more specific the customer service criteria are, the clearer your team will be and the more likely they will be to meet the expected standards.

Assessment criterion 1.3 Describe measurement criteria to monitor customer service performance

So, the team members know what is expected of them. They can start to use their customer service skills with confidence. As their team leader, you will support them and monitor their performance. Monitoring requires you to be clear from day one exactly what criteria you are using to measure their performance. Let's look at different ways performance can be monitored and measured against the standards.

In the case of specific and easily quantifiable criteria for customer service standards, for example:

- to answer all calls within three rings
- to respond to all customer queries within 24 hours
- to respond to all customer complaints within days.

it is easy to measure whether the criteria have been met – you simply need to check actual quantities against targets.

You may need to set up a procedure to gather the data and monitor the performance of individuals, for example:

- to observe team members at least once during the week
- to listen in to a number of calls
- to examine computerised call records.

It may be more difficult to measure more general criteria or improvements in the quality of customer service, for example:

- to improve the customer experience
- to exceed customers' expectations
- to put the customer first.

These may be aspirational aims, but they can still be measured.

One way to measure an improved customer experience could be to compare the number of loyal, returning customers each month. An increase in the take-up of customer loyalty schemes could indicate customer satisfaction. Over time, if sales of products or demand for services increase, this could show better customer experience. Other quantifiable measures could be a month-on-month reduction in the number of complaints, increased footfall, more enquiries and new customers recommended by word of mouth.

It is always wise to conclude that improved customer service is one factor, but there may be other things that influence these figures, for example seasonal sales, discounts, a decrease in the competition. It is always an option to ask customers for feedback. This can be done indirectly by using a mystery shopper who will pretend to be a customer to test the quality of the service offered. This gives an element of objectivity but will provide only a snapshot of service on a particular occasion. You can ask customers to give feedback directly, either verbally or anonymously via a suggestion box or online survey. Each of these techniques is reliable up to a point and they all have their down sides too. Customers may not wish to offend if asked for feedback face to face. Surveys and suggestion boxes require busy customers to spend time they may not have.

Customer complaints are also a useful form of feedback and give valuable insights into areas for development.

Internal customers can be useful in giving feedback as it is in their interests to improve quality within the organisation. Consider how this could be gathered in a sensitive way so as not to undermine good relationships between colleagues and departments.

Feedback from employees is also valuable. Some organisations reward employees for ideas which lead to improved service. Employees follow company procedures and are usually very aware of the ones that don't work. They know exactly which aspects of their daily routine give them the most problems and cause the most problems for customers.

Your team members could be your biggest asset when measuring customer service performance. Take the opportunity to listen to them and observe them dealing directly with customers.

The case study below provides an opportunity for you to read about a team leader or team leading scenario. The case study highlights some of the issues discussed. You can use this to reflect on the situation and answer some questions. You do not have to write down your answers unless your tutor or assessor has asked you to do so.

CASE STUDY 1

Rachel is a team leader in a busy discount fashion store. She supervises a team of sales assistants. Although the store has a Customer Service Promise to give every customer the best possible service, no one has ever explained what this might mean in practice.

Rachel briefs her team every morning, allocating job roles and reinforcing the team's sales targets. She reminds the team to treat customers politely, with a smile, and send them to her if they have any queries or problems.

Every month Rachel has a performance review with each of her team to discuss sales targets and any problems. They often complain that customers can be rude and difficult, especially when using the fitting rooms. Rachel is very sympathetic and agrees with her team that the general public are never easy to deal with and that she will do her best to rotate staff so that no one person has to work in the fitting rooms for longer than two hours at a time.

What do you think?

1. Is Rachel aware of the store's requirements for customer service?
2. How else might she explain the expected standards for customer service to her team?
3. What do you think might be causing the problems with customers in the changing room area?
4. How could Rachel monitor customer service performance in this area?
5. What might she find if she did?
6. How might this lead to improvements?

DEVELOPMENT ACTIVITY 1 with your virtual adviser

I am here to demystify the assessment criteria and help you relate what you have learned to your own job role. We will look at what you are currently doing and how you can develop your skills and have a real impact in your workplace.

Draw a simple table with three columns. In the first column write **Where am I now?** and, as if you were explaining to me, make a few notes about your strengths and weaknesses when establishing and communicating customer service standards. Be specific and provide some examples. Be honest with yourself – this is not part of your assessment, and identifying weaknesses is the first step to making improvements.

The questions below may help you.

Where am I now?
Tell me how you find out about customer service standards and how you explain them to your team.

1. What are the legal requirements and industry guidelines that you must comply with?
2. How do they benefit your customers? Internal? External?
3. How would you find out if the legislation or guidelines had changed or been updated?
4. What promises does your organisation make to its customers?
5. What are the standards of customer service expected from you and your team?
6. How do you explain the standards to your team?
7. How do you monitor their performance in relation to customer service?

Now, in your second column, write the heading **Improvements** and in the third column **Action**.

Improvements and action

Are there any areas where your skills could be improved?

What action do you think you could take to make those improvements happen?

Some of the changes you have identified might affect the way things are done in your organisation and you may need to discuss them with your line manager. Some changes can be made by you. Remember, small changes can make a big difference.

When you plan to make a change, remember to make your new objectives SMART!

You can discuss the notes you have made with your assessor. They may provide evidence of your competence.

Learning outcome 2 – Be able to support staff in meeting customer service standards

In this section we will explore each of the assessment criteria in more detail to develop your knowledge and understanding.

Assessment criterion 2.1 Identify staff and other resources to meet customer service standards

In the introduction to this unit, we looked at some of the customer service skills you and your team need to meet customer service standards. Your team will probably be made up of individuals with different strengths and weaknesses. One team member may have in-depth product knowledge while another person may be relatively new to the organisation and still learning. One member of the team may be exceptionally good at engaging customers in conversation and building a rapport, another may be less confident but may be calm and effective in stressful situations.

If you and your team are running a stall at a trade exhibition, you may need to identify combinations of team members for different shifts so that you have a good balance of skills. You may want to prioritise those with good product knowledge and pro-active customer contact skills to maximise this opportunity to engage with new customers. You know your team, so you can choose the best people for the job while creating opportunities for other team members to develop their skills.

Once you've chosen your team, you need to give them the resources they require to do the job properly. There's no point turning up at the trade exhibition without the right quantities of leaflets, brochures, sample products, or equipment to show your promotional DVD. So plan ahead. Consult the team to find out what they need in terms of time and materials to do the job. Use the team's knowledge and experience to establish what resources customers expect. Your team's feedback is probably the most valuable information for improving the customer's experience. In your plan, allow time for supplies to arrive. And always have a contingency plan in case things don't work out!

Assessment criterion 2.2 Communicate roles and responsibilities to employees and provide support

When communicating roles and responsibilities, it is easy to focus on the practical tasks and overlook opportunities to talk about customer service. Take an example of receiving a delivery. There are a number of jobs that need to be done:

1. Space needs to be cleared in the warehouse to receive the delivery.

2. A qualified forklift driver needs to check the truck and have it ready to unload.

3. The delivery needs to be signed for, checked, unpacked and put into stock.

What if we were to identify our customers and what their needs might be:

1. The driver will benefit if:
   − the access route is clear and he can get in and out easily
   − the goods-in area is cleared before the delivery arrives
   − someone is authorised to sign the paperwork
   − he is spoken to politely and even offered a cup of tea.

2. The sales team will benefit if:
   − someone tells them new stock has arrived
   − they can inform any customers who have pre-ordered items.

3. The admin/finance office will want to:
   − see clearly checked delivery notes to tally with orders
   − update stock records.

4. The store manager may want to:
   − give other work to the warehouse team following the delivery.

5. The customer will be delighted if:
   − they are informed as soon as their order is in stock.

Now the list of roles and responsibilities has changed considerably. The customer is now firmly at the centre of this process.

The way you communicate roles and responsibilities to your team provides an opportunity to reinforce good customer service and develop the customer service skills in your team. To build a confident team with good customer service skills means giving them the chance to succeed. They need to know about levels of autonomy and what authority they have and what they cannot do. For example, they may be able to sign for the delivery, but if the driver wants to take an order for next month, they may have to refer this to you, their team leader. They need to know that if things are difficult or they are uncertain how to proceed, there is always someone they can contact who will give them the support they need.

Assessment criterion 2.3 Describe how to resolve customer service queries within own organisational policy

Even within an organisation with clear customer service standards and procedures, there will always be queries that need to be resolved. Customer queries can be seen as problems and difficulties or as opportunities to 'go the extra mile'. Take the issue of responsiveness. Your organisation may promise to deliver customer orders within 3–5 working days. A customer may phone up and ask for their order to arrive the next day due to exceptional circumstances. It is unlikely that the customer service assistant will have the authority to guarantee next-day delivery there and then over the phone. They may have to refer the issue to you, their team leader, or a specialist, and then phone the customer back.

As with any customer service query, there will be several possible solutions to explore:

1. Say no. It may be essential to say no, if the goods are not in stock, if they are brought in from another depot, if the warehouse cannot physically turn the order round in time due to other commitments. However, a 'no' will upset the customer. They may feel they are dealing with an unmovable system rather than human beings. So if it has to be 'no', your team member will need the skills to apologise and explain the reasons.

2. Say yes. It may be disruptive and cause problems in the warehouse and it may prove costly in terms of additional delivery charges. But you may consider that the benefits of having a delighted customer outweigh these costs.

3. Say yes, if… Alternatively, you could negotiate a compromise. Say you can deliver the next day but as you would need to use a special delivery service the customer would need to pay the additional charge.

So, in resolving any customer service query, you may need to look at all the possible solutions and then choose the option that best suits the needs of the customer and your organisation. Whatever solution you choose, remember to contact the customer as soon as possible and let them know.

In choosing a solution, remember the overall customer promise made by your organisation. Have you said you will put the customer first? Have you promised to deliver the best possible service? Have you implied you will do everything in your power to give them the best customer service experience? This may be the time to prove it!

The case study below provides an opportunity for you to read about a team leader or team leading scenario. The case study highlights some of the issues discussed. You can use this to reflect on the situation and answer some questions. You do not have to write down your answers unless your tutor or assessor has asked you to do so.

It is the time of year when last season's clothes need to be put into the sale and the store needs to be reorganised to accommodate the new season's stock. This is a busy time and the reorganisation has to cause a minimum of disruption to normal trading as possible.

New display areas need to be created. Rachel asks for volunteers from the team to do this work but when everyone volunteers, to be fair, she picks the two team members who put up their hands first.

The display area goes up slowly and it looks a bit of a mess, so Rachel asks two more experienced team members to take over, sending the original pair to cover the fitting room area. While they are there, a customer has tried on a coat but, before she buys, wants to get a second opinion from her friend who will be in town at the weekend. She asks if they can hold the coat for her until Saturday. The team members know that the store is busy and don't want to bother Rachel with the query, so they apologise, saying the store will hold an item for 24 hours only. This does not encourage the customer to buy; instead she leaves the store and is not sure whether it's worth returning on Saturday if the coat may or may not be in stock.

What do you think?

1. How did Rachel approach the task of identifying staff for specific tasks?

2. What effect would this have on the whole team?

3. How else could she have done this?

4. When she sent two team members to the fitting rooms, what other support could she have given them?

5. How else could the team members have dealt with the customer query?

DEVELOPMENT ACTIVITY 2 with your virtual adviser

I am here to demystify the assessment criteria and help you relate what you have learned to your own job role. We will look at what you are currently doing and how you can develop your skills and have a real impact in your workplace.

Draw a simple table with three columns. In the first column write **Where am I now?** and, as if you were explaining to me, make a few notes about your strengths and weaknesses when supporting staff in meeting customer service standards. Be specific and provide some examples. Be honest with yourself – this is not part of your assessment, and identifying weaknesses is the first step to making improvements.

The questions below may help you.

Where am I now?
Think about how you identify staff to meet customer service standards, how you support them and how you resolve customer queries.

1. What criteria did you use when you last chose staff for a particular customer service role?

2. How did you ensure the team had all the necessary resources?

3. How did you explain their roles, their responsibilities and the limits of their authority?

4. What support did you make available to them?

5. What customer queries have your team dealt with or referred to you?

6. How have you resolved them?

7. When have you 'gone the extra mile' to ensure a customer's expectations have been exceeded?

Now, in your second column, write the heading **Improvement** and in the third column **Action**.

Improvements and action
Are there any areas where your skills could be improved?

What action do you need to take to make those improvements?

Some of the changes you have identified might affect the way things are done in your organisation and you may need to discuss them with your line manager. Some changes can be made by you. Remember, small changes can make a big difference.

When you plan to make a change, remember to make your new objectives SMART!

You can discuss the notes you have made with your assessor. They may provide evidence of your competence.

Learning outcome 3 – Be able to monitor and evaluate customer service performance, systems and processes

In this section we will explore each of the assessment criteria in more detail to develop your knowledge and understanding. You have established what your customer service standards are, explained them to your team, supported the team in meeting the standards and now it's time to see whether the team are performing well and whether systems and processes deliver the service customers expect.

Assessment criterion 3.1 Monitor customer service performance against established criteria

Monitoring is an activity that takes place day to day while your team are engaged in working with customers. First, you need to know what you are looking for (in section 1.3 we looked at different criteria for measuring performance). Once you know what you are looking for, you need to identify how to find it.

During day-to-day operations, this will generally involve some simple observations of your team interacting with customers and discussions with team members and customers. The aims of monitoring day-to-day activities are to:

- gather information on customer service
- identify and deal with problems as they happen
- identify potential problems and avoid them
- encourage and support your team.

The method you use to monitor customer service will depend on the criteria and how they can be measured. The range of criteria involving numbers or quantities can be monitored with a simple count. If a call centre operator must answer 12 calls an hour, you can easily check whether they are on track by checking the numbers. If the criterion is more about the quality of the customer's experience, this has to be monitored by observation or by gathering feedback from employees and customers.

Customers are used to completing surveys or rating their experiences. If you buy anything online, you will be familiar with customer satisfaction surveys. If you travel, go on holiday, stay in a hotel, visit a tourist attraction, you will nearly always be asked to rate the service you received. If you shop in certain supermarkets, the chip 'n' pin machine may prompt you to give feedback on your service.

Imagine you are selling your product online. You will want feedback on each stage of the process or each point of customer contact with your organisation. For example:

- attractiveness of the website
- website easy to use
- order acknowledged
- speed of delivery
- good product knowledge for queries
- good experience dealing with staff
- queries and complaints handled well.

You will need to ask questions based on each of these areas and ask customers to give them a score. This will enable you to measure more easily and see how you have improved from year to year.

Feedback comments are not as easy to analyse but they do give a more specific idea of the customer's needs. You may want to use a combination of the two methods. Customers can also give feedback in other ways. In sectors such as food and drink, hairdressing and taxi driving, feedback is often given in the form of a tip. If customers are not happy, they may never return. This type of feedback is not useful to an organisation that wants to improve. A customer who doesn't return to a restaurant never says whether it was the food, the long wait, the atmosphere, the price, the staff or whether they have just moved house. It is difficult to interpret a customer's motives and impossible to decide which area of the business to improve.

It is equally difficult to assume that a customer who returns is a happy customer. Research shows that customers are busy and haven't got the energy to switch from your organisation to a competitor. They may do so only if they are upset.

If you want to know whether your customer is happy, and if you want to know which area of the business to improve, you really have to ask the customer. Consider the advantages and disadvantages of the following:

● Asking for feedback face to face – it's instant so the customer won't have forgotten, but will they be too polite to say what they really think?

● A written questionnaire. Customers can consider their answers, but only a few will have the time to complete it and fewer will return it.

● An online survey. Like the written survey, this gives customers some anonymity so they may be more honest. Not everyone will complete it, however.

It is essential to gather feedback from customers even if it is not always reliable or guaranteed to return. It would be difficult to evaluate your customer service without it.

Another equally valuable source of feedback is your team. They deal with customers every day. They hear what customers want. They know what makes customers happy, they know what upsets customers. Your team are your eyes and ears. They also know exactly which systems and procedures, dreamed up by people who don't deal with customers, work and which ones don't. Feedback from your team is your most valuable asset in evaluating customer service – speak to them, listen to them!

Assessment criterion 3.2 Analyse feedback from staff and customers on the quality of customer service

Having gathered feedback from your customers and your team you now need to analyse it. The next step is to break it down into a number of different areas, for example if you are managing a team in a taxi service, you might ask for customer feedback on the following points of service:

● How easy was it to find the contact number?

● How was the experience of booking a taxi?

● Did your taxi arrive when we said it would?

● How polite was your driver?

● How would you rate your driver's knowledge of the area?

By breaking down the feedback for each of the processes or each time the customer engages with the service you offer, you can target individual areas for improvement.

There are tools to help you analyse feedback depending on the scale of the project. A large organisation may outsource this work or have a specialist within the organisation to analyse feedback electronically. Using a spreadsheet allows you to analyse your data effectively and gives you different options for displaying the data. Comparative tables and charts will help you visualise your data and make it more accessible to others when you come to make your recommendations (see Table F17.1 and Figure F17.1 below).

Table F17.1: Customer survey results shown in a table

Customer survey:	Taxi cabs					
Point of service	Excellent 5	V Good 4	OK 3	Poor 2	V Poor 1	No. of replies
Finding the number	15	29	46	8	2	100
Booking a taxi	51	32	14	3		100
Waiting for taxi	9	13	35	38	5	100
Driver courtesy	25	36	31	8		100
Driver knowledge	68	31	1			100

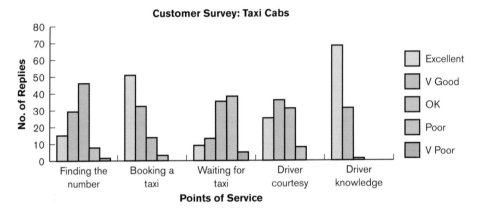

Figure F17.2: Customer survey results shown in a bar chart

Assessment criterion 3.3 Evaluate customer feedback and identify areas for improvement

Now that you have gathered your feedback and matched it to the different points of service, you can easily see:

● which areas are doing well

● which areas need improvement.

Looking at the data that has been analysed in Table F17.1 and Figure F17.1, you can see straightaway that one area of excellence is driver knowledge. Do you think this is more obvious when displayed as a chart (Table F17.1)? This is an area of strength and can be given as positive feedback to the team. The area that seems to be in most need of improvement is the time customers wait for a taxi.

By looking at the data you have been able to evaluate the strengths and weakness of the organisation. Further investigation may be needed before you recommend improvements and this is where your team are so valuable. They can tell you why the customer is waiting so long. Is the operator making unrealistic promises? Are there too few cars/drivers to cope with the demand? Are customer expectations too high? Are traffic conditions slowing the service?

The action you recommend to improve the service will change depending on the reasons for poor performance. You need to investigate this thoroughly before you can invest time and money in making changes. There is a useful guideline called the Pareto Principle, which states that the perfect ratio of change to effort should be in the region of 80:20. So, if you are going to recommend effective improvements you should choose ones that will improve the service by 80 per cent with a 20 per cent investment. It is less than ideal when you are putting 80 per cent of your time, money and energy into something that will yield only a 20 per cent improvement.

So make sure you ask the right people the right questions, and spend time analysing and evaluating the results.

Assessment criterion 3.4 Recommend changes to customer service processes or standards based on performance evaluation

When it comes to recommending improvements, you want to be heard and you want your ideas to be taken on board. But every organisation is different in terms of size, responsiveness to change and culture.

If the CEO or head of your organisation is not open to change, improvements are unlikely to happen. The head of an organisation sets its values and its culture. Without a good customer service culture or commitment to continuous improvement, nothing will change. And in today's market, organisations run in this way are less likely to survive. More progressive organisations are pro-active in seeking suggestions for improvements from employees. They set up quality forums, have customer service champions and establish channels of communication for employees to contribute their ideas.

Your organisation could lie anywhere between these two business models and you may have to consider how best to make your suggestions heard.

Even in the most progressive organisations there can be line managers who block changes, so it is good to identify who in the organisation has the authority and the enthusiasm to make your improvements happen.

Then consider how to get the information across. Yet another email or report can get lost or ignored in someone's inbox. Giving a presentation at a meeting will have a greater impact, allowing you to explain your ideas, show visual evidence and answer questions.

If the improvements are agreed, think carefully about how you introduce change to your team. They may welcome it with open arms or they may need to be supported through the process of initial resistance, flat-out refusal, then grudging acceptance before they take it on board and embrace the change wholeheartedly. Hopefully, if you have communicated the customer service standards to the team right from day one, and supported them in meeting the standards, asked for their feedback and suggestions, then they will be right with you when improvements are made. And whether the improvements are

- training for the team to improve their customer service skills
- training for an individual team member
- changes to systems and procedures

the transitions will be smoother, greeted more positively and have a greater chance of success.

Finally, the focus of customer service should not just be on sales and marketing and attracting new customers. The benefits of continuously improving customer service to existing customers are many:

- Happy customers are more likely to return and to recommend others, thus leading to increased business.
- Staff who deal with happy customers are more likely to be motivated, happier and more productive.
- Everyone has more time to focus on business growth if they spend less time dealing with complaints and litigation.

The case study below provides an opportunity for you to read about a team leader or team leading scenario. It highlights some of the issues discussed. You can use this to reflect on the situation and answer some questions. You do not have to write down your answers unless your tutor or assessor has asked you to do so.

CASE STUDY 3

Rachel has had so many employees complain that they do not like working in the fitting rooms that she has decided to spend a day working alongside her team to find out what the problems are.

As well as observing the fitting room area, she has devised a short questionnaire to find out about the customers' experiences.

Her first impressions are that the staff are polite to customers but quite clearly bored. The customers come out of the fitting rooms often disappointed that they have not found anything they like. The feedback from the customers is not positive and covers a range of areas of dissatisfaction. The recurring themes are:

- fitting rooms too cramped – 4 comments
- fittings rooms too gloomy – 6 comments
- staff miserable – 12 comments
- treated as a potential shoplifter – 15 comments.

To change the actual fitting rooms Rachel would have to make a recommendation to Head Office and she knows budgets would be tight. There may be ways of brightening the place up without a major store refit.

She has observed the bored faces of the staff, so is not surprised by the feedback, but she did not expect the feedback about being treated as a potential shoplifter. Now she looks around the store and is aware of the many signs asking customers not to take bags into the fitting rooms and only three items at a time.

What do you think?

1. What are the advantages and disadvantages of the two methods that Rachel has chosen to monitor customer service?

2. The questionnaire she has used asks for customer comments. Why might this work better than a score rating system in this situation?

3. If you were Rachel, how would you improve each of the areas? Which improvements would you implement first on the basis of the Pareto Principle, i.e. which are the simplest to do that will have the biggest effect?

DEVELOPMENT ACTIVITY 3 with your virtual adviser

I am here to demystify the assessment criteria and help you relate what you have learned to your own job role. We will look at what you are currently doing and how you can develop your skills and have a real impact in your workplace.

Draw a simple table with three columns. In the first column write **Where am I now?** and, as if you were explaining to me, make a few notes about your strengths and weaknesses when monitoring and evaluating customer service. Be specific and provide some examples. Be honest with yourself – this is not part of your assessment, and identifying weaknesses is the first step to making improvements.

The questions below may help you.

Where am I now?
Think about how you monitor and evaluate customer service.

1. How do you monitor the performance of your team?
2. How do you monitor customer satisfaction?
3. What tools do you use to analyse the feedback?
4. What have you judged to be strengths and weaknesses in
    - your team's performance?
    - your systems and procedures?
5. What improvements have you recommended?
6. How effective is the process of evaluation? Does it really get to the heart of any problems?

Now, in your second column, write the heading **Improvements** and in the third column **Action**.

Improvements and action
Are there any areas where your skills could be improved?

What action do you need to take to make those improvements?

Some of the changes you have identified might affect the way things are done in your organisation and you may need to discuss them with your line manager. Some changes can be made by you. Remember, small changes can make a big difference.

When you plan to make a change, remember to make your new objectives SMART!

You can discuss the notes you have made with your assessor. They may provide evidence of your competence.

TEST YOUR KNOWLEDGE

Here are some questions to test your knowledge and understanding of the issues explored in this unit. You can write the answers down or discuss them with your assessor. They could provide good evidence for your NVQ.

1. What legal and regulatory requirements exist in your sector to protect or provide a better experience for customers? AC 1.1

2. What are your organisational standards of customer service? (Customer Promise, Customer Charter, Customer Service Standards, Mission Statement, Operating Procedures, verbal or written) AC 1.1

3. How do you explain those customer service standards to your team and let them know what is expected of their performance? AC 1.2

4. How do you measure the customer service performance of your team? AC 1.3

5. What staff do you need and what other resources do you need to meet your customer service standards? AC 2.1

6. How do you explain roles and responsibilities to your team? AC 2.2

7. What support do you make available to the team so that they can meet the customer service standards? AC 2.2

8. Give three examples of the kind of customer service queries you have had and how you have resolved them. AC 2.3

9. Name two ways you can monitor customer service performance against established criteria. AC 3.1

10. How and when would you capture feedback from: AC 3.2

    Staff:..

    Customers:...

11. Describe how you analyse and evaluate customer feedback. AC 3.3

12. Give two examples of feedback you have received and the improvements to service that you suggested as a result. AC 3.3

    Feedback ....

    Improvement...

    Feedback ....

    Improvement...

13. What other changes have you recommended based on your evaluation of customer service performance? AC 3.4

Further information

Institute of Customer Service website, including a glossary of terms used in the workplace
www.instituteofcustomerservice.com

BSI Group
www.bsigroup.co.uk

Businessballs – A free training website for businesses
www.businessballs.com

Pulling it all together and gathering evidence

You and your assessor will need to agree the most appropriate sources of evidence. Here are some suggestions:

- An electronic portfolio: you could upload your evidence to an e-portfolio package or simply store the evidence in electronic format.
- A paper-based portfolio: you could build a folder with hard copies of your evidence.

Types of evidence:

- Observation: a record by your assessor when observing you briefing your team on customer service standards.
- Work product: copies of work produced by you that demonstrate your competence, for example questionnaires or survey you have devised, feedback received, analysis of feedback, presentation or report of your recommendations.
- Discussion: a record of you and your assessor discussing customer service standards, how you support you team in meeting them, how you monitor their performance, evaluate customer service and recommend improvements.
- Questioning: a record of your assessor asking questions to test your knowledge.
- Personal statement, reflective account or case study based on the activities in this unit: this should have sentences which start with 'I …' and should tell a story giving real-life examples.
- Witness testimony from your line manager confirming your competence, in writing or recorded as a discussion with your assessor.

It is a good idea to include a range of evidence from different sources. Your evidence should cover a period of time and not be a 'one-off'. However, try to keep the evidence to a minimum. Your assessor can make a note of product evidence they have seen so it can be left in the workplace.
Remember:

Less is more – quality not quantity!

Be holistic – can you use this evidence again for other units?

EVALUATION

What have you learned from completing this unit?

What new skills and techniques are you using?

How has this affected the people you work with?

How has your organisation benefited? How might it benefit in the future?

INDEX

Your notes, ideas and reflections

Your notes, ideas and reflections

Your notes, ideas and reflections

Your notes, ideas and reflections

Your notes, ideas and reflections

Your notes, ideas and reflections

Your notes, ideas and reflections

Your notes, ideas and reflections

Your notes, ideas and reflections

Your notes, ideas and reflections

Also available from Hodder Education

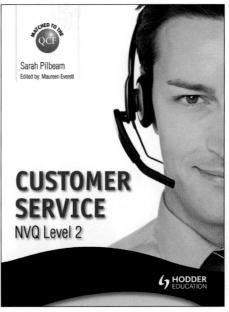

These textbooks offer full support to students in completing their Level 2 NVQ in Customer Service quickly and easily.

All NVQ jargon and the NVQ process is covered in full, with clear explanations so students know exactly what they need to do. For each unit there is a simple explanation of the kind of evidence they need to provide and ideas about how they might generate this evidence in their own jobs. All the knowledge and understanding that make up the course are also covered, so students won't get stuck in the time between assessor visits.

Written to the latest QCF standards by experienced external verifiers and covering the core units, the books include plenty of Case Studies describing real-world Customer Service examples, Development Activities and Knowledge Tests. These will help students to progress in their knowledge and understanding so they can attain the best possible grades in the shortest possible time.

OCR Customer Service Level 2 NVQ

ISBN: 978 1444 15150 3

This book is endorsed by OCR for use with the OCR Level 2 NVQ in Customer Service.

Customer Service Level 2 NVQ

ISBN: 978 1444 15743 7

This book is suitable for students completing the NVQ with any awarding body.

Order from www.hoddereducation.co.uk

Also available from Hodder Education

Written to the QCF 2010 standards, these textbooks cover the core and most popular optional units of the NVQ Level 2 in Business and Administration. Written by experienced authors and overseen by a senior assessor, these books maximise your chances of success by clearly linking the assessment requirements to the relevant knowledge and understanding. Numerous activities and tasks will help you to remember and further understand the clearly explained concepts.

Assessment requirements are clearly linked to relevant knowledge and understanding. Written with editorial input from a senior assessor.

Language, level and approach specifically targeted at NVQ level 2 students.

OCR Business and Administration NVQ Level 2

ISBN: 978 1444 12374 6

This book is endorsed by OCR for use with the OCR Level 2 NVQ in Business and Administration.

Business and Administration NVQ Level 2

ISBN: 978 1444 14420 8

This book is suitable for students completing the NVQ with any awarding body.

Order from www.hoddereducation.co.uk

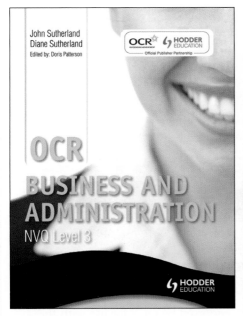
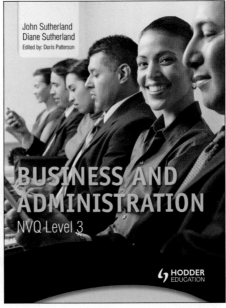

Also available from Hodder Education

  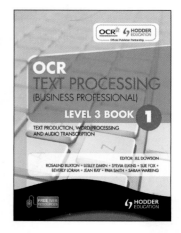

Text processing: text production, word processing and audio transcription

OCR Text Processing (Business Professional) has been endorsed by OCR for use with the OCR Text Processing (Business Professional) 2008 specification and consists of a series of textbooks at all three levels of this popular qualification. Written by an expert team and edited by the chief examiner, this resource will consolidate all of the required knowledge and then allow a student to practise the skills that will ultimately be assessed. This preparation will be of great benefit to students and tutors.

Recall text, templates and audio files for transcription are provided online to support the exercises.

OCR Text Processing (Business Professional) Level 1, ISBN 978 1444 10789 0
OCR Text Processing (Business Professional) Level 2, ISBN 978 0340 99185 5
OCR Text Processing (Business Professional) Level 3, ISBN 978 1444 10790 6